AF842806

Privatization and the New Medical Pluralism

Privatization and the New Medical Pluralism

Shifting Healthcare Landscapes in Maya Guatemala

Anita Chary and Peter Rohloff

LEXINGTON BOOKS
Lanham • Boulder • New York • London

Published by Lexington Books
An imprint of The Rowman & Littlefield Publishing Group, Inc.
4501 Forbes Boulevard, Suite 200, Lanham, Maryland 20706
www.rowman.com

Unit A, Whitacre Mews, 26-34 Stannary Street, London SE11 4AB

Copyright © 2015 by Lexington Books

All rights reserved. No part of this book may be reproduced in any form or by any electronic or mechanical means, including information storage and retrieval systems, without written permission from the publisher, except by a reviewer who may quote passages in a review.

British Library Cataloguing in Publication Information Available

Library of Congress Cataloging-in-Publication Data

Privatization and the new medical pluralism : shifting healthcare landscapes in Maya Guatemala / edited by Anita Chary and Peter Rohloff.
pages cm.
Includes bibliographical references and index.
ISBN 978-1-4985-0537-6 (cloth : alk. paper) -- ISBN 978-1-4985-0538-3 (electronic)
1. Medical care, Cost of--Guatemala. 2. Privatization. 3. Integrative medicine. I. Chary, Anita. II. Rohloff, Peter.
RA410.55.G9P75 2015
338.4'33621097281--dc23
2015027861

∞™ The paper used in this publication meets the minimum requirements of American National Standard for Information Sciences Permanence of Paper for Printed Library Materials, ANSI/NISO Z39.48-1992.

Printed in the United States of America

Contents

Preface

Anita Chary and Peter Rohloff

Maya communities of Guatemala have long been major sites for anthropological study. From 1944–1954, under the democratically elected governments of Presidents Arévalo and Árbenz, anthropological studies by regional scholars flourished as scholars and society struggled to "[understand] the indigenous reality with the goals of integration into modern capitalism" (Perez de Lara, 1987, p. 16). These efforts were heavily influenced by the integrationist anthropologies of *indigenismo* in Mexico, a political ideology which sought to construct a coherent national history and to assimilate indigenous populations into national life (Beltran, 1992; Marzal, 1981; Weaver, 2002). Much of this work was conducted under the auspices of the Guatemalan National Indigenist Institute (*Instituto Nacional Indigenista*), founded in 1945, which regularly published original and reprinted works on Maya folklore, rituals, epistemologies, and ontologies (Guidinelli, 1981; Naranjo, 1978; Rodríguez Rouanet, 1969). At the same time, from the 1940s onward, foreign researchers, most from the United States, increasingly began to focus on Maya communities of Mexico and Guatemala, studying the social dynamics, politics, and economies of Maya towns and villages, Maya ritual life and kinship, and Maya people's complex interactions with the state (e.g., Nash, 1967; Redfield, 1950; Smith, 1990; Tax, 1963; Vogt, 1976; Vogt, 1994).

Scholarly interest—and, particularly, international interest—in the Maya continued, and indeed increased, during the Guatemalan civil war and state-sponsored genocide of Maya peoples from 1960–1996. From this period emerged a large amount of scholarship analyzing the historical events that culminated in the war (e.g., Grandin, 2000; Schlesinger & Kinzer, 2005), victims' and witnesses' lived experiences of trauma (e.g., Carlsen, 1997; Carmack, 1992; Menchú & Burgos-Debray, 1983; Montejo, 1987; Sanford, 2003; D. Stoll, 1999), and postcolonial processes of reconciliation within a fractured nation (e.g., Jonas, 2000; Nelson, 1999; Smith & Adams, 2011; Warren, 2001). Notably, the war also catalyzed a tradition of engaged anthropology in Guatemala, perhaps best emblematized by the Guatemala Scholars Network, which formed at the peak of wartime violence in 1982. Through the Guatemala Scholars Network, researchers, advocates, and activists—Guatemalan and non-Guatemalan alike—publicized the struggles of Maya communities through press releases, popular media, and documentary films. A central tenet of the Guatemala Scholars Network has also been working towards social justice in Guatemalan society—for example, serving as expert witnesses in courts and connecting communities to journalistic and nongovernmental resources. This tradition of public engagement has continued in the postwar period, as anthropologists and other researchers have documented new forms of suffering, injustice, and violence related to neoliberal political and economic reforms, narcotrafficking and the United States-backed War on Drugs, transnational migrations, ongoing exploitative mining operations, and the recent trial of former military dictator and genocidaire Efraín Ríos Montt (e.g., Burrell, 2014; Dougherty, 2011; Foxen, 2008; Little & Smith, 2009; McAllister & Nelson, 2013; Metz & Webb, 2013; O'Neill & Thomas, 2011; Stuesse et al., 2013).

Despite a robust legacy of scholarly advocacy, activism, and ideologies of solidarity and accompaniment in general Mayanist anthropology, scholarship on health and healthcare has lagged behind the rest of the field. This is not to suggest that health, illness, and health disparities have not been a subject of study in Guatemala. Indeed, Guatemala has a robust tradition of medical anthropology, dating back to the 1930s and 1940s (e.g., O. Stoll, 1938; Wisdom, 1952). As outlined by Bruce Barrett (1997), in the twentieth century, studies of medical anthropology in Guatemala historically "followed two broad paths" (p. 580). The first of these focused on "pure" anthropology, dedicated to documenting and analyzing traditional Maya healing modalities (for extensive reviews of this early literature, see Cosminsky & Harrison, 1984; Harrison & Cosminsky, 1976). The second of these involved "applied" work intended to bridge the gaps between approaches to healing among public health practitioners and the rural indigenous communities targeted by their interventions. Of these, the best-known example is perhaps Richard Adams' (1952) work with the famous nutrition trials sponsored by the Institute for Nutrition of Central America and Panama (INCAP). Indeed, most of the applied studies continued to come from anthropologists affiliated with INCAP or, later, with other development organizations (e.g., Adams & Rubel, 1967; Burleigh, Dardano, & Cruz, 1990; Pebley, Hurtado, & Goldman, 1999; Scrimshaw & Hurtado, 1988; Solien de Gonzalez, 1966). The substance of this applied work generally consisted of documenting local cultural understandings and translating them for outsiders involved in health interventions.

These two schools of thought reflected broader trends in early medical anthropology, which predominantly focused on analyzing the internal coherence of non-Western cultural healing systems (e.g., Rivers, 1924) as well as lending insights to biomedicine and public health through "clinically applied" studies (e.g., B. Paul, 1955; see also Sargent & Johnson, 1996). However, even as medical anthropology as a field increasingly embraced "critical" perspectives focusing on the political economy of health beginning in the 1980s and 1990s (see Baer & Singer, 1995), medical anthropology of Guatemala did not follow suit (with a few exceptions, such as Berry, 2006; Green, 1989; Hinojosa, 2004; Maupin, 2008, 2009). Rather, studies of medical anthropology in Guatemala have largely continued to focus on the "cultural"—ethnomedical healing systems, alternative nosologies of Maya people (e.g., Eder & García Pú, 2003; Harvey, 2008; Hawkins & Adams, 2007; Mosquera Saravía, Gaspar Salvador, & Sucuquí Mejía, 2001; Mosquera Saravía & Kolstrup, 2006)—or "applied" development-type work (e.g., Arvelo, Degollado, Reyes, & Alvarez, 2013; Burleigh et al., 1990; Pebley et al., 1999; Scrimshaw & Hurtado, 1988; Thompson, et al., 2007; Weller et al., 2002).

These analytic perspectives, while an excellent starting point, are no longer adequate to describe experiences of health and illness given the many changes currently transforming Guatemala's healthcare systems in the postwar period. The public health system, which has always been underfunded and inadequate, is evolving as it increasingly contracts out health services to nongovernmental organizations. The nongovernmental and private sectors are rapidly expanding. Private foundations and corporations are assuming a growing role in dictating the health agenda. And these dynamics have important effects for Maya people.

Our perspective, and our desire to research and publish this volume, is in no small part informed by our clinical work in the nongovernmental sector, where we have been privileged to interact with indigenous patients and to listen to their stories and health narratives for more than 10 years now.[1] For example, we remember Silvia, a middle-aged Kaqchikel woman with stomach cancer, whose family sold most of their belongings to pay for a (botched) surgery in a private clinic and who came to us for help shortly before she died. We remember Mariela, a young Kaqchikel mother who sought us out due to confusion about the conflicting recommendations she had received from various pharmacists and private doctors regarding her infant daughter's diarrhea. We also remember Juan, a K'iche' father who proudly recounted to us how, through persistence and creative networking, he had managed to get his son a life-changing cleft palate operation with a visiting surgical mission team.

This volume develops a critical analytic framework within which to understand stories like these. In our work in Guatemala, we have witnessed the devastating impact of poverty, societal neglect, and lack of access on healthcare outcomes for Maya people. However, we have also been struck by a pragmatic openness to biomedicine and to new resources, remarkable creativity in health-seeking tactics, and hope and persistence in the face of adversity. In addition to offering an important case study of healthcare privatization in the global context, we aim to fill a gap in the contemporary medical anthropological literature in Guatemala with this volume. In this volume, we situate Maya people's lived experiences of health, illness, and inequality within national and global policies; unpredictable flows of resources; a dizzying, chaotic array of healthcare institutions; and shifting boundaries between public and private sectors. This landscape creates both new disjunctures and new connections between patients, communities, and practitioners. Novel configurations of healthcare resources, interventions, and strategies of governance are emerging.

Ultimately, we hope that this volume will encourage ongoing engaged scholarship and activism in healthcare, in solidarity with Maya people.

NOTE

1. Both editors of this volume work for Wuqu' Kawoq | Maya Health Alliance, which provides free health services in rural indigenous communities of Guatemala in Mayan languages.

Acknowledgments

Many people and institutions have helped make this book possible. We are deeply indebted to the patients and staff of Wuqu' Kawoq | Maya Health Alliance, who encouraged us to reflect about the issues described within. Bret Gustafson, Carolyn Sargent, Brad Stoner, and Kedron Thomas offered valuable advice throughout the development of this project. We also received helpful feedback from participants in a panel about healthcare in Guatemala at the Society for Applied Anthropology Annual Conference in Albuquerque in 2014 as well as from participants of the Medical Anthropology Reading Group at Washington University in St. Louis. Several anonymous reviewers provided thoughtful commentaries and insights that greatly improved the manuscript. Carolyn Smith and the editors of Lexington Books were extremely helpful with the preparation of this volume. At Washington University in St. Louis, the Global Health Center of the Institute for Public Health as well as the Medical Scientist Training Program provided generous support for the publication of this volume.

Introduction

Peter Rohloff and Anita Chary

Julia, a 38-year-old Kaqchikel-speaking Maya woman from a rural farming community, first noted the painless black spot on her left foot in 2008. She thought nothing of it initially, assuming she must have gotten a scratch she hadn't noticed. Over the next several months, however, the spot gradually enlarged and began to bulge out from the top of her foot. Concerned, she consulted with her husband and extended family, who encouraged her to make the half-day trip to the nearest public rural health post. There, the nurse on duty told her that she probably had cancer and needed to travel to the private cancer hospital in the capital, Guatemala City. She scribbled out a brief referral on official letterhead and handed it to Julia.

It took Julia several weeks to muster courage and to save up money to travel to the cancer hospital. She had never been to that part of the city before, and the fact that she could neither read nor speak Spanish made the trip particularly intimidating. Julia arrived at the cancer hospital early in the morning and waited in line with hundreds of other expectant patients. Finally, she was able to see a doctor. He told her that she would need a biopsy, and then she would probably need surgery and medications to treat what he also thought was cancer. She had a hard time understanding everything he said, as he spoke rapidly in Spanish. However, she had no trouble understanding the initial cost estimate for treatment that he prescribed. Even after a trip to the social work office to ask for a price reduction, the staggering figure was easily equivalent to several months' worth of her family's income for the first treatment alone.

When Julia got back home late that night, she and her family talked over their options. Only by selling off their land could they afford the treatment costs, and that would mean not being able to grow enough food to feed the family. Furthermore, the money they would obtain would not be sufficient to cover all the additional expenses of travel and lodging for the long trips to Guatemala City. Together, they agreed that they would not pursue treatment; they would trust in God that things would take care of themselves.

Over the next few years, the tumor on Julia's foot grew and grew, eventually reaching the size of a large melon. She could no longer walk, and the mass festered and grew black. Julia began to have fevers at night and developed a cough. Now desperate for a solution, she and her husband began to investigate their options. She consulted with a surgeon who ran a private clinic in a nearby town. He urged her to have the leg amputated, a service which he readily provided for a considerable fee. He also informed her that her condition was incurable and strongly recommended that she not seek further care elsewhere, although he would, of course, be happy to provide ongoing follow-up. Unsatisfied with this response, she sought additional opinions at two short-term medical missions visiting towns near her own. However, she was turned away from both missions because her problem was "too complicated" for the volunteer doctors from the United States. Through word of mouth, Julia discovered that a nongovernmental organization (NGO) the next town over had recently begun supporting patients with difficult medical problems. She and her family decided to travel there for help. The staff at the NGO were sympathetic to her dilemma and worked to coordinate and finance a repeat consultation—ironically, back at the cancer hospital where she had first traveled years earlier. There, she finally received chemotherapy, but her cancer had metastasized by this point and proved difficult to treat. She died two years later.

GUATEMALA "AT PEACE"

Guatemala is a country of striking social disparity. In particular, it is a country marked by a pattern of sustained violence perpetrated against a rural indigenous Maya population majority. This violence reached its modern apogee during the 36-year civil war (1960–1996), particularly the years 1982–1983 under the presiding president, General Ríos Montt, whose infamous "scorched earth" tactics destroyed hundreds of villages and killed and displaced hundreds of thousands of indigenous inhabitants (Oficina de Derechos Humanos del Arzobispado de Guatemala [ODHAG], 1998). This genocide, however, was only the latest and bloodiest episode in a long history of anti-indigenous Guatemalan state policy, including multiple iterations of forced labor and land expropriation schemes throughout the twentieth century (Carey, 2001, 2006; Carmack, 1992; McCreery, 2003; Smith, 1990).

After decades of military rule through the Cold War era, Guatemala finally reemerged with an elected, albeit weak, civilian government in 1986. Shortly thereafter, in 1995, the Guatemalan congress ratified ILO Convention 169 on the Rights of Indigenous and Tribal Peoples. Subsequently, the armed conflict between military and guerilla forces was brought to a closure with the historic signing of the Peace Accords in 1996. A major subsection of the Peace Accords was a document entitled the *Agreement on Identity and Rights of Indigenous Peoples*.[1] This document provided wide-ranging provisions for reversing the marginalization and discrimination against indigenous persons, including provisions for improved healthcare, land rights, and education, as well as the status of indigenous languages, spirituality, and cultural beliefs. It seemed, therefore, that the time was ripe for a new democratic and multicultural aperture in the Guatemalan polity.

However, in the ensuing years, hopes for substantive, sustained improvements in quality of life for Guatemala's indigenous peoples largely evaporated. The reasons for this are numerous, but two are particularly salient. First, the civilian governments that assumed responsibility for carrying out the provisions of the Peace Accords were strongly influenced by neoliberal policy reforms, which emphasize free markets, privatization of social services, and a minimal role for government in economic regulation (D. Harvey, 2005). Neoliberal policies in Guatemala were exemplified by the international trade treaties such as the Central American Free Trade Agreement, which was ratified in 2006. These international trade agreements have had far-reaching consequences (Jansen, Morley, & Torero, 2007). To give just one very important example, they have greatly exacerbated food insecurity by flooding local markets with imported grain staples (Gauster & Sigüenza, 2008).

Second, the relatively weak (and increasingly outsourced and privatized) central government apparatus was unprepared for the challenge of the postwar surge in racketeering, urban violence and narcotrafficking. Indeed, the annual homicide rate in Guatemala now exceeds the violent death rate during the civil war (O'Neill & Thomas, 2011), and, in 2011, burgeoning levels of insecurity and violence earned Guatemala a spot on the list of the world's least peaceful nations, compiled by the Institute for Economics and Peace (IEP) (IEP, 2011). Faced with the pressing and politically urgent issues of crime and urban violence, it has been difficult to sustain public interest in advancing the causes of indigenous peoples who, for the most part, reside in rural parts of the country, with which the bulk of Guatemala's urban polity has little contact (Rohloff, Kraemer Diaz, & Dasgupta, 2011). Taken together, therefore, many scholars of Guatemala have expressed the sentiment that disparities for indigenous peoples in Guatemala have actually worsened since the signing of the Peace Accords (Chase-Dunn, 2000; Little & Smith, 2009; Robinson, 2000, 2003).

PRIVATIZATION OF HEALTHCARE IN GUATEMALA

Attempts to modernize Guatemala's healthcare system date to the 1940s and the brief democratically-elected presidencies of Arévalo and Árbenz (1945–1954), which offered a respite from prior military rule. Both leaders' social welfarist agendas contributed to the development of a national healthcare system. Following the general trend of progressive governments in Latin American at the time, Guatemala's modern healthcare system was structured around a social security model, designed to provide healthcare benefits to workers employed in the formal economy and "backed up" by a Ministry of Health (MOH)-administered safety net for those without formal employment.[2] Although only a small fraction of the population worked in the formal economy and was therefore covered by social security, the political aspiration was nevertheless one of universal health coverage through gradual growth of the nation's modern economy (Bustamante & Méndez, 2014). However, these aspirations were never realized. Árbenz's term ended in a CIA-backed coup in 1954, which reestablished military dictatorship and eventually led to protracted civil war (Schlesinger & Kinzer, 1982). The resurgence of military rule immediately after the restructuring of the public healthcare system, and its continuation over several decades of civil war, worked to prevent expansion of the formal economy into rural and indigenous areas of the country. Low investment in rural infrastructure, such as roads and clinics, security concerns for health personnel working in rural areas during the war, and lack of culturally- and linguistically-appropriate services for indigenous populations all simultaneously limited health services offerings through the MOH system (Glei, Goldman, & Rodríguez 2003; Hurtado & Sáenz de Tejada, 2001; La Forgia, Mintz, & Cerezo, 2005; Maupin, 2009). Additionally, as Guatemala's small formally-employed middle class did not substantially grow after the coup (Way, 2012), social security healthcare coverage remained low.

This is the background against which a discussion of the contemporary healthcare landscape for indigenous people in rural Guatemala must be viewed. In the immediate postwar period, the MOH was tasked with fulfilling several of the provisions of the Peace Accords that specifically referenced the overwhelming lack of healthcare services in rural Guatemala. At the time of the signing of the Peace Accords, the social security system covered only 13 percent of the population, almost exclusively in urban, nonindigenous areas. Furthermore, best-case estimates of the MOH's capacity were that it provided services only to 25 percent of the population and that around 45 percent of the population had no health coverage at all (Pan American Health Organization [PAHO], 1998; United Nations Development Programme [UNDP], 2010). It was therefore apparent that the MOH would be unable to meet the demand for a rapid increase in public health coverage in rural communities (La Forgia et al., 2005). Furthermore, in line with trends in global health policy, structural adjustment programs prohibited increased public healthcare expenditures in Guatemala. The World Bank and International Monetary Fund imposed these programs, strategies of neoliberal market-driven governance, upon many low- and middle-income countries throughout the 1980s as conditions of international debt rescheduling.[3] Structural adjustment required governments to limit public spending on social services, including healthcare; concomitantly, they promoted private and non-governmental sectors as ideal purveyors of care and encouraged redirection of international aid to NGOs rather than governments (Pfeiffer & Chapman, 2010). In response to the requirements of structural adjustment, in the late 1990s, spurred by seed funding from the Inter-American Development Bank, the Guatemalan MOH began to expand healthcare coverage through subcontracting and outsourcing arrangements with nongovernmental organizations. This arrangement, which became known as the Program for Expansion of Coverage (PEC), grew rapidly in the first decade of the twenty-first century to include contracts with nearly 90 national NGOs, providing a basic minimum package of mostly maternal-child health services to 3.2 million persons free of charge (La Forgia et al., 2005).

The PEC privatization scheme was possible in the first place because of the strong presence of civil society and nongovernmental organizations in Guatemala. International business and development organizations maintained a presence in Guatemala throughout the entire twentieth century (Way, 2012). However, these organizations grew especially from the 1960s onward, spurred on both by external Cold War anti-communist financing initiatives, such as the Kennedy administration's Alliance for Progress, as well as by a ground-swell in religiously-motivated community organizing, as exemplified by the Catholic Action movement (Rohloff et al., 2011). Although growth of the nongovernmental sector slowed during the height of the armed conflict, it exploded in the deregulated post-Peace Accords era. An estimated 10,000 to 15,000 NGOs now operate in the country (Sridhar, 2007), as compared to only 700 in 1992 (Solis, 1996), reflecting broader trends worldwide over the last several decades. Notably, recent surveys estimate that somewhere from 45–60 percent of NGOs in Guatemala operate health programs (Alvarado Browning, Carrera Guerra, & Giron, 1998; Carrera Guerra, 2002; Foro de Coordinaciones de ONG de Guatemala, 2002).[4]

Coincident with the rise in nongovernmental activity, Guatemala has also experienced unprecedented growth in the private, for-profit medical sector. A recent United States Agency for International Development (USAID) report, for example, showed that some 80 percent of all healthcare expenditures in Guatemala are privately financed (USAID, 2008), giving Guatemala the lowest ratio of public to private healthcare expenditures in Central America. More than 80 percent of physicians in Guatemala work within the booming metropolitan area of Guatemala City (González, 2011), and many of these physicians have close ties to United States or European academic medical institutions. While they may provide a limited amount of service work in the public urban institutions, they largely devote themselves to operating fee-for-service private clinics. As a result of this rapid growth in the private sector,[5] Guatemala is increasingly becoming a popular destination for both international medical tourism (Johnson, 2009) and clinical trials (Perez-Martini et al., 2012). The expansion of private clinical services has also been accompanied by rapid growth in both the manufacturing capacity and sales volumes of the biomedical pharmaceutical industry (Davies, n.d.; Ministerio de Economia de Guatemala [MINECO], n.d.) as well as a market of non-traditional parapharmaceutical products (T. S. Harvey, 2011; Herbalife, n.d.).

INDIGENOUS HEALTH IN THE POSTWAR PERIOD

For the rural indigenous population in Guatemala, the effects of these post-war trends in healthcare privatization have been mixed. Privatization of basic MOH functions through PEC has unequivocally increased rural healthcare coverage, as noted above. From 1995 to 2007, for example, official statistics report that the percentage of the Guatemalan population without any health coverage fell from 46 percent to 6 percent (UNDP 2010). These numbers for absolute coverage are impressive, although they are likely overestimates.[6] Additionally, external evaluations of PEC have shown improvements in some basic process indicators in rural areas served by subcontracting NGOs, especially child vaccination rates and prenatal care (Danel & LaForgia, 2005).

At the same time, however, a core feature of PEC was a restructuring of the role of local primary care and community health workers. In particular, the availability of curative services at the community level was severely curtailed in favor of more immediate referral to higher levels of medical care. To offer just one example, prior to PEC, indigenous lay midwives had broader powers to perform prenatal examinations and diagnose and treat complications of pregnancy. In the post-PEC era, midwives are primarily viewed as links in the referral chain: they are expected to recognize and refer much more often than to treat (Chary, Kraemer Díaz, Henderson, & Rohloff, 2013; Radoff, Thompson, Bly, & Romero, 2013). This has inevitably undermined the authority and effectiveness of traditional health practitioners as providers of rural curative services, and hence eroded the social safety net to some degree (Maupin 2008, 2009, 2011; Rohloff et al., 2011). The restructuring of roles for frontline health staff under PEC was also accompanied by retractions in public rural infrastructure: the number of rural health posts (staffed at least by nurses or medical students) adjusted for population decreased more than 20 percent between 1990 and 2006 (UNDP, 2010).

Indigenous activists and community leaders often allege that PEC has led to an inflexible bureaucratic fixation on "coverage" through provision of basic preventive care—almost exclusively for pregnant women and young children—that is not responsive to local priorities or community needs. From this viewpoint, as a health package, PEC actually undermines the pro-indigenous, communitarian provisions of the Peace Accords precisely by attempting to address them (La Forgia et al., 2005; Rohloff et al., 2011). Many NGOs that subcontract with PEC have found the amount of funding available to them to be insufficient for the job at hand, especially since these have not generally been adjusted for inflation from year to year (La Forgia et al., 2005).[7] Similarly, many NGOs that included innovative health or advocacy services in their pre-PEC programming have found contractual and financial obligations under PEC too inflexible for them to continue these services to their constituents (Cardelle, 2003; see also Maupin, this volume). Taken together, all of these features together have led us to propose that the privatization of MOH services under PEC should be considered a provision not of a "*minimum* package" of basic healthcare but, rather a "*minimal* package" of too few services (Rohloff et al., 2011).[8]

With no reliable local option for basic curative services, and with the authority and capacity of traditional ethnomedical practitioners increasingly undermined, it is not surprising that the indigenous population is increasingly turning to private biomedical institutions—including not only nongovernmental organizations, but also for-profit fee-for-service institutions—for a large portion of their care. Indeed, fully 53 percent of all medical consultations by indigenous persons now occur in private settings (USAID, 2008). Remarkably, household out-of-pocket expenses for medical care more than doubled between 1999 and 2005 and account for virtually all of the current growth in national healthcare expenditures, as other forms of private and public financing have remained essentially unchanged over this period. Particularly impressive has been the growth in out-of-pocket payments for pharmaceuticals. Household spending on pharmaceuticals has grown at a nearly constant rate of 10 percent per annum during the last decade and represents a full 70 percent of this 480 million dollar per year pharmaceutical economy (USAID, 2008).

INDIGENOUS HEALTH AND THE "NEW MEDICAL PLURALISM" IN CONTEMPORARY GUATEMALA

Medical pluralism, the existence and active use of multiple healing systems within a society, occurs in a variety of contexts worldwide and is a core topic in medical anthropology (Leslie, 1980). Early anthropological studies of medical pluralism sought to analyze patients' therapeutic choices in contexts where local healing systems such as shamanism, herbalism, and midwifery came into tension with biomedicine, particularly as the latter became more widespread in non-Western societies (for a review, see Kroeger, 1983). Scholars often focused on the divide between "ethnomedicine" and "biomedicine" to gain insight into how medical decision-making reflected processes of sociocultural change and identity formation (Kroeger, 1983).

In Guatemala, studies of healthcare decision-making have followed these general historical tendencies of the field of medical anthropology, focusing on the issues of cultural continuity and change at the interface between biomedicine and indigenous healing systems. For example, numerous scholars have examined how rural Maya people navigate between a vibrant array of local healers—herbalists, midwives, medicine men, and bonesetters, among others—and why they tend to prefer these traditional healers to biomedical practitioners for particular health problems (Cosminsky 1982; Mosquera Saravia, Gaspar Salvador, & Sucuqui Mejia, 2001; Mosquera Saravia & Kolstrup 2006). This literature has stressed how Maya people's alternative nosologies, desires for autonomy, and goals of cultural revitalization influence their preferences for indigenous healing over biomedicine (Berry, 2010; Eder & García Pú, 2003; T. S. Harvey, 2013; Hawkins & Adams, 2007; Hinojosa, 2004).

However, in contemporary Guatemala, and especially in the wake of the surge in privatization and "NGO-ization" of the healthcare sector, these traditional anthropological analyses of medical pluralism and indigenous healing seem increasingly dated. Healthcare decision-making in Guatemala does not occur only along a dichotomous ethnomedical-biomedical line. This volume contends that increasingly, and especially in the case of complex chronic diseases, Maya people must decide between multiple *biomedical* practitioners and systems, as well. While scholars studying medical pluralism recognize a multiplicity of ethnomedical healing systems, the internal variations within biomedicine have been understudied (Kleinman, 1995). Guatemala presents a striking case of the diversity of biomedical institutions, many of which may very well constitute their own medical "systems." Healthcare privatization has encouraged a proliferation of community health workers, health promoters, health guardians, pharmacists, pharmaceutical representatives, nurses, and physicians, who are affiliated variously, and sometimes simultaneously, with the private, public, or NGO sectors. Healthcare privatization has also intensified the involvement of local and foreign donors and philanthropists in determining the priorities and structures of care. This is the context in which we must situate the health decision-making, illness narratives, and medical practice of indigenous Guatemalans. As this volume argues, privatization has fostered a "new" medical pluralism, in which multiple biomedical systems compete and interact while the authority of traditional ethnomedical resources is on the decline. As explored in more detail by the chapters in this volume, these dynamics have multiple implications for health-seeking behaviors and health systems, and more broadly, for health equity and social inequalities.

THIS VOLUME

Privatization and The New Medical Pluralism explores the ground-level effects of healthcare privatization in Guatemala for indigenous Maya through a close analysis of the country's multiple transforming healing systems. The contributors connect lived experiences of healthcare privatization to broader themes of multiculturalism, indigeneity, and critical studies of global health in order to provide an updated and contemporary understanding of medical pluralism in an unequal society. The "new" medical pluralism concerns not only the tensions and exchanges between ethnomedicine and biomedicine, but also the implications of the multiple competing biomedicines that emerge in a highly privatized environment. The work complements existing literature evaluating the effects of privatization in Guatemala from the standpoint of system-wide measures (La Forgia et al., 2005), while also permitting comparison with other recent studies documenting the effects of health reform in other parts of Latin American and the Caribbean (Belmartino & Baris, 2000; Mulligan, 2014; Muntaner, Guerra Salazar, Benach, & Armada, 2006; Schneider, 2010; Scott, 2010; Vargas, Vazquez, Mogollon-Perez, & Unger, 2010) and particularly in countries undergoing a postwar or democratic transition (Han, 2012; James, 2010; Smith-Nonini, 2010).

This volume is divided into three sections, which explore changing aspects of Guatemala's healthcare landscape in the context of privatization. The first of these, "The Public-Private Interface," brings together three chapters that examine shifting relationships between the civil, public, and private sectors. It begins with Jonathan Maupin's study of the Behrhorst Foundation, which began in the 1960s as an autonomous NGO with a holistic approach to improving health in rural Guatemala. Historically, the Foundation was most famous for training networks of indigenous community health promoters and developing economic and land tenure programs. This social and structural approach to health led the Foundation to initially resist participation in PEC in the 1990s. Maupin traces the political pressures and economic challenges that over time led the NGO to adopt government contracts, which have not only restricted the scope of the Foundation's programs to a package of healthcare services, but also has shifted the mission of this once independent NGO away from social welfare to more technocratic service provision.

Shom Dasgupta-Tsikinas and Paul Wise pick up where Maupin leaves off by analyzing the coupling of basic rural healthcare services to conditional cash transfer (CCT) programs within public-NGO sector partnerships of PEC. They identify a maternalist bias inherent to the CCT mechanism, which privileges the welfare of children and accounts for women's needs only if they are mothers. CCT programs also reinforce ideologies that make indigenous women, as mothers, ultimately responsible for any failures in child health, even if such failures inhere as a result of curtailed curative services. Dasgupta-Tsikinas and Wise describe how a network of rural health promoters resists such ideologies and attempts to restore societal caregiving functions to children with special needs, who are excluded from PEC services.

Alejandra Colom's chapter explores how various sectors engage with the pressing public health issue of adolescent pregnancy. Colom contrasts civil society advocacy for female adolescents' sexual and reproductive rights with private-public partnerships that attend to the needs of adolescent females only if they are mothers or mothers-to-be. Specifically, she examines the role of the Guatemalan private sector's corporate social responsibility (CSR) initiatives in promoting the Thousand Days Initiative (TDI), a worldwide effort to reduce chronic malnutrition in infants. Colom highlights how this philanthropy-driven initiative frames pregnant indigenous adolescents primarily as mothers and as vehicles for ensuring the futures of young children, rather than as subjects with sexual and reproductive rights who merit their own care.

These chapters highlight a transformation of the interface between the public, civil, and private sectors. In some ways, the boundaries between these sectors are becoming less distinct as public-private partnerships and government-contracting of NGOs become the norm in healthcare administration and delivery. However, it is apparent that certain institutions exert more influence than others. The NGO sector, historically, has been recognized for its creativity and adaptability to needs at the local level. These capacities as well as social reformist agendas are circumscribed as NGOs participating in the PEC and CCT programs become more accountable to those "above" them—here, the state—rather than to the beneficiaries of their services, or those "below" (cf. Schuller, 2012). Though NGOs are often thought to fill in for weakened states (Fisher, 1997), in Guatemala, the authority of the state is strengthened through NGO contracting. That is, even when the state is removed from the actual delivery of services and provides very limited infrastructure, it defines agendas and significantly shapes ideologies about how and to whom to provide healthcare. This finding reflects analyses about how states do not necessarily withdraw or become "small" under neoliberal policies, but rather simply govern through other means, usually through an intensification of bureaucratic and surveillance procedures (Mulligan, 2014; Peck, 2010; Pierson, 1996). Simultaneously, Colom's chapter demonstrates an increased role for the private sector, particularly CSR initiatives, in prioritizing social issues and steering governments and public opinion towards particular interventions, a phenomenon that has been observed in critiques of development (Mosse, 2013) and global health (Biehl & Petryna, 2013). In this context, interventions that are palatable to or arouse sentiment among a conservative philanthropic elite are more likely to be funded or prioritized. Not inconsequently, CSR organizing around the TDI in Guatemala was also closely tied to a prominent role for wide-scale distribution of various sponsoring companies' existing nutritional or food brands to beneficiaries (e.g., Ministerio de Desarrollo Social [MIDES], 2013), a form of "philanthrocapitalism" described in other contexts (Birn, 2014). Importantly, both chapters 2 and 3 explore the disempowering effects of the emerging social consensus between the public, private, and civil sectors for women, who become interpellated as conduits of social policy, an instrumental means to an end of ensuring healthy children. Both chapters do, at the same time, highlight critical ground-level awareness among civil society groups who resist these hegemonic ideologies and attempt to reconfigure care and social services at grassroots and policy levels.

Part two, "Commoditizing Care," turns to the marketplace of healthcare seeking, offering both patient and provider perspectives. David Flood and Peter Rohloff's chapter provides accounts of indigenous diabetics' pathways to care. Because routine diabetes care is not available through the public sector, diabetics must seek care within a proliferating market of private for-profit biomedical and naturopathic providers. Accessing private-sector care often results in bankruptcy, leading to perceptions that diabetes is a disease only for those who can afford it. Patients' limited understandings of diabetes and its chronicity also present an opportunity for profiteering among private practitioners, who market branded polypills and other designer drugs or promise cures for diabetes with packaged parapharmaceuticals. In this environment, patients and family members come to interpret the cost of care as a proxy for quality.

Rachel Hall-Clifford describes the pyramid scheme of Omnilife, a parapharmaceutical advertised to cure a variety of illnesses, which has grown in popularity throughout Latin America in recent years. The rural indigenous poor, Hall-Clifford argues, are doubly affected by the Omnilife pyramid scheme, which both recruits them as low-level vendors with promises of huge profits and simultaneously misinforms them as consumers of the products. Maya vendors market Omnilife to their fellow community members in hopes of improving their own economic status through sales, acting as pro-capitalist entrepreneurs. Drawing from an ethnographic study of health seeking behaviors surrounding children's acute diarrheal illnesses, Hall-Clifford shows how children's caregivers aspire to purchase Omnilife for its perceived efficacy as well as the high social status it confers as a relatively expensive consumer good.

These chapters point to a phenomenon documented in other privatized healthcare settings: the commoditization of healthcare (Commission on Social Determinants of Health [CSDH], 2008; Han, 2012; Mulligan, 2014; Scott, 2010; Stoeckle, 2000; Whyte, 2014a; Wilson, 2010). Indigenous patients now find themselves exposed to the full, unsubsidized market price of the fee-for-service system. In cases of catastrophic illnesses, many poor households, such as that of Julia, may consider selling off assets—especially agricultural land—to subsidize healthcare expenses. This can lead to severe household instability in the short-term and financial ruin in the long-term. Those seeking care for minor or acute illnesses, for which treatment is largely unavailable through the public sector, also face economic constraints accessing private sector care. Such experiences of paying for healthcare through private sector facilities result in local conceptualizations of health itself as a consumer good available only to those who can afford it. At the same time, however, the experience of paying for care fosters consumer desires to participate in the marketplace and what in some cases is arguably an empowering sense of "choice" between practitioners or products. What accompanies these sentiments is a perception that the higher the cost of a health service or good, the higher its quality.

Both chapters also point to an emerging market of non-traditional parapharmaceuticals (cf. Whyte, 2014a). While some might label these products as complementary and alternative medicine (CAM), a term that typically refers to holistic or integrative healing practices or products, we find it important to make a distinction: these products are advertised and aggressively marketed as "natural" and "herbal" cures for a variety of ailments, but they are in fact composed of highly processed ingredients and tend to be manufactured by overseas corporations. These items are non-traditional in that they are not endorsed by formal biomedical regulatory agencies, nor do they resemble "traditional" indigenous ethnomedical remedies based on local herb and plant formularies. However, because vendors describe the products as "natural," a term also applied to ethnomedical herbal treatments, they capitalize on local historical preferences for non-chemical medicines and will likely continue to successfully garner attention and sales in Guatemala. These products are understudied in Guatemala and elsewhere and represent a fruitful direction for future scholarship.

Part three, "Navigating Resources," examines how indigenous health seekers and providers negotiate an array of biomedical resources, which have proliferated in the wake of healthcare privatization and NGO sector growth. Carla Pezzia's chapter features the experiences of Maya people seeking out mental healthcare in Panajachel, a prime tourist and volunteering destination of Guatemala. Because mental health services and pharmaceuticals are largely unavailable through local public health facilities, public sector practitioners either recruit patients into their private fee-for-service clinics or refer them to pharmacies to fill prescriptions. In these ways, public health facilities pipeline mental healthcare seekers to private resources. Patients unable to afford private sector options sometimes attempt to seek out services offered through NGOs and clinical rotation programs, but these tend to be transient and unpredictable. As such, hoping for luck and cultivating relationships with foreign volunteers and NGO staff become dual strategies to obtain mental healthcare.

Anita Chary highlights similar dynamics as she explores the health seeking pathways of Maya women with advanced cervical cancer. Because oncology services are not available through the public sector, women with cervical cancer often end up "shopping" for the best deal for treatment between biomedical practitioners. This practice of visiting multiple providers for the same illness is normalized as commonsensical within an environment of competing for-profit private providers, whose therapeutic recommendations often differ, and NGOs, which sometimes offer subsidized care under the rubrics of service and humanitarianism. In some cases, women "choose" a provider wisely or attach themselves to the right NGO patron—perhaps more accurately, they "luck out"—and access appropriate care. Others suffer poor health outcomes when inadequate medical regulations, profit motives, and/or humanitarian desires to alleviate suffering lead providers to perform non-standard contraindicated procedures.

Nora King, Anita Chary, and Peter Rohloff complement the other chapters of part three with a description of how indigenous lay midwives leverage the biomedical resources and social capital increasingly available to them through private- and NGO-sector sources. Though national health policymakers and anthropologists have historically understood lay midwives as ethnomedical and non-biomedical, this chapter highlights how Maya midwives increasingly engage with public, private, and NGO-sector biomedical providers and resources to define the scope of their practice—including ethnomedical and biomedical repertoires—on their own terms. Lay Maya midwives take advantage of flows of aid from the Global North to the Global South, collaborate with humanitarians who target them for health interventions, and network with local private practitioners in order to professionalize and assert their roles as essential community health providers and government liaisons.

These chapters illustrate the entrepreneurialism required of indigenous health seekers and healers in an environment of diverse and unpredictable health resources. For health seekers with complex chronic conditions such as mental illnesses and cancer, the public sector offers so little that it ultimately serves as a pipeline for referring patients to private sector resources (cf. Adams, 2013). Pezzia's and Chary's chapters, as well as Julia's case herein, demonstrate that responsibility for "completing a referral" from the public sector in the era of privatization is devolved entirely to the patient and their family. Once in possession of a referral slip, patients must navigate rural highway networks, overcome cultural, language, and literacy barriers, and shoulder all costs of transportation, lodging, and lost wages in order to successfully engage a higher level of public medical care. Consequently, it is no wonder that few bother to or can afford to "be referred" and instead, they turn to the chaotic "patchwork" of civil society and private organizations that have sprung up in the postwar period (Rohloff et al., 2011). However, navigating this "patchwork" can be quite confusing and difficult in its own right. As described at the opening of this chapter, Julia, for example, turned to multiple different private organizations before ultimately finding support for her condition. Notably, in the interim, she fell prey to a private practitioner who extracted fees from the family but foreclosed the possibility of more definitive care. Successfully making one's way through these competing resources requires boldness and a high degree of cultural capital (cf. James, 2010; Nguyen, 2010), which many do not possess. Those who are persistent, pro-active, and self-enterprising are more likely to be successful. However, creative navigation of multiple medical resources does not alone guarantee that one will access appropriate care; rather, crucial are what Susan A. Whyte (2014b) refers to as the "contingencies" of finding the right provider at the right place at the right time as well as the "contingent sociality" of reaching out for health resources through the right social networks. The influence of luck and civil sector patron-client relationships on healthcare access and health outcomes also cannot be overstated; indeed, these findings have been reported in other "aid-saturated" contexts such as Uganda (Scherz, 2014; Whyte, 2014b) and Haiti (James, 2010; Schuller, 2012).

Just as the cacophony of resources can present opportunities for health seekers, it can do so for indigenous healers, as well. Local healthcare workers who figure out how to successfully navigate the terrain of international aid and burgeoning private resources can accumulate financial and social capital, better positioning themselves as healers while simultaneously setting up continued opportunities for their professional success and livelihoods. This dynamic has also been explored by Prince (2014) among community health workers participating in HIV/AIDS programs in Kenya. Once again, such engagement requires entrepreneurialism and enterprise, the archetypical features of the sector of subjects who prosper under market-driven governance (Ong, 2006).

Taken together, the contributions to this volume delineate a clear picture of how privatization has reconfigured Guatemala's healthcare landscape in recent years. Neoliberal rearrangements at the interface between public sector and NGO-led healthcare systems, the declining authority of traditional ethnomedical resources, and a proliferation of multiple competing biomedicines have shaped what we term the "new" medical pluralism, whose features are intimately connected to market-driven governance. In this setting, indigenous Guatemalans increasingly view health as a commodity or consumer good, and use cost heuristically as a convenient—although as many of the contributors' cases studies show, not always accurate—proxy for quality. Although cost may be perceived as an indicator of quality, this does not mean that cost is manageable. Indeed, many treatments are well out of financial reach, so individuals must expend considerable social capital and time in the search for a new "deal"—which may be free or lower cost services from an NGO, a different private clinic with a different pricing structure, a new pharmacy carrying a different branded or generic line, or a vendor of parapharmaceuticals offering a cure once and for all.

Finally, these accounts reflect a point made by Whyte (2014b) about health-seekers in fragmented, multisectorial healthcare landscapes: they do not simply access care, but "achieve" it. In the face of persistent everyday marginalization, Maya people respond "tactically" (de Certeau, 2011). They creatively resist and subvert the forces arrayed against them, and they seek out resources for themselves and their families through multiple healing systems and sectors of healthcare. Scholars of Maya spirituality and religious syncretism document similar behaviors and willingness to layer new forms of knowledge and practice onto older systems when doing so appears to have clear benefits (Wantanabe, 1990; Cook & Offit, 2008). Similarly, we propose that Maya people follow these additive patterns of dialectical engagement with multiple health systems as they seek care and resources in the context of the "new" medical pluralism. Their pathways to care may appear haphazard within a fragmented landscape, but their engagements with the new medical pluralism are rational and strategic.

PRIVATIZATION AND THE NEW MEDICAL PLURALISM IN GLOBAL CONTEXT

There is an extensive literature on the effects of health system reform in Latin America and elsewhere. Many scholars document and lament the ways in which privatization has often not had the intended consequences of improved access and efficiency, but rather produces social inequalities and restricts healthcare access (e.g., Castro & Singer, 2004; Fort, Mercer, Gish, & Goyd, 2004; Kim, Millen, Irwin, & Gershman, 2000; for a review, see Pfeiffer & Chapman, 2010). For example, in the post-socialist context occasioned by the collapse of the Soviet Union, anthropologists have documented an erosion of the social safety net and an increase in healthcare inequity when privatization occurred in the vacuum created by a collapsing or eroding welfare state (Janes, Chuluundorj, Hilliard, Rak, & Janchiv, 2006; Keshavjee, 2014). Scholars have raised similar criticisms in Latin American contexts where neoliberal reform has included scaling back or privatizing existing public healthcare systems, as in Chile in the 1980s (Unger, De Paepe, Cantuarias, & Herrera, 2008) or Puerto Rico in the 1990s (Mulligan, 2014), or where reform has involved converting public to private insurance models, as in Argentina, Colombia, and Mexico (Abadia & Oviedo, 2009; Scott, 2010; Waitzkin, Jasso-Aguilar, & Iriart, 2007; see also Armada & Muntaner, 2004). In Chile and Colombia, particularly, which have high rates of social security coverage and official aspirations to universal coverage; attempts to control national social security costs through privatization have had extensive negative social effects (Bustamante & Méndez, 2014; Unger et al., 2008).

While we share in some of these criticisms, in our view, Guatemala, as an extreme example of a rapidly privatizing, underfunded Central American healthcare system, represents a very different case. Healthcare privatization in Guatemala has changed some of the ways in which inequities and inefficiencies are refracted through the social order, but it has not introduced widespread social inequalities in access to healthcare. This is because in Guatemala, privatization has not been closely linked either to a retraction of the welfare state per se, nor to a redesign or restructuring of an existing public primary care system or social insurance option. Prior to health system reform and the move towards privatization, Guatemalan health economics was characterized by extremely low penetration of social security insurance (due to endemic informal employment), a poorly functioning safety net, and an underfunded MOH (Rohloff & Kraemer Diaz, 2013). Furthermore, social security restructuring has been marginal in most Central American countries, where rates of social security coverage are much lower than in other Latin American countries (Fiedler, 1996; Mesa-Lago, 2012). This context is significant, because national discussion of healthcare privatization in Guatemala has ended up focusing exclusively on the privatization of *healthcare delivery*. This makes privatization not simply a neoliberal project, but also, essentially, a very socially conservative project (see Dasgupta-Tsikinas & Wise, this volume). In other contexts—Chile, Argentina, Colombia, Costa Rica, Brazil—healthcare privatization has simultaneously involved discussion about *healthcare financing*, which has explicitly included the expansion of health insurance coverage to new beneficiaries (Bustamante & Méndez, 2014; La Forgia, 2005; Mesa-Lago, 2007). Even Mexico, which has historically had a very low social security coverage rate, has made expansion of a safety net insurance plan a major part of its recent health system restructuring efforts; a majority of the population is now insured, and out-of-pocket healthcare costs are falling (Bustamante & Méndez, 2014).

This is not so in Guatemala, where discourse about social welfare options *never substantially existed* prior to the current era of privatization (Segura-Ubiergo, 2007). As such, privatization has not necessarily introduced widespread social inequalities in access to public healthcare. Rather, the social inequalities resulting from privatization in Guatemala are of a different sort and scale, because among the poor, privatization offers apertures for obtaining care to some health seekers, but not others. Julia's experiences of accessing cancer treatment illustrate these points well. Her pathway to healthcare in post-reform Guatemala involved a non-transparent array of healthcare institutions, charitable organizations, and complex financial and personal risks. However, it is difficult to argue in a straightforward way that privatization negatively impacted her health trajectory. This is because, again, the situation in Guatemala prior to neoliberal reform and privatization was not one of affordable, publicly-financed care, with a transition to private, expensive care. Rather, it was one of *no care.* This phenomenon is similar to that described by contributors to Prince and Marsland's (2014) excellent volume on public health in Africa, where in nations such as Uganda and Kenya, the healthcare landscape has transitioned directly from a nonfunctioning or minimally functioning public system to a rapidly flourishing "aid-saturated" and "donor-directed" pluralistic one (see also Benton, 2015; Whyte, 2014b).

For patients like Julia, an expanding private sector has created new challenges and hazards, but it has also opened up novel avenues for previously inaccessible care. After giving up on visiting the oncology referral hospital, Julia received costly and sub-standard care with a local private physician. However, as she lived near a town with a flourishing NGO sector, she resourcefully visited medical missions and NGOs until she encountered an NGO that supported her through chemotherapy and provided her with palliative care. As this volume suggests, therefore, from a theoretical perspective, it is not enough to decry the phenomenon of privatization and the proliferation of multiple biomedicines. Rather, we must engage in detailed and reflective ethnography and multidisciplinary analysis as we attempt to spell out the ground-level effects of the health system transition.

The perils of this transition are quite evident in multiple ways, as contributions to this volume enumerate. First, as healthcare encounters increasingly come to revolve around the buying and selling of commodities and services (see Flood & Rohloff; Hall-Clifford), practitioners' motivations to accrue revenue can quickly become dominant. Individuals seeking healthcare may fall victim to predation (see Chary; Pezzia, this volume). Second, the attenuation of public health infrastructure in favor of government subcontracting to private enterprise, and the resultant blurring of public-private boundaries, has the tendency to shift civil society "to the right" as it increasingly accepts oversight by and operates on the terms dictated by neoliberal government, abandoning or deemphasizing prior activist or communitarian tendencies (see Maupin, this volume). This process has met with little resistance from healthcare activists, because healthcare activism in Guatemala is largely restricted to discourse within and about Guatemala's small and relatively fortunate middle class and its coverage by the social security system (Godoy, 2013).[9] In contrast to other contexts where expectations of the state persist even where state services have been and continue to be nonfunctional (e.g., Geissler, 2015), in Guatemala, public imagination of the feasibility of state social service provision is fairly low (Sieder, 2011). This is yet another important illustration of how the spectrum of social discourse in postwar Guatemala is alarmingly narrow, a concern raised in broader discussions of indigenous rights and multiculturalism (del Valle Escalante, 2009; Hale, 2006). Finally, privatization has encouraged new forms of social inequality: for the poor, accessing healthcare has become increasingly dependent on health seekers' proactive entrepreneurialism as well as on a panoply of institutions offering unpredictable and often uncoordinated services. Healthcare is inequitable and only available to some—to those who live in the right places, to those with cultural and social capital, to those who are bold, savvy, or lucky (see Chary; Pezzia, this volume).

On the other hand, the hidden potentials of the health system transition are important to consider. Although privatization shifts risk to individual actors under the guise of "responsibility," it may also open up opportunities for new forms of community activism and entrepreneurial flexibility (Chary, Messmer, et al., 2013; Ong, 2006). These possibilities are especially rich in Guatemala, which has a long tradition of indigenous Maya activism and still a small, committed civil society sector with a social justice agenda. Indeed, many of this volume's contributors document ways in which small grassroots organizations subvert the larger hegemonic healthcare discourse, along the way managing to advance local conversations about care delivery and quality (see Colom; Dasgupta-Tsikinas & Wise, this volume). Similarly, previously marginalized traditional ethnomedical practitioners are discovering new social capital through their engagements with the global flows of aid (see Dasgupta-Tsikinas & Wise; King, Chary, & Rohloff, this volume). Countless individuals with pressing healthcare needs find assistance through informal and semiformal civil society arrangements, or through clever utilization of private-sector services, all of which previously did not exist (see Chary; Flood & Rohloff; Pezzia, this volume). There is an urgent need for an ongoing engaged scholarship and "developmental" activism, which will help to define and shape these potentialities as, together, we work forward in Guatemala towards new collective futures.

NOTES

1. All components of the Peace Accords are accessible electronically at http://www.usip.org/publications/peace-agreements-guatemala.

2. Guatemala's Social Security Institute (IGSS, the *Instituto Guatemateco de Seguridad Social*) was founded in 1946. The "safety net" system, the MOH (known in Spanish as MSPAS, or the *Ministerio de Salud Publica y Asistencia Social*) was founded nearly simultaneously, in 1944 (Rivera Alvarez, 1985).

3. Structural adjustment policies were introduced in Guatemala in the early 1980s, and government implementation of structural adjustment measures increased in the late 1980s and early 1990s (Jonas, 2000).

4. These surveys do not indicate the percentage of NGOs that are national versus international.

5. Reasons for the rapid growth of the private health sector are complex, and there are no straightforward accounts explaining this phenomenon. Private health sector growth likely emerged as a market response to economic deregulation, the postwar

upturn in the economy, and the absence of public sector services, which together created both capacity and a felt need for other healthcare options.

6. PEC coverage numbers are calculated based on theoretical coverage, rather than the actual number of individuals served. For example, if an NGO has a subcontract to provide health services to 10,000 individuals, all 10,000 are counted as "covered" by the subcontract, whether or not they actually access services.

7. Indeed, the MOH budget in general has not kept up with inflation and is lower now, in per capita terms, than it was twenty-five years ago (UNDP, 2010).

8. It is worth noting that as this book goes to press, the MOH is severely curtailing PEC contracts due to persistent issues of MOH underfunding and corruption. In 2014, 220 PEC contracts with NGOs were canceled, leaving 2.6 million formerly covered Guatemalans without healthcare. In 2015, the MOH announced that within the upcoming fiscal year, it would reduce the number of PEC contracts by 80 percent (Arévalo, 2015). The attorney for human rights has decried the current healthcare crisis in Guatemala as "an unprecedented situation that has never occurred in the country" (Espina, 2015).

9. Guatemala's social security healthcare system covers 18 percent of the nation's population (Lao Pena, 2013).

I

The Public-Private Interface

ONE

Strategic Alliances

The Shifting Motivations for NGO Collaboration with Government Programs

Jonathan Maupin

Over the past two decades, an increasingly popular form of healthcare privatization worldwide has been governmental-contracting of non-governmental organizations (NGOs) to extend access to health services in areas not covered by the state. Framed by neoliberal reforms, which call for the retraction of the state in the provision of social services in favor of private sector involvement, government-NGO collaboration is proposed as a way of improving the equity, efficiency, and quality of services in underserved areas (Harvey, 2005; Malena, 1995; World Bank, 1993) and achieving the Millennium Development Goals (Loevinsohn & Harding, 2005). The perceived value of contracting NGOs resides not only in policymakers' and government officials' perceptions of their flexibility, efficiency, responsiveness to local needs, and identification with the populations they serve, but also as a mechanism to facilitate processes of democratization and decentralization (Bebbington, 1993; Frantz, 1987; Hommes, 1995; LaForgia, Mintz, and Cerezo, 2005; O'Donnell, 1994; Reilly, 1995). Recent cross-national reviews of cases as diverse as Bangladesh, Bolivia, Cambodia, Haiti, and India suggest that contracting out primary healthcare services can improve health indicators (Liu, Hotchkiss, and Bose, 2008; Loevinsohn & Harding, 2005).

Critics of this type of privatization have argued that the incorporation of NGOs into the delivery of public health services not only transfers state responsibility to the private sector, but also transforms NGOs by distorting their agendas and potentially increasing state control (Gideon, 1998; Hulme & Edwards, 1992; Migdal, 1988). A central tension in government-NGO collaboration is the extent to which collaborating NGOs are able to maintain a "liberationist" strategy, which focuses on social and political strategies to incite wider structural changes, or if NGOs must adopt more "technical" and "developmentalist" strategies, which treat health issues as technical problems and focus on implementing development projects to address them (Cardelle, 2003; Gideon, 1998). Privatization through governmental-contracting also opens space for the emergence of new "entrepreneurial" NGOs created to pursue government contracts. This not only diversifies the NGO sector, but also forces established NGOs to adopt more technical and developmentalist strategies to compete for government contracts or risk marginalization (Arellano-López & Petras, 1994; Cardelle, 2003; Pearce, 1997).

In Latin America, several countries have pursued models of government-NGO collaboration in healthcare delivery as part of neoliberal economic and political reforms promoting privatization of state health services. While several evaluations suggest that contracting NGOs to provide primary care services improves access, efficiency, and efficacy (Danel & La Forgia, 2005; Liu et al., 2008; Loevinsohn & Hardin, 2005), Gideon (1998) and others highlight how this process impacts the NGO sector by fostering the creation of new entrepreneurial NGOs throughout Latin America, forcing autonomous NGOs to abandon their autonomous and liberationist strategies, and bolstering support for neoliberal economic reforms (Arellano-López & Petras, 1994; Pearce, 1997; Smith-Nonini, 2010). Despite these risks and limitations of NGO-state collaboration, NGOs are continuing to participate in government-sponsored programs. This holds true not only among the newly-created entrepreneurial NGOs, but also among previously autonomous and social-change-oriented NGOs, which initially opposed participation in government-contracting systems.

To examine the factors underlying motivations for collaboration, and the implications for NGO and government relationships, I focus on a case study from Chimaltenango, Guatemala: the *Fundación para el Desarrollo Guatemalteca* "Carroll Behrhorst" (hereafter referred to as the Fundación).[1] The Fundación is one of the longest operating NGOs in Guatemala, and its history demonstrates the changing relationships between NGOs and the state through varying political and economic contexts. Once epitomizing the liberationist and autonomous model of NGO development, and initially rejecting participation in the Guatemalan government's NGO contracting system, the Fundación now collaborates closely with governmental institutions to provide health services to a large population. The case of the Fundación provides a unique opportunity to examine the processes influencing the shift from autonomous and liberationist strategies to an entrepreneurial and cooperative agenda, as well as the paradoxical expansion of state control over the NGO sector through healthcare privatization in Guatemala.

THE EXPANSION OF COVERAGE PROGRAM

In 1997 the Guatemalan government implemented the *Programa de Extensión de Cobertura* (Program for the Expansion of Coverage) (PEC). PEC emerged from the 1996 Peace Accords, which mandated the creation of a new healthcare delivery system to improve access and coverage for underserved rural and indigenous populations (Maupin 2008, 2009, 2011). To do this, the government contracts NGOs to provide a basic package of mostly maternal and child health services to jurisdictions of approximately 10,000 individuals.

PEC expanded rapidly after its introduction. Starting as a pilot program in 1997 in three departments, with fourteen contracts and seven NGOs covering 460,000 rural Guatemalans, PEC was expanded to the national level in 1998. By 2012, 68 NGOs held 376 contracts covering an estimated 4.3 million inhabitants, or roughly 54 percent of the rural Guatemalan population (Lao Pena, 2013). Political support for PEC has varied over time, impacting government investment and NGOs' productivity. From 2000–2004, Alfonso Portillo Cabrera's government administration invested little in the program, and the number of subcontracts to NGOs remained stable at eighty-eight. The Oscar Berger administration (2004–2008) doubled the PEC budget from 12.14 to 24.44 million USD, increased the population covered from 3.2 to 4.3 million, and formalized the contracting process. Support wavered during the Álvaro Colom administration (2008–2012). Colom used PEC primarily as a mechanism for implementing the *Mi Familia Progresa* (My Family is Advancing) conditional cash transfer program (see Dasgupta-Tsikinas and Wise, this volume). Colom's administration viewed NGOs' healthcare delivery as unsustainable, and instead promoted services by MOH mobile health teams (Lao Pena, 2013). As a result, the PEC budget declined and the population covered decreased. The current Otto Pérez Molina administration (2012–2016) reversed this trend, increasing state funding for PEC to approximately 47.84 million USD in 2013. This investment has been tied to the Pérez Molina administration's major health initiative, *Hambre Cero* (Zero Hunger), which aims to reduce food insecurity and improve nutrition for young children throughout the country (see Colom, this volume).[2]

The profile of NGOs participating in PEC has also shifted, as the government has implemented stricter requirements over time. In the early stages of PEC, many "Astroturf" NGOs formed solely for the purpose of obtaining government contracts, as opposed to grassroots organizations that declined to participate (Cardelle, 2003). In contrast, current PEC

NGOs must be local; have at least three years of operation, with at least one year of experience providing health services; have an annual budget over the last three years of at least 250,000 quetzales (roughly 32,000 USD); and have an average budget execution rate over this time of 75 percent.

NGO PARTICIPATION IN THE PEC

Historically, the NGO sector in Guatemala has been strongly anti-statist and autonomous. The sector first emerged in the 1960s, through funding from international organizations such as USAID and through religious institutions such as the Catholic Church, although several independent small-scale organizations also took shape (Davis & Hodson, 1982). NGOs at this time represented the "niche" model, providing services that the state failed to deliver (Cardelle, 2003). These early NGOs were not necessarily antagonistic to the state, but they were largely independent of any state supervision and many, particularly in the 1970s, had a social change and liberationist agenda focused on addressing social inequalities (Beck, 2014; Cardelle, 2003). The growth of the NGO sector also coincided with wider socio-economic movements reflecting the "rural awakening" of the 1970s (Davis & Hodson, 1982). This process peaked following a large earthquake in 1976, which not only resulted in an increase in the number of aid organizations and international funding, but also exposed the inability of the state to mobilize resources or respond to community needs. While many NGOs founded during this time focused on direct provision of specific aid to affected communities, others increased their focus on social change as the pathway to development. There was also greater coordination in the NGO sector, with national and regional associations emerging in the late 1970s (Beck, 2014; Davis and Hodson, 1982; Rohloff, Kraemer Díaz, & Dasgupta, 2011).

The socio-political violence at the height of the civil war effectively extinguished the NGO movement. While the violence is often framed within a Cold War dichotomy of counterinsurgency, state oppression also sought to quell the "rural awakening" in rural indigenous communities, and liberationist NGOs became suspect (Davis & Hodson, 1982; Schirmer, 1998). In 1981, military president Lucas García declared 250 cooperatives illegal because of supposed "Marxist inspirations." Some NGOs did collaborate with the military during the 1980s to provide humanitarian assistance, particularly religious organizations sympathetic to Efrain Ríos Montt's (1982–1983) melding of evangelical Christianity and counterinsurgency (Garrard-Burnett, 2010; Sanford, 2003). The majority of NGOs, however, either fled the country or reduced their operations (Davis & Hodson, 1982).

With the return to civilian rule in 1986, NGOs resumed their efforts, funded by new international resources aimed at strengthening civil society. Peace negotiations in the early 1990s created greater socio-political space, resulting in an increased number of NGOs with diverse agendas working in the country (Howell & Pearce, 2001). While the increase in external funding allowed many NGOs to continue their focus on social change, the decentralized model of political and economic reform outlined in the Peace Accords also opened new spaces, and economic incentives, for NGO-state collaboration through the PEC contracting system.

When PEC was introduced, the established NGO sector largely rejected the notion of collaboration and some even challenged the constitutionality of the ability of the MOH to contract private providers to provide public services. Autonomous and liberationist NGOs largely refused to participate in PEC, fearing a potential loss of autonomy; restricted content of the basic package of services; lack of financial sustainability; and focus on short-term goals rather than long-term development (Camey Huz, 2000; Cardelle, 2003). These NGOs were able to refuse to participate due to other sources of international funding that provided them with financial security. This lack of participation from established NGOs, however, created a vacuum where new government-friendly "Astroturf" NGOs were created by MOH staff to pursue PEC contracts. Of the 103 NGOs contracted in 1998, fifty were created by MOH staff, while only eight of the thirty-one NGOs in the four departments reviewed by José Cardelle (2003) had any history of working in healthcare. Unlike the NGOs that initially rejected PEC, NGOs that participated were more developmentalist and "entrepreneurial." That is, they focused on pursuing contracts as an economic strategy and viewed modernization projects as the model for development. Based on this, Cardelle (2003) argues that collaboration with the state did not represent the creation of a new NGO logic, or shift in institutional strategies, so much as the creation of a new type of NGO. This process has occurred throughout Latin America (Arellano-López & Petras, 1994; Pearce, 1997).

The ability of autonomous and liberationist NGOs to sustain their independence from the state depended upon financial sustainability. Changes in international economic contexts may encourage previously autonomous NGOs to pursue government contracts as a source of revenue. The extent to which this has occurred in Guatemala is uncertain, however, as there is little information on the types of NGOs currently participating in PEC. The case study presented here addresses this issue by detailing the internal and external processes fostering a shift in institutional strategies, from independence to cooperation, as well as the implications of participation in PEC for state-NGO relationships in the current context of privatization. This case study emphasizes NGO negotiation between liberationist philosophies and economic necessities as well as the need for NGOs to seek 'strategies alliances' to maintain institutional sustainability.

THE FUNDACIÓN BEHRHORST

Autonomy and Liberationist Development

Founded in 1962 by Dr. Carroll Behrhorst, the *Fundación Guatemalteca para el Desarrollo* "Carroll Behrhorst" is one of the longest operating and best-known NGOs in Guatemala. Initially, the Fundación focused on the provision of culturally appropriate curative services to the large and predominantly Kaqchikel Maya population in the Department of Chimaltenango through establishing a small hospital and clinic. At the time, Chimaltenango was characterized by high poverty rates, infectious diseases, and little access to biomedical services. In this sense, the Fundación reflected the "niche" model of NGOs, as it emerged in response to the lack of public health services (Cardelle, 2003).

By 1963, Behrhorst radically revised his philosophy regarding health and development, realizing that curative services themselves would not address the underlying factors causing poor health among the rural population. The emerging strategies of the Fundación prioritized a social and economic justice agenda emphasizing community participation and empowerment (Behrhorst, 1975). Epitomizing the liberationist and autonomous strategies, Behrhorst (n.d.) outlined his view of development:

> [T]he basic goal [of health development programs] must be the empowerment of the people, particularly the poor . . . and this must mean the endowment of economic and political power. . . . Seeds for struggle must be sown and the people made capable of expressing their demands on the system so that processes can be realized that improve their relative status in society. (p. 4)

This model of empowerment was not anti-statist, however, and though there was little collaboration with the government, there was not direct confrontation either. Rather, the Fundación focused on addressing local and regional social and economic structures through community participation and integrated development programs, including agricultural, land reform, and water programs. The Fundación also implemented one of the first community health worker programs in Guatemala, through which rural Maya individuals received training in curative and preventative medicine to practice in their respective communities (Behrhorst, 1975). The training in preventative medicine focused in part on the social inequalities that contributed to inequitable health conditions. As a result, many promoters became involved in wider social and economic movements emerging at the time. Funding for the Fundación came largely from international sources, including the Lutheran Church and World

Neighbors. In 1967, the Behrhorst Clinic Foundation, later renamed Behrhorst Partners for Development (BPD), was founded in the United States. The primary function of BPD was to raise funds to support the work of the Fundación in Guatemala. Although the Fundación did charge for all clinical services, patients were charged based on their ability to pay, so these charges were largely symbolic rather than a source of financial sustainability. Therefore the viability of Fundación programs depended heavily on BPD and other international sources of revenue (Behrhorst, 1983).

The Fundación reached its peak in the late 1970s and was identified as one of the top 10 community development programs worldwide by the World Health Organization in 1975 for its model of integrated development and community participation (Newell, 1975). However, the violence of the civil war severely impacted the Fundación. Although the Fundación formally declared itself politically neutral, it did collaborate with the government in rural health and education programs during this time, leading some to characterize it as an instrument of the state (Perera, 1995; Sanford, 2003). Dr. Behrhorst saw collaboration with the state as the only pathway to reach rural communities affected by the violence (Garrard-Burnett, 2010). However, this collaboration did not spare the Fundación, as nearly one-third of its health promoters were either killed or disappeared, one of its doctors was assassinated, and Behrhorst himself fled the country following death threats. The Fundación continued operating during the violence, but ceased all of its socio-economic development programs. By 1983, the philosophy of the Fundación became one of auto-financing and curative care (Muller, 1991). Not only did the violence make any form of community development dangerous, the general reduction of international funding during this time also restricted the potential for development projects. Behrhorst's death in 1990 also caused a decrease in funding, as international donations and patient visits to the Fundación were often tied to his charismatic persona (Muller, 1991). As a result, by the early 1990s, the Fundación focused on providing curative services rather than adhering to the liberationist community-based strategy it held prior to the violence. However, the Fundación at this point was also completely staffed and operated by Guatemalans, which was always a primary goal of Behrhorst for the sustainability of the organization.

Seeking Alternatives

This restriction of services continued throughout the 1990s and into the early 2000s. The Fundación continued to rely on charging for curative services for income while also receiving money from BPD. However, BPD began funding other small-scale NGOs in the Chimaltenango region as well as its own independent programs, resulting in a decline in institutional funding. To compensate for the reduction in funding, the

Fundación pursued new strategies, including the provision of specialized care at higher costs and focusing on its lucrative pharmacy business.[3] New institutional procedures, such as requiring uniform use over *traje* (indigenous clothing) made the Fundación less distinguishable from other private hospitals in town. Many of the founders critiqued these changes as threats to the original philosophy of the Fundación.

Another revenue-generating strategy was participation in Pro-Redes, a Guatemalan NGO network funded by USAID, in coordination with the MOH. Operating from 2000 to 2004, Pro-Redes was designed to expand coverage to indigenous areas not covered by PEC while also testing several innovations in service delivery that could be applied to national programs, particularly regarding the training and supervision of community health workers (CHWs) (Burleigh, n.d.). Another goal of Pro-Redes was to improve the transparency and bidding process of PEC, create networks of NGOs, and increase the technical and administrative capacity for NGOs to manage PEC contracts. As a result, Pro-Redes helped establish a national federation of NGOs in Guatemala, ASOREDES, comprised of 8 NGO networks and over 150 NGOs nationwide. Pro-Redes was not an alternative to PEC, but rather served as a pilot to test specific innovations that were later integrated into PEC.

Members of the Fundación administration, however, did not associate Pro-Redes with the government or PEC, and made a sharp distinction between the two and their decision to participate in the former. When I interviewed the director of the Fundación, Dr. Ortega,[4] in 2003, he responded:

> No, we don't participate in [PEC]. They asked us to participate, but we said no because it was the government. Everyone knows that the government does not pay, and the financing is corrupt. . . . The government lacks legitimacy, and it makes threats against other NGOs who do better work.
>
> When [PEC] started, a lot of NGOs got together and we had meetings to talk about it. We decided that it was not a good model. It was not designed well for Guatemala. All the money for [PEC] comes from foreigners, and those foreigners told Guatemala that they would give them tons of money, but that they would have to implement [PEC] exactly how they wanted it to be done. And so Guatemala adopted [PEC] but they had no part in its structure or design. It wasn't designed with the needs of the communities in Guatemala in mind. It was done for political needs and not in consideration of the needs of the communities.
>
> We also didn't participate because we don't want to be associated with the government, because of the stigma. The government doesn't pay on time, and so NGOs are always having to work without services. So then the NGOs look bad to the communities, they lose their status and people think that it's the NGO's fault that they aren't doing their work or providing any help.

Dr. Ortega's comments thus reflect broader critiques of PEC by NGOs at the time, which focus on the lack of participation by Guatemalan representatives in the design of the program; the uniform and restricted content of the basic package of services; and issues of government funding (Camey Huz, 2000; Cardelle, 2003). In contrast to PEC, Dr. Ortega identified three factors that made Pro-Redes a better option. First, Pro-Redes received its funding from USAID, which provided more assurance and continuity. Second, in Pro-Redes, the Fundación was the administrator of all its funds and projects, giving it more flexibility. Third, Pro-Redes addressed the needs of the community, allowing for increased support for CHWs. Finally, he noted that the director of Pro-Redes, Dr. Burleigh, had worked with Dr. Behrhorst at the Fundación and so she knew the "real meaning" of health and development.

Strategic Alliances

The mid-2000s signaled a significant shift for the Fundación. During this time BPD and the Fundación formally split, ending over thirty-five-years of relatively secure international funding. The number of patients at the clinic also continued declining, and, in 2004, Pro-Redes ended. The confluence of these factors left the Fundación with few resources to continue its normal operations. In 2004, the Fundación entered into a contract with the government to serve as a PEC provider for the municipality of Acatenango in the Department of Chimaltenango, the same municipality it had covered through Pro-Redes. Over the next few years, the Fundación expanded its work with PEC so that by June 2014 it had 10 contracts, providing coverage to nearly 120,000 residents in 152 rural communities with over 700 institutional and volunteer workers.

When I interviewed Dr. Ortega again in 2014, I asked what made them decide to participate in PEC, given his previous statements. He responded:

> We worked with [Pro-Redes] eighteen months, and afterwards, Pro-Redes ended their work in Guatemala. And we ended up with the institutional capacity; trained personnel, community centers with furniture, medicine, chairs, beds, medical equipment, equipment to measure blood pressure, stethoscopes, equipment to examine the throat, hearing, et cetera. . . . After working in Pro-Redes, we started to work in [PEC]. This was the great advantage, that we were well organized with our community personnel to be able to integrate ourselves, coordinate our work with the MOH, that is, [PEC].

Rather than an economic argument, Dr. Ortega at this time explained the decision to participate in terms of the training and organization they received through Pro-Redes, a factor that reportedly led several NGOs to join PEC (Burleigh, n.d.).

When I asked Dr. Ortega about his original concerns about participating in PEC, he recounted:

> In the beginning, in 1997, we got together, around 28 organizations from Chimaltenango, to go against [PEC]. . . . Why? Because we, for a time, thought that the MOH was not giving the health promoter, who we had trained for years, their rightful place. . . . The promoters that [Behrhorst] trained were leaders in their communities. They know the problems of their communities. They speak the language of their communities. . . . And so they were closer to the reality and could relate the changes in life to improve their communities.
>
> When [PEC] came, it didn't speak about health promoters. It spoke of health guardians. . . . And these people that started to work as health guardians were not prepared like the promoters that we had earlier. And so this was an obstacle for us, that they didn't give a space to the promoter or its original philosophy. Instead, they picked people and gave them a very superficial training and they could be community facilitators. But they did not have a sufficient training. This was one of the reasons why we didn't start with them.

This response, in part, reflects the changes initiated by the Pro-Redes program, in which CHWs were given more training, responsibilities, and supervision. In the subsequent changes to PEC, the community facilitators, which Dr. Ortega directly compared to the old health promoters, were provided with more medical training and were more involved in the delivery of health services in their communities. Thus, for Dr. Ortega, their participation in PEC was both because they were organized, trained, and ready to participate as well as the fact that the MOH made changes to the program to resolve disagreements in philosophy and practice.

Dr. Ortega emphasized that participation in PEC has drawbacks as well, particularly the lack of secure and prompt payments from the government. In 2013, delays in the disbursement of funds severely curtailed the work of PEC at the national level for several months. These delays place considerable stress on NGOs, which are required to cover at least one month of budgetary costs, although long-term delays force many to suspend services. Yet, when asked if participation was worthwhile, Dr. Ortega stated, "Yes, it's worth it. If the government fulfills its promise, it's worth it." However, the Fundación is not necessarily looking for new contracts with PEC. According to Dr. Ortega, they have been offered more jurisdictions, though he "said no, because there are more problems [due to] the lack of payments. It is better to stay with what we have. We have enough problems."

The Fundación's participation in PEC has been met with criticism by several of the original founders, however. In informal conversations, these critics have argued that the current administration is "killing" the philosophy of Dr. Behrhorst and erasing the history of the institution.

They call for the Fundación to return to its original emphasis of community health and development. In response, Dr. Ortega replied:

> It's logical. [Behrhorst], in the 60s and 70s, came with sufficient funding for his health programs in Guatemala. The workers who were here in this time, they weren't struggling, they weren't worried about if the workers have their salary or not. No, they were working with the international aid that [Behrhorst] brought. There wasn't any preoccupation about the sustainability of the Fundación for its programs. That wasn't a problem here. Because of this, in the statutes, the word "sustainability" doesn't appear. And those with this old ideology, they say "the gringos, they're obligated to bring money to the Fundación." . . . They don't have an evolution of ideas. . . . This is their ideology. It's a paternalistic ideology. They only want to receive the programs.

In contrast to the original founders, Dr. Ortega does not find a contradiction between the mission, vision, or philosophy of the Fundación and their participation in PEC. In fact, he argued that participation in PEC allows the NGO to continue fulfilling Behrhorst's philosophy by enabling them to collaborate with the government to provide integrated health services. "So, I am filling a void," he stated, "where I don't have money to cover what [Behrhorst] did through the health promoters. . . . It is true that it is a program of the government, but the philosophy of the institution is the same."

However, philosophical match is not the only reason for participation, as highlighted by his critique of the founders: "They didn't want me to work with the government. But they didn't say, 'Doctor, don't work with the government. I'll find projects in another part for you to manage.' They only give critiques, but they don't do anything that benefits the Fundación." Dr. Ortega suggested that he would be open to alternatives, but that no one has identified potential sources of funding to secure the sustainability of the Fundación. His critique of the "antiquated ideologies" and expectations of international aid highlight his strategy to pursue "strategic alliances," whether with the government, private entities, or other organizations in order establish institutional sustainability. Collaboration with the government, then, is a strategic economic alliance justified by a re-framing of institutional philosophy.

Recently, the Fundación has extended this tactic by forming a "strategic alliance" with the Guatemalan Institute of Social Security (IGSS), a government healthcare system that covers those employed in the formal economic sector, or about 18 percent of the Guatemalan population, through a network of clinics and hospitals separate from MOH facilities (Lao Pena, 2013). As the population eligible for IGSS services has increased, IGSS has contracted private hospitals or NGOs to provide services. In this model, the Fundación provides pediatric care, maternal health services (including deliveries and surgeries), and internal medicine consultations. In 2013, IGSS patients accounted for nearly one-third of the Fundación's total ambulatory care volume and three-quarters of hospitalizations, while the number of surgeries has nearly tripled. The dramatic increase in patients received through IGSS thus provides a significant economic resource for the Fundación, which now relies primarily on these service provision contracts for institutional sustainability.

CONCLUSION

In this chapter, I have used the example of one well-known NGO to describe the historical contingencies of state-NGO collaboration and relationships in Guatemala. While the history of the Fundación is unique, it demonstrates the historical processes underlying shifts in institutional strategies and highlights the changing relationships between previously autonomous NGOs and the state within the current context of healthcare privatization through NGO contracting. The Fundación, which initially resisted participation, reflects the changing type of NGOs participating in PEC, as well as the increasing tendency for private contracting to change the missions of NGOs to become less socially and politically oriented. This account shines light not only on the situation in Guatemala, but also on regional and global trends in healthcare privatization through NGO-state collaborations in the context of neoliberal reforms in two major ways.

First, the case study of the Fundación demonstrates the susceptibility of autonomy and liberationist strategies to changing political and economic contexts. Sustained autonomy requires a political context that permits or tolerates a degree of social activism outside of the state. Moreover, economic independence is necessary for NGOs that resist collaboration or maintain their social change agendas. As few NGOs are able to operate on a model of auto-financing, external investments are often necessary to achieve and maintain this economic sustainability. For the Fundación, international funding in the 1960s and 1970s provided the opportunity to pursue liberationist strategies that challenged regional social and economic structures. Like many autonomous NGOs, the Fundación rejected participation in PEC in the late 1990s. While NGOs justified this rejection in terms of institutional strategies and the limitations of the state, the ability to refuse collaboration was possible because of the continuation of international aid and the opportunities provided by alternative programs, such as Pro-Redes. The termination of Pro-Redes, decrease in international funding, and declining patient base forced the Fundación to seek new "strategic alliances" to secure financing. The decision to participate in PEC, then, was a necessary economic strategy for institutional sustainability. The Fundación's liberationist strategies declined following the violence, and then the decrease in international and local funding forced the Fundación to further change its institutional strategies towards a more entrepreneurial and developmentalist orientation.

Second, the case of the Fundación demonstrates the paradoxical extension of state control even in the midst of the withdrawal of the state as an active service provider. The notion of privatization, particularly in the neoliberal paradigm, classically implies the complete withdrawal of the state from the delivery and management of social services (Harvey, 2005). However, the reality described in this case study is that, as Jean Perrot (2006) suggests, government contracting of private entities does not entail the complete removal of the state from social services, and in fact may create new mechanisms for state regulation of both health systems as well as civil society. While contracting may result in mutual dependence, as NGOs rely on the government for funding and governments rely on NGOs for service delivery (Coston, 1998), the role of the government in setting national health priorities, budgets, the scope and scale of services, and performance measures effectively extends its influence over a previously autonomous NGO sector (see Dasgupta-Tsikinas and Wise, this volume). That is, even as the state withdraws from service delivery, it continues to set the agenda for development (Vaux, 2001), and constrains NGO activities in new ways to conform to the state's agenda (Gideon, 1998; Smith-Nonini, 2010).

In PEC, for example, the content and scope of the basic package of services focuses primarily on maternal and child health through increased surveillance of health conditions and preventative services. While providing important services in communities that previously lacked access, this "*minimal* package" (Rohloff et al., 2011, p. 430) not only excludes a significant proportion of the population, it also fails to address the underlying causes of morbidity and mortality in rural Guatemala. The focus on preventative services, increased surveillance, and basic curative services effectively diverts attention away from identifying the social, economic, and political structures that create and sustain systemic inequalities causing poor health in rural areas. PEC functions as a means for the Guatemalan state to both generate a sense of "consensus" by demonstrating concern for and a willingness to collaborate while at the same time serving the "coercive" function of constraining NGO activities by "rendering technical" (Li, 2007) the causes of and solutions to poor health, a point Linda Green (1989) has also made regarding primary healthcare programs in Guatemala. As James Ferguson (1990) details, this type of development serves as an anti-politics machine, as it makes the content of health services and transfer of healthcare delivery to the private sector appear apolitical; it deflects questions of existing inequalities, while at the same time extending government control and influence over the NGO sector and rural areas previously less regulated.

NGOs participating in PEC are complicit in this process. While the Director of the Fundación framed PEC as a mechanism through which to continue the philosophy of Dr. Behrhorst by providing health services in rural communities, this accommodation obscures the original emphasis on empowerment and social change as well as the actual role of NGOs in PEC. As I have detailed elsewhere (Maupin, 2009), participating NGOs serve largely as administrators for the delivery of the basic package of services and there is little integration of these services, employees, or recipients within existing programs. Additionally, the increasingly strict performance measures for participating NGOs constrain their activity to providing the specific programmatic elements contained in the basic package of services (see also Dasgupta-Tsikinas and Wise, this volume). Rather than addressing underlying causes of poor health, NGOs must become more technical and developmentalist by focusing on achieving measurable improvements in specific variables, such as immunization rates, growth patterns, and prenatal care visits (Ebdon, 1995; Hulme & Edwards, 1992). Moreover, as Dr. Ortega stated, the expansion of PEC also serves to deter NGOs from pursuing independent programs, further restricting the potential for alternative models that pursue social change agendas. The privatization of health services through PEC has therefore, in some ways, expanded the role of the state in defining the nature and scope of rural health programs throughout Guatemala and has circumscribed the role of NGOs to the provision of restricted services that effectively stifle efforts at social change.

For individual NGOs such as the Fundación, however, financial and institutional sustainability is largely tied to its continued formation of strategic alliances with governmental and semi-private organizations, such as PEC and IGSS. Declines in international donations, patients, and alternative programs have created a new context in which the Fundación must collaborate with state institutions in order to survive. Continuation of this collaboration is uncertain, however, as the political support for PEC continues to fluctuate. In July 2014, the government revoked 220 PEC contracts with 18 NGOs, effectively ending health coverage for approximately 2.6 million residents. The Guatemalan government continued to dismantle PEC in 2015, and at the time of this writing the Fundación had recently lost its contracts. The rationale underlying the decision to cancel NGO contracts with PEC is not clear. In informal conversations, several colleagues in Guatemala suggested the 2015 national elections as a prime motivator, while others mentioned institutional corruption within PEC (see Espina, 2015). At the moment there is no clear alternative to PEC, although the PEC director, Nicté Ramírez, proposed replacing PEC NGOs with mobile MOH units (Arévalo, 2015), a proposal similar to that of Álvaro Colom's government (Lao Pena, 2013). While the legal debate over the cessation of PEC continues, uncertainty and political instability will continue to drive NGOs such as the Fundación to seek new strategic alliances as they seek to adapt to Guatemala's rapidly changing healthcare landscape.

NOTES

1. This research is based on extensive ethnographic research with the Fundación since 2002, but is also informed by a larger personal relationship with the Fundación. Dr. Carroll Behrhorst is my grandfather, a factor that granted me access to administration, board members and staff, Dr. Behrhorst's archives, as well as a unique perspective on the long-term history of the Fundación framed by family members in the U.S. and Guatemala. This relationship also presents a potential bias, however, particularly regarding the ways in which individuals drew upon Dr. Behrhorst's philosophy and legacy in order to contextualize contemporary processes and strategies. This issue is particularly poignant currently, as various factions within the Fundación draw upon the past in different ways to promote alternate visions of the future and current strategies, a factor which I address, albeit briefly, in this paper.

2. Additionally, the Pérez Molina administration began very preliminary attempts to shift PEC's specific focus on maternal and child health towards addressing other health needs associated with the changing epidemiological profile of the country (see Lao Pena, 2013; although see Dasgupta-Tsikinas and Wise; Flood and Rohloff, this volume, for critiques of PEC).

3. For more information about pharmacies as a first line of health care resort, see Hall-Clifford; Pezzia, this volume.

4. A pseudonym is used here in order to protect anonymity.

TWO

"Mi Familia Pobreza"

Conditional Cash Transfers and Maternal-Child Health in Rural Guatemala

Shom Dasgupta-Tsinikas and Paul Wise

Ever since the signing of the Peace Accords in 1996, which put an end to Guatemala's long civil war, the country has experienced a rapid acceleration of the privatization, decentralization, and marketization of government functions and social programs (Chase-Dunn, 2000; Robinson, 2000). In the arena of public health, the extension of these processes was formalized through the creation of the Program for Expansion of Coverage (PEC) in 1997 (see Maupin, this volume). Through PEC, the government contracts nongovernmental organizations (NGOs) to provide basic health services to rural segments of the population. More recently, large-scale conditional cash transfer (CCT) programs have scaled up throughout rural Guatemala utilizing the PEC infrastructure.

This chapter examines the deployment of CCTs in Guatemala. Based on fieldwork conducted in San Lucas Tolimán, we highlight two ideological critiques of the CCT mechanism. First, CCT devolves responsibility for child health to women, as mothers, while simultaneously disregarding their own welfare needs. Second, the PEC-deployed CCT allows for the fetishization of technical elements of aid related to child malnutrition. We then explore efforts of a health promoters' network working with special needs children as an example of community-based resistance to the CCT program's bureaucratic model of care.

CONDITIONAL CASH TRANSFERS: GLOBAL CONTEXT AND GUATEMALA'S PROGRAMS

In response to global debt crises of the 1970s and 1980s, international lending institutions such as the International Monetary Fund and the World Bank attempted to encourage economic growth by promoting neoliberal economic reforms—i.e., anti-inflationary monetarism and privatization of public enterprises to reduce fiscal deficits. Scholars have extensively documented the widespread immiseration of populations in developing countries that resulted from these reforms (Gershman & Irwin, 2000; Harvey, 2005; Molyneux, 2007; Pfeiffer & Chapman, 2010; Stiglitz, 2002). In response, international economic development policymakers subsequently crafted more flexible economic approaches, which concede that social deficits—and not just fiscal deficits—must be addressed as part of the policy agenda. This has led to the incorporation of novel anti-poverty approaches into government policies (Hujo & Gaia, 2011; Pantelić, 2011), which Maxine Molyneux (2007) and others have called "the New Social Policy."

One increasingly popular anti-poverty approach, which has gained traction particularly in Latin America, is the CCT program (Fiszbein & Schady, 2009). CCTs provide periodic cash transfers to mothers of young and school-age children who comply with specific requirements—specifically, of accessing basic maternal and child healthcare as well as children's school enrollment and attendance. In general, a CCT program identifies eligible beneficiaries through a combination of regional targeting and proxy means tests for poverty (Fiszbein & Schady, 2009; Stampini & Tornarolli, 2012).

Globally, CCT programs have had positive social effects, such as improvements in poverty rates; increases in household expenditures on food; improvements in dietary quality and nutritional status; decreases in child labor; and improvements in school enrollment (Cecchini, Leiva, Madariaga, & Trucco, 2009; Fiszbein & Schady, 2009; Pantelić, 2011). Mexico's Progresa/Oportunidades program is one example of a successful program. In addition to being one of Latin America's largest CCT programs, it is an important comparison for this chapter since it represents the model on which the Guatemalan program has been based. Progresa/Oportunidades cash transfers have permitted beneficiary women to increase opportunities for productive economic activities (Pantelić, 2011). Furthermore, the program has substantially decreased child labor, decreased the prevalence of childhood stunting, and improved overall school enrollment and attendance (Fizsbein & Schady, 2009; Molyneux, 2006, 2007).

Guatemala's national CCT program, Mi Familia Progresa (MFP), was implemented in 2008. In contrast to the Mexican programs, which were implemented in an environment of careful experimentation and regular evaluation (Dubois & Rubio-Codina, 2012; Molyneux, 2006, 2007), the Guatemalan version was implemented with a one-size-fits-all strategy that enabled a very rapid rollout and scale-up. This rapid expansion was largely enabled by the preexisting PEC NGO network, which also was tasked with implementing and supervising the core CCT conditionalities. By the end of its first year, MFP had distributed 13 million USD to nearly 300,000 beneficiaries (Gaia, 2010); by 2011, MFP had distributed 272 million USD to around 900,000 beneficiaries (Gutiérrez, 2011b).[1]

Under MFP cash transfers were initially available for three groups of individuals: (a) women with children under age six, conditional on accessing prescribed health and nutrition services; (b) pregnant and lactating women, again conditional on healthcare accessing behaviors; and (c) women with children aged six to fifteen years of age, conditional on minimum school attendance rates. In 2009, MFP added an additional transfer targeted at specific communities with the highest rates of acute child malnutrition (Gaia, 2010). In 2012, with a new presidential election, the program was renamed Mi Bono Seguro (MBS), and a cash transfer for families with children with disabilities ages zero to fifteen was added upon proof of accessing rehabilitation and therapy services at privately administered rehabilitation centers (Grave, 2013; Ministerio de Desarrollo Social [MIDES], 2014).

One unique feature of Guatemala's CCT program compared to the countervailing Mexican example is that rapid scale-up proceeded through the existing privatized network of PEC NGOs. The wholesale provision of rural health services by government-aligned NGOs is a major shift in the civil society landscape. As Maupin details in this volume, PEC subcontracting has encouraged a gradual shift away from the more autonomist stance taken by a historically activist civil society towards a more technocratic administrative role. This has led to an increasingly conservative approach to social welfare, further reinforced by Guatemala's long-standing political history of authoritarianism and oligarchy (Chase-Dunn, 2000; Robinson, 2000) and by a boom in conservatively-aligned corporate philanthropy initiatives (see Colom, this volume).

As one first-level instance of Guatemala's unique political conservatism regarding social welfare, most CCT programs in Latin America have included cash transfers of more than 20 percent of estimated monthly household expenditures among target beneficiaries. In contrast, Guatemala's current CCT programs transfer less than 10 percent of the minimum average household expenditure among those living in extreme poverty (Gaia, 2010; Stampini & Tornarolli, 2012). Since initial implementation, there have been no adjustments for inflation or other factors, such as employment, income, or family size. So constituted, Guatemala's CCT programs represent a "minimalist" initiative (Gaia, 2010). They do not address unequal political-economic structures or ensure the "supply-side" adequacy of the social welfare and public health functions that CCT programs are designed to increase demand for. Against this background, we now turn to ethnographic data to describe the on-the-ground activities of and ideologies promoted by CCTs.

HEALTHCARE INFRASTRUCTURE IN SAN LUCAS TOLIMÁN

The ethnographic data herein are based on participant observation conducted in the municipality of San Lucas Tolimán, where we have collectively nearly two decades of experience working with health promoters and rural health programs in a variety of clinical and administrative capacities. San Lucas Tolimán is in the majority indigenous department of Sololá, which has been prioritized for CCT programs since their inception in Guatemala in 2008. Reflecting this timeline, our observations in the present chapter are informed by field experiences between 2009 and 2011, which correspond to the peak years of CCT scale-up in the area. San Lucas Tolimán's CCT program is operated by a government-contracted NGO participating in PEC. The NGO offers a package of preventive health services to women and children at rural government-operated health posts and, every two months, administers cash transfers to women who arrive with required documentation of accessed health services and children's school attendance.

In parallel to the PEC NGO, an alternative network of twenty to thirty health promoters affiliated with the local Catholic mission runs a community health program serving most of San Lucas Tolimán's rural outlying settlements. These promoters are mostly women—mothers or grandmothers—and all are bilingual in Spanish and Kaqchikel Maya. For several decades, they have provided basic preventive and health education services. Although from diverse backgrounds, they have all participated in a three-year, peer-to-peer training program on community leadership, health promotion, and public health. A hospital in San Lucas Tolimán built by the local Catholic mission serves as a referral center for patients, and the hospital's physician and medical director clinically supervise the health promoter program. In the last five years, strong working relationships with other NGOs in Guatemala and international academic institutions have provided enhanced financing and operational support.

UNDERLYING IDEOLOGIES AND CRITIQUES OF CCTS

The Maternalization of Poverty

As MFP expanded throughout rural Guatemala in early 2009, a new health education poster appeared on the walls of health post waiting rooms in rural San Lucas Tolimán. Two mother-child dyads—cut out from stock images provided by the local PEC NGO—were juxtaposed on a large piece of colored cardstock: under the heading "Healthy Child" (*Niño Sano*) appeared a woman in form-fitting pants and blouse, effortlessly balancing a smiling child on her hip; next to this image was a Maya woman—identifiable as such by her traditional blouse and woven skirt—accompanied by an unhappy child, this time under the heading, "Sick Child" (*Niño Enfermo*).

Beyond obvious racialized bias about Maya women as inadequate mothers, the poster's incorporation of affect reflects a broader tendency within CCT programs to attribute children's health outcomes to the individual-level characteristics of mothers. The Maya woman—who in almost every rendition of the poster is wearing a generic blouse, suggesting that she is too poor to acquire a more expensive, hand-woven blouse that would represent her ethnic and geographic identity—displays a flat or depressed affect. The poster projects a technocratic view of Maya women as passive, inert, and unmotivated—perhaps unable—to act on behalf of their children's health: the ideal recipient of an aid package.

In contrast to this view, the local Kaqchikel Maya lexicon sharply underscores that depressed affect is the *result* of poverty rather than its cause. Rather than using the nominal "meb'a'," which denotes "poor" in standard Kaqchikel Maya, people from San Lucas Tolimán routinely complicate standard interpretations of poverty as a socioeconomic experience by referring to the extremely poor in their communities using the verb "-b'ison," which literally means, "to be sad." When we have asked for clarification of the usage of "nb'ison" (literally, "she is sad") in this context, our informants detail the particular social and financial circumstances—for example, an alcoholic or deceased husband, or being disowned by family members—that led to an individual or household's impoverishment.

The poster's reduction of ethnicity, socioeconomic class, and health outcomes to personal, individuated attributes, responsibilities, and affect elides the structural nature of poverty and inequality. It therefore constricts the range and scope of possible mechanisms to address poverty. The public assistance function of CCT programs delegates responsibility for achieving coverage and adequacy of social welfare functions, and for improvements in social welfare outcomes (including clinical and public health outcomes), to women *qua* mothers. Poverty and social welfare outcomes are thus rendered a private, maternal affair.

Scholars have developed this criticism of CCT (and the New Social Policy broadly) in other contexts as well. As Molyneux (2006) argues, CCT extends the focus of economic development policy to the level of the individual beneficiary, with the objective of individual "empowerment," read as "the acquisition of capabilities and changes in subjectivity that enable agency to be exercised" (p. 429). This discourse, in the end, devolves responsibilities to the individual, both for the management of social vulnerability (i.e., via accessing welfare services), as well as for potential improvements in social welfare outcomes. Despite this language of empowerment, since beneficiaries are often unable to extract themselves or other household members from the so-called "vicious cycle" of poverty, the status of CCT "beneficiary" is converted into a static social, economic and cultural category (Pantelić, 2011).

Here we dwell for a moment on the title of this chapter, "Mi Familia Pobreza." When CCT programs were first being rolled out in San Lucas Tolimán, substituting the active "Progresses" (My Family Progresses) for the nominal "Poverty" (My Family, Poverty), was a common joke among community leaders and health promoters. In light of the above discussion, what at first seemed just to be a cynical joke became a sociologically significant malapropism. CCT's beneficiaries are interpellated as developmental subjects because they are mothers, a role assumed both biologically and socially; because they have "families"—that is, children in specific age ranges; and, most importantly, because they belong to a rural class of people who, within Guatemala's logic of poverty management, are denominated as "living in conditions of ['extreme'] poverty" (Gaia, 2010; Presidencia de la República, 2008). Indeed, the phenomenological manifestations of MFP we have observed—impoverished Maya women standing in lines stretching out the door at rural health posts, waiting for the opportunity to prove their scrupulous fulfillment of various conditionalities—suggest that becoming and remaining a beneficiary of MFP requires that impoverished women assume and perform a role within a field of social relations that emphasizes their ongoing poverty. In this way, MFP solidifies women's experiences of caregiving and poverty into a stable, self-evident social class.

CCT programs also further perpetuate gender bias both by devolving all responsibility for child health to women as mothers and by reinforcing a discourse that marginalizes women's own welfare needs. Molyneux (2006), for example, argues that CCT programs in Mexico and Brazil render women a mere "conduit of [social] policy" (p. 439). In this view, CCT programs entail a differential "construction of need" (p. 438), treating children as citizens having needs and rights, capabilities, and life chances, and their mothers as simply having responsibilities—particularly, to ensure the welfare of their children and families. CCT programs thus essentialize women as mothers, first and foremost, in order to efficiently improve the social welfare outcomes of children.

This maternalist bias is evident in the language of the legal documents that serve as the basis for Guatemala's CCT programs. President Álvaro Colom's government created MFP under an executive order, which specified the program's original objectives as: "to improve the quality of life of families living in conditions of poverty; improve the levels of school attendance of children between six to fifteen years, and to protect the health and nutrition of children younger than six years and of pregnant and lactating women" (Presidencia de la República, 2008). In this executive order, women—the direct beneficiaries of MFP's cash transfers—are only specified as recipients of social welfare services that complement the program insofar as they assume the reproductive roles of promoting their children's wellbeing. Furthermore, as Colom's political opponents called for increased transparency around funding during MFP scale-up, continued justification of the program centered on "the necessity of elevating the levels of school attendance and to achieve the education and integral development during childhood and adolescence" (Presidencia de la República, 2009), with no mention of objectives of improving women's welfare outside the context of motherhood.

Similarly, President Otto Pérez Molina's government launched MFP's successor program, Mi Bono Seguro, as an initiative stemming from the Law for Healthy Maternity and the Thousand Days Initiative. The latter is an international infant and child nutrition program that defines conception to a child's second birthday as a critical period for the prevention of childhood malnutrition (MIDES, 2014; United Nations International Children's Emergency Fund [UNICEF], 2013; see also Colom, this volume). In these ways, Guatemala's CCT programs reflect broader legal and programmatic formations that institutionalize the historical biases of "maternal-child health" and "sexual and reproductive health" (Frenk, Gómez-Dantés, & Langer, 2012; Turshen, 1989). Women's social welfare and public health needs are reduced to the requirements of maternity and lactation, biosocial functions that are seen as deriving their value and importance from their role in ensuring the health, nutrition and developmental outcomes of infants and children.

FETISHIZATION AND CHILD MALNUTRITION

One afternoon, a group of health promoters from the alternative parish program mentioned above and I [SD] turned onto a street leading to the local PEC NGO health post in Chi'npe. There, we had planned to meet up with a senior parish health promoter, a middle-aged woman named Ya' Ab'äj, who had scheduled a series of home visits. Outside the door of the health post, twenty women stood with their young children in a line; one of the women, Sandy, the mother of a one-year-old boy with Down syndrome whom we planned to visit later that day, was chatting with our contact towards the front of the line. After a short exchange with Sandy, Ya' Ab'äj came to greet us. She reported that Sandy, like the other women, was waiting to have her son weighed to fulfill MFP conditionalities. Sandy was worried that she would miss her home appointment with us, and she was anxious for us to see her son because he seemed to have come down with a bad cold. She had asked Ya' Ab'äj if we would be willing to wait until she was finished with the "well-child checkup" and associated paperwork.

Sandy's concerns index a problematic dynamic inherent to CCT programs in Guatemala: the way outcomes are measured. In 2009-2010, the first large-scale, official evaluation of MFP was conducted. Some metrics reported in this evaluation are straightforward and align well with basic health and social objectives, such as vaccination coverage for children under 2 years of age (Gutiérrez, 2011a, 2011b, 2011d). At the same time, however, a disproportionately large amount of the evaluation is dedicated to other outcome measures which seem of dubious relevance, and which suggest a fetishization of techniques and procedures of aid.

For example, a principle outcome in this evaluation is beneficiary mothers' remembering to bring their children's "*carnet,*" a folded paper card used to track physical growth and document fulfillment of CCT conditionalities. The report identifies as especially problematic the failure of MFP to improve beneficiaries' utilization of the *carnet* (Gutiérrez, 2011a). It is concerned that failure to bring the *carnet* to visits may create future difficulties in assessing compliance with co-responsibilities, "for example, monitoring of growth" (Gutiérrez, 2011a, p. 37). Notably and ironically, however, during the same time period in which failure to bring paper registration cards to visits was identified as a concern, the report states that MFP had "no impact" (Gutiérrez, 2011b, p. 22) on the extremely high prevalence of stunting among beneficiaries' children. In fact, stunting among beneficiaries' children under two years increased from 50–59 percent to an astounding ~76–84 percent between 2009 and 2010 (Gutiérrez, 2011c).

In short, what matters to MFP and its evaluators, as evidenced by the fetishization of the *carnet,* is not good growth per se but, rather, good *monitoring* of growth. This is best reflected in how MFP beneficiaries and providers differentially approach monthly growth-monitoring sessions. At times, during routine social and clinical visits to patients, we have found houses empty, only to be informed by neighbors that the families we intended to see would be spending the day waiting in line at the health post not to get their children assessed, but *to have their carnets stamped* as proof that they are meeting the requirements for cash transfers. At the same time, we have observed health staff on multiple occasions refusing to examine visibly malnourished children if mothers do not bring the *carnet*.

In other words, as the preceding vignette and discussion illustrate, healthcare providers' preoccupation with growth supervision is not coupled to preoccupation about growth outcomes. In these cases, the *carnet,* originally intended to serve as a tool for monitoring child growth, becomes self-justifying and self-referential, and supplants and displaces the real and original concern for child health. This fetishization of a technical object betrays a bureaucratic, developmentalist prioritization of techniques of subjectivization over demonstrable improvements in social welfare outcomes—or, for that matter, the adequacy of the functions and services required to improve them (Scott-Smith, 2013; Vaux, 2001). Indeed, the so-called "well-child check up," the cornerstone of preventive care and surveillance for children, is reduced by PEC-funded and CCT-administering NGOs to little more than poorly performed, serial measurements of weight and height, accompanied by stamping of the *carnet*, and, unless precluded by rolling stockouts and personnel furloughs, administration of age-appropriate vaccines.

The critiques of CCTs outlined in this section—the maternalization of poverty, and fetishization of child health—are recognized and resisted by the alternative parish health promoter program of San Lucas Tolimán. We now turn to cases of how this group of health promoters engages with children with special needs to demonstrate how their work resists the effects of privatization of public health functions and, through a critical re-valuation of practices of caregiving, fills in the gaps and, per Salmaan Keshavjee's terminology (2014), the "blind spots" created by fetishized technologies of aid.

CAREGIVING, PRIVATIZATION AND HEALTH-SEEKING TACTICS

"Mothers of the Family" and "Special Children"

In November 2011, I [SD] sat with a group of health promoters as they took a short break after home visits in the community of Chi'npe. We had spent the last several hours visiting patients with "chronic diseases," a term which, until now, the program had used with reference to adults with noncommunicable diseases. However, in reviewing Chi'npe's list of patients with "chronic diseases," Ya' Ab'äj, the senior health promoter from the town, noted that their child malnutrition project had recently encountered several young children who were not responding appropriately to an otherwise successful targeted nutritional supplementation algorithm. As a health promoter employed simultaneously both by the parish health program and the local PEC/CCT NGO, Ya' Abäj expressed frustration that one of her most challenging malnutrition cases had been written off by local CCT administrators as falling outside their programmatic scope:

> I don't want anyone to think that I am not doing my work because some children, they require extra support, they require more visits to their home, and nobody pays attention to them. . . . As a mother (*madre de familia*), I understand the baby's mother, I go to weigh him anyway, but the doctor just took one look at the child and said, "Oh, he is just a 'special child,' we cannot help these cases." Now the baby's mother

> asks me, but her baby just keeps losing and losing weight . . . maybe we can help the baby's mother more through this [parish] program.

Several in the group nodded in agreement, and they took turns naming children from their own sectors who presented a similar challenge. One of the program's leaders added each one to the list of "chronic disease" patients from Chi'npe and, turning to me, asked, "Do you think we can help these special children (*niños especiales*)?"

Ya Ab'äj's use of *madre de familia* indexes a reappropriation of a set of values and practices that CCT programs in Guatemala have systematically instrumentalized and obscured from public scrutiny. As a mother herself, Ya' Ab'äj expresses solidarity in her attentiveness to the needs of mothers of "special children." Laying claim to her caregiving work *as a mother*, she applies the concerns of motherhood to her experience as a health promoter, thereby expanding caregiving's sphere of influence beyond the narrow field of play created by CCT programs, in which motherhood is reduced to a "private" affective domain in which one works out the "responsibilities" and "conditionalities" of the developmental subject. To the contrary, as Ya' Ab'äj insists, attentiveness, responsibility, responsiveness, and competence are core values that inform pro-social caregiving functions (Held, 2006; Tronto, 1993). Precisely *because she is a mother*, Ya' Ab'äj claims, she can protect, heal, nourish and empower the most vulnerable members of her society or community.

Furthermore, Ya' Ab'äj's usage demonstrates how motherhood—a subjectivity forged through private practices of caregiving—can become a political position. Her invocation of the concerns and values of caregiving permits the health promoters' identification of "special children" as a particularly vulnerable population requiring specialized attention. It implies a resistance to the technocratic, process-driven specializations of child growth monitoring that dominate the CCT environment—where some severe cases of child malnutrition now fall "outside the scope" of child health and nutrition programs. The PEC and CCT framework of contracting governmental functions to civil society perpetuates a necropolitical status quo: at best, "special children"—and the intensive caregiving practices required for their mere survival—are made invisible; at worst, these children are denied basic protections, rights and entitlements—they enjoy no "public" status, and their lives are rendered "disposable" (Giroux, 2008).

The example of Sandy, from the earlier anecdote, is critical here, since it further illustrates the necessary ambivalence and adaptive response of caregivers towards a social welfare system that has deemed their children's needs and wellbeing as "outside its scope." Sandy does not harbor any illusions in this regard, but she also does not retire helplessly to abandonment. Rather, she responds to her situation strategically, or in de Certeau's (2011) terms, "tactically"; that is, her actions are influenced, but not wholly determined, by the structures and rules of the health programs in her orbit. Sandy fulfills the growth monitoring and other "well-child checkup" conditionalities of the CCT program to remain a beneficiary, while at the same time pragmatically using her social capital to "shop around" and procure other healthcare services (see also Pezzia; Chary, this volume).

Sandy's tactics are novel in several ways. First, she continues to participate in the CCT program not as a healthcare consumer but rather as an entrepreneur. Having been already disappointed like many other mothers of "niños especiales," she does not rely on the CCT program to meet her son's complex needs. Rather, she participates—and has her *carnet* stamped—only as a means to secure ongoing access to income, however meager and intermittent. In literally the same moment, however, she secures access to "real" healthcare elsewhere. In seeking healthcare outside of the local PEC/CCT framework, she skillfully undermines the raison d'être of CCT programs—that is, increasing demand for PEC services—while cleverly securing the small cash benefit.

The Case of Danilo and Eufemia

Danilo is a nine-year-old boy from Chi'npe with malnutrition, profound developmental delay, and cerebral palsy. He was first brought to our attention by Ya' Ab'äj in 2011 as one of a dozen or so "special children" who had been denied participation in MFP. By the time we met Danilo and his mother, Eufemia, the boy was in the throes of severe malnutrition: his swallowing mechanism had become so weak and uncoordinated that he could not consume enough food to meet his caloric needs.

During this time, the local PEC/CCT team came to the home and weighed him with a portable hanging scale in the narrow doorway leading to the front room where Danilo and his parents shared a double bed. While doing so, the team warned Eufemia that they could not come to every single house to make sure eligible children complied with MFP's growth monitoring requirement, requesting instead that she make the trip to their health post in the future for check-ins. Eufemia corrected the team: her child was actually too old even to participate in the growth monitoring components of MFP; because of his severe malnutrition and growth restriction, the team had mistakenly assumed that he was young enough to qualify. Shrugging, as if to express relief that, by virtue of his age, Danilo was "outside their programmatic scope," the team quickly asked if there were any qualifying children in the home. Eufemia mentioned that her grandson was four years old and that, therefore, her daughter-in-law did qualify for MFP. The team turned their attention to this child, jotted down growth parameters, and quickly left, repeating their admonition to remember to show up for health post check-ins on their way out the door.

Danilo's dismissive abandonment by the PEC/CCT team—the only segment of the health system that could have reasonably and efficiently responded to his acute needs—is not unique. This social abandonment is part and parcel of the dynamics that underlie the subcontracting and privatization of social welfare services. The very nature of the subcontract drives a bureaucratic fetishization of contract deliverables—deliverables whose scope becomes increasingly and necessarily narrow due to the budgetary constraints imposed by cost-containment and efficiency. A "niño especial" like Danilo is the responsibility of no particular institution, and no public or private institution is held accountable for his health and welfare: he is associated with no measurable outcomes, no stamped *carnets*, and no "well-child checkups." At the same time, he is, from the standpoint of public health infrastructure, "covered," in that he pertains to a given subcontracted NGO's catchment area and therefore is also no longer the responsibility of any higher-level health institution either.

A few weeks after Ya' Ab'äj took us to see Danilo for the first time, she coordinated a follow-up visit. As the group of health promoters approached the dusty lot in front of the house, I [SD] could see Eufemia standing anxiously in the doorway waiting for us. Once inside, we realized the reason for her worry. After a recent episode of acute diarrhea, Danilo was gaunt from dehydration, his lips cracked and bloody. We explained to Eufemia that he needed to be hospitalized immediately. She wept as she explained that she had already called the social worker at a child sponsorship NGO in a nearby town that provided some support for Danilo. The social worker had arranged for transportation the following morning to be evaluated for placement of a feeding tube by a private gastroenterologist in Guatemala City who donated a few consultations a month to the NGO's clients.

I expressed my concern that it was very unlikely that such a medical procedure could be safely or successfully performed until Danilo was stabilized and rehydrated with hospital-level care and several weeks of nutritional rehabilitation. Eufemia thanked us profusely for our generosity and efforts to help her son, but explained that she preferred to pursue the opportunity to see the gastroenterologist. She told us that she was already prepared to leave the next morning for the appointment and that she would stay up all night feeding her son capfuls of oral rehydration solution, giving me the impression that she had done this many times before. As expected, however, on the following day, we learned that the gastroenterologist had refused to clear Danilo for the procedure and had sent him quickly back home.

Ya' Ab'äj and her team continued to provide support. On our next visit, we learned why Eufemia had been so insistent on visiting the gastroenterologist, even though hospitalization would have been more appropriate. She told us that, several months prior, she had had a conversation with her husband about Danilo's severe malnutrition. She became visibly agitated as she recounted her husband's response. He had told her that she was lazy and gullible, that she just didn't want to take care of Danilo anymore, and that she preferred to let unknown doctors in an unknown hospital perform an operation and kill him so that she would not be burdened by him anymore. Tears rolled off her cheeks onto the dirt floor as she dropped her gaze to the bed, where Danilo was sleeping quietly. "He is not a burden for me," she told us. "He is my baby. I love him. He keeps me company, even if he can't speak. He keeps me company, what would I do without him? I don't want him to suffer; I don't want him to die. I was afraid."

Noteworthy about these interactions with Eufemia is that she proves herself incredibly resourceful, capably navigating a landscape of competing social welfare and healthcare services. Like Sandy, she is able to identify points of social contact that she can mobilize to provide her son with access to services that are in very limited supply, and she effectively cobbles together a tenuous support network. Ultimately, however, this network—a parish health promoter program working in her community, a sponsorship NGO from a neighboring municipality, and a private physician in Guatemala City—is completely decentralized, and each component of her network demonstrates slightly competing interests. The result is a predictable failure in coordination mediated by a lack of mutual responsibility and responsiveness between potential caregiving partners. Despite each entity's competence within their corresponding domain of social welfare or healthcare services, their lack of coordination renders their collective action ineffective and grossly incompetent. As Eufemia gets desperate about Danilo's condition and feels increasingly isolated, she too becomes clumsy in selecting and deploying her tactics of caregiving. Rather than "shopping around" (i.e., availing herself of newer, more immediate offers of assistance) she insists on making her own decision, however ill-advised, and in spite of the availability of other competing offers of support.

When Eufemia's emotional abuse at the hands of her spouse is revealed, her sudden resoluteness becomes more intelligible. In a move analogous to the maternalization of poverty, Danilo's father devolves all responsibility to Eufemia for what she had previously understood as a shared or collaborative project—that is, ensuring the well-being of their children—while simultaneously freeing himself of accountability for Danilo's rapidly deteriorating condition. In accusing Eufemia of wishing ill on her son, Danilo's father also symbolically devalues her dedication and the immense effort required to meet their son's intensive caregiving needs, essentially making all of her work invisible. The techniques of privatization and the instrumentalization of motherhood are suddenly caricatured as grotesquely violent when deployed, ironically, in the traditionally private sphere of the home.

Two weeks after Danilo's failed gastroenterology appointment, Ya' Ab'äj's team finally was able to arrange for a consultation at a pediatric nutritional rehabilitation center. Danilo was admitted to the facility, where he stayed as an inpatient for nearly four months. The health promoters from Chi'npe arranged transportation for Danilo's parents to visit him every two weeks during his hospitalization. Upon discharge, Eufemia reported that Danilo's swallowing had become stronger and more coordinated. Ya' Ab'äj's new, biweekly logs for Chi'npe's "special children" confirmed that Danilo was able to continue gaining weight and was beginning to eat without assistance. The health promoters have since designated "Special Children" as a priority project.

CONCLUSION

This chapter provides a detailed reflection on the implementation of conditional cash transfers in Guatemala, which have proliferated rapidly through a semi-privatized scheme whereby programming and monitoring of CCT conditionalities are administered by NGOs. Our observations of CCT programs in one community, San Lucas Tolimán, underscore how these private-public partnerships shift the responsibility for societal welfare to women *qua* mothers. At the same time, they promote a fetishization of techniques of aid without meaningfully addressing poor child health outcomes in either political or economic terms. Additionally, and very importantly, under this mechanism, children with extraordinary medical needs are deemed outside the purview of the NGO's contract with the government and are increasingly abandoned.

These observations highlight one of the central dangers of implementing social welfare and public health functions through the private sector, whose agenda is increasingly defined by the government. As Maupin describes in this volume, the spectral interpenetration of government into NGO sector health services tends to move the entire civil society domain "to the right." This movement to the right is augmented and exacerbated by Guatemala's long history of political conservatism, which has also limited the spectrum of what is considered socially possible (see Colom, this volume). Prior to privatization, many civil sector organizations throughout rural Guatemala provided personalized and alternative services, which served as a critique of and response to deficiencies or particularities of governmental services. However, increasingly these NGOs are subcontractors; in other words, they *are* the government. In this way, CCT programs in Guatemala can be read as reinforcing the status quo, reducing the diversity of resources and opinions that operate within the rural healthcare landscape. These dynamics also provide some explanation for the current considerable enthusiasm for CCT and similar programs by oligarchical institutions in Guatemala, because they allow a re-entrenchment of old conservative values under a nonthreatening veneer (see Colom, this volume), helping to ensure that Guatemala remains a "not-so-neo neoliberal state," to use Ferguson's (2010) formulation in describing South Africa.

The alternative parish health promoter program of San Lucas Tolimán offers a striking counterexample to our discussion of CCT programs. It illustrates that, in rural Guatemala, there still exists both political space and pressing need for alternative visions of civil society. Danilo's case in particular illuminates the latent opportunities within this sector for the elaboration of progressive, pro-social alternatives (cf. Ferguson, 2010; Ferguson, 2013). Here, health promoters sponsored by a private, Catholic charity provide extraordinary attention to "special children" and other members of their communities, resisting the effects of the privatization and bureaucratization of social welfare functions. Because the logic and grounded practices of caregiving govern the health promoters' community health programming, their approach to the provision of public health and social welfare functions remains thoroughly pro-social. Rather than counting *carnets* stamped and checkups performed, they visit sick individuals at home, arrange tertiary care referrals, and accompany patients and their families during long trips to specialty appointments. The health promoters lament the deaths of "niños especiales" who had received services through their child malnutrition and growth monitoring program, and when composing their annual report, the program's leaders include the deaths of "niños especiales" within the overall under-five mortality data, even though these have been the only childhood deaths registered in the program during the last several years. Each case is scrutinized as a sentinel death by the leadership committee, and the resultant dialogues are seen as opportunities to improve their capacity to fulfill public health functions. For the parish health promoters, fulfilling the needs of the most vulnerable individuals—especially those who fall outside the "scope of practice" of large-scale programs—takes on a vital urgency and primacy, becoming in essence a new definition for and challenge to the dominant paradigms of public health.

Fostering the growth and stability of the kinds of "networks of care" comprised by organizations like the rural health promoters of San Lucas Tolimán will require establishing and maintaining "translocal alliances" (Ferguson & Gupta, 2005), as evidenced by their collaborations with other NGOs and international institutions. This has, in some ways, been made possible by the flows of resources from Global North to Global South encouraged by healthcare privatization at a global scale (see also King, Chary, & Rohloff this volume). If such networks of care aspire to something more than haphazard responses to the lacunae in social welfare and public health functions—that is, if they are to thrive *in spite of* those lacunae, and ultimately transcend them—they must be able to tactically adapt and deploy the techniques and mechanisms of the regnant political economy, but also recognize the inherent limitations of such approaches.

More importantly, however, such networks of care must be able to posit and cultivate techniques and practices of a more humane and prosocial form of governance: one based on caregiving (Ferguson, 2010, 2013). In particularly, we propose that the value of the caregiving functions must be acknowledged and adequately compensated (Held, 2006; Tronto, 1993). Monetary valorization of caregiving functions is a pressing strategic intervention that must proceed, albeit cautiously at first, to correct the moral deficiencies of the deeply marketized status quo: this would entail, for example, recruiting especially skilled caregivers to serve as health promoters, and favorably compensating health promoters who demonstrate competence in these specialized, priority caregiving functions. These represent first steps towards working out pragmatic and effective programs that can mobilize the techniques, practices and values of caregiving to remake and build translocal communities where justice, care and other public goods take precedence over privatized interests in everyday moral economies.

NOTE

1. Given the lack of budgetary transparency in Guatemala, the source of this 272 million USD has been a source of considerable political controversy. Guatemala's budget for healthcare spending remains the lowest in Central America (World Bank, 2013). From 2008 to the peak CCT spending year of 2010, the MFP budget increased from 0.03 to 0.35 percent of the GDP, whereas public health spending only increased from 0.9 to 1.1 percent of GDP. In other words, one could argue that the CCT programs are symptomatic of misplaced funding priorities and of moving limited social welfare funds from one program to another. Indeed, in 2010, several vital public ministries, such as the Ministries of Public Finance and Agriculture received less funding than MFP (Benavides, 2013; World Bank, 2013). Another cynical but convincing explanation is that CCTs allow Guatemalan politicians to appropriate public funds to advance their own populist political careers, whenever the CCT mechanism can be manipulated to appear as a "gift" from the ruling political party.

THREE

Forced Motherhood in Guatemala

An Analysis of the Thousand Days Initiative

Alejandra Colom

In 2011, Eladia, a young Maya adolescent, sought services to begin the process to place her soon-to-be-born child up for adoption. A neighbor had raped her and Eladia had moved to another town to hide her pregnancy. She felt that her parents would never believe her story. Because her Spanish was rudimentary, an interpreter from a governmental office was requested to translate during her meeting with the social worker from the National Council for Adoptions. While the social worker stepped out to get some forms, the interpreter told Eladia that it was her duty to keep the child because "that was what women did." The interpreter also refused to translate those options that would allow Eladia to begin the adoption process as soon as she gave birth. Eladia left the session in tears. After giving birth, when she sought services to help her overcome trauma, she was offered counseling to help her "embrace her maternity."

(Excerpt from author's fieldnotes)

In Guatemala, one out of every five children is born to an adolescent female (Instituto Nacional de Estadística [INE], 2014).[1] According to Guatemala's Observatory of Reproductive Health (OSAR), between January and August 2014 alone more than 24,000 births were recorded among mothers under age twenty (Observatorio de Salud Sexual y Reproductiva [OSAR], 2014a). Of these, nearly 1,300 were mothers ages fourteen and younger, all of which indicate instances of statutory rape per legal definitions (OSAR, 2014b; Noticias Juridicas, 2013). Notably, these numbers reflect only those adolescents who sought public health services; many more go without healthcare altogether. Alarmingly, national surveys demonstrate that over the past ten years, the total fertility rate among female adolescents under sixteen has increased (INE, 2011a). These fertility trends are particularly salient in indigenous areas of Guatemala, where poverty, sexual violence, and the historical normalization of early unions drive adolescent females into motherhood, exacerbating their experiences of economic insecurity and low educational attainment (Population Council 2012, 2013).

In recent years, a variety of nongovernmental organizations (NGOs) have formed to promote gender equality and protect adolescent females from sexual violence, pregnancy, and its life-long consequences (Berger, 2006). Most of the energy behind these NGOs has come from an emerging civil society network—mostly female physicians, reproductive health professionals, and graduates of youth leadership programs. Some of these actors provide services such as legal counseling, education, or health for adolescent females, while others assume advocacy roles promoting the rule of law (e.g., Fundación Sobrevivientes, 2011; Mujeres Transformando el Mundo, 2014).

Such growing activism around reproductive rights in Guatemala reflects trends in Latin America more generally (Morgan & Roberts, 2012). However, in Guatemala, efforts to promote adolescent reproductive rights are continually undermined by a paternalistic and inefficient legal system, by the prevailing conservative ideologies of politically-influential elites, and by a disinterested private philanthropy sector. In this chapter, I juxtapose the progress made in favor of adolescents' reproductive rights with that of the Thousand Days Initiative (TDI), a global nutrition intervention that focuses on ensuring child health from fetal conception to two years of age. In 2012, the TDI was endorsed by the *Pacto Hambre Cero* (Zero Hunger Pact), a national plan to reduce childhood malnutrition, and was rapidly and enthusiastically embraced by elites, private businesses, and philanthropic foundations.

In my analysis, I highlight the role of private actors and institutions in promoting the TDI while remaining silent on the issue of adolescent sexual and reproductive rights. In Guatemala, a nation with one of the highest rates of income inequality in the world (World Bank, 2014a), elite families who control the most lucrative industries wield significant influence over the social development agenda. In recent years, in line with global trends, much of this control has been rebranded through the establishment of affiliated charitable foundations or corporate social responsibility (CSR) initiatives. As the Guatemalan state increasingly relies on the private sector to provide basic social welfare services, in line with neoliberal economic reforms and healthcare privatization (see this volume's introduction), it is increasingly important to pay attention to the politics promoted by these corporate entities. As I will explore, private-sector actors and institutions supporting the TDI promote an agenda that privileges the lives of infants and young children over those of adolescents like Eladia, who are conceptualized only as mothers or mothers-to-be, perpetuating a moral regime that reduces women, including young adolescents, to reproductive roles.

The contrasts between the marginalized struggles of adolescent rights advocates and private-sector foundations' championing of the TDI reflect what Morgan & Roberts (2012) refer to as "reproductive governance," or "the mechanisms through which different historical configurations of actors—such as state, religious, and international financial institutions, NGOs, and social movements—use legislative controls, economic inducements, moral injunctions, direct coercion, and ethical incitements to produce, monitor, and control reproductive behaviors and population practices" (p. 241). I argue that the TDI normalizes pregnancy among adolescent women, and its implementation through government and private-sector-endorsed programming gives its mother-centric agenda a significant competitive advantage over civil society programs that envision adolescents as rights-bearing subjects. Therefore, I extend the analytical focus of reproductive governance to include acts of omission (i.e., choosing to remain silence on adolescent reproductive rights). In the "zero-sum" limited-resources environment of aid discourse and private philanthropy, choosing to care for one issue can preclude caring for other issues.

Within this contested environment, reproductive rights advocates, such as those mentioned above, have recently developed the concept of "forced motherhood." This concept, which I explore throughout this chapter, signifies how adolescent females are coerced into motherhood. Forced motherhood captures local dynamics of reproductive governance, of which Eladia's case provides a direct example, where social service providers and presiding judges pressure victims into raising children born in a context of sexual violence. Forced motherhood is also promoted indirectly through the societal normalization of early unions and forced marriage, intimate partner violence, and limited access to information on reproductive rights and services (Max Agüero, del Valle Quinteros, & Angela Gálvez, 2004). This chapter foregrounds another indirect mechanism of forced motherhood: TDI programs that reduce adolescent females to a reproductive role. Indeed, by shifting limited funding resources, TDI programs paradoxically ensure that adolescents are only able to access reproductive health services by *already being pregnant.*

This chapter is based on a review of print and online materials of NGO and state programs focused on preventing early pregnancies in Guatemala, as well as government and CSR or philanthropic materials regarding strategies to combat chronic child malnutrition.[2] The review was complemented with semi-structured interviews with senior staff of NGOs tasked with protecting victims of sexual violence as well as leaders of proposed reforms to strengthen the legal framework to protect victims. Data were also gathered from attendance at and review of notes from meetings and working groups, including the Working Group to Prevent Early Pregnancies. The research also relies on ethnographic data from 120 young indigenous women, ages fifteen to twenty-six and representing seven Mayan language groups, who participated in reproductive rights workshops.[3] I focus specifically on the experiences of indigenous Maya adolescents in Guatemala, and henceforth, this is implicit wherever the word "adolescent" is used, unless noted to the contrary. Although some of the phenomena discussed in this paper are also relevant to the lives of poorer nonindigenous adolescents (Menjívar, 2011), the indigenous population is heavily and differentially affected, a phenomenon common throughout other Latin American countries as well (Comisión Económica para América Latina y el Caribe [CEPAL], 2011; Ishida, Stupp, Turcios-Ruiz, William, & Espinoza, 2012).

THE CONTEXT OF EARLY MOTHERHOOD IN GUATEMALA

Pregnant adolescents in Guatemala face a series of challenges concerning their health, education, and general wellbeing (Max Agüero, 2004; Colectiva por el Derecho a Decidir, n.d.). Despite growing awareness of the risks of early unions and pregnancies and their implications for women's quality of life as well as population health overall (Cleland, Conde-Agudelo Peterson, Ross, and Tsui, 2012), strategies to deal with adolescent pregnancy are not yet a priority. Interviews with young women and advocates for reproductive rights illustrate how, for adolescent females, marriage and pregnancy in rural indigenous areas are infused with varying degrees of coercion.

Julia is a twenty-one-year-old who I met through a community education program for young women. She does not plan to marry yet. This upsets her mother, Cecilia, who thinks that Julia will not be able to find a husband. Cecilia was married at age thirteen to a man ten years her senior. Julia recounts how her mother became a wife after being "stolen"—that is, raped—while returning from the corn mill. The perpetrator then went to Cecilia's parents' house to make the union official. Julia explained that, until recently, she had not associated the tradition of "stealing" females with sexual violence (see Forster, 1999 and Menjívar, 2011 for further discussion of "stealing" brides). "It still happens," she said, "and some parents accept giving their daughters away."

Julia was able to complete her secondary education through a scholarship. Her growing understanding of sexual violence transformed her perception of what forms of marriage are acceptable. She considers herself fortunate because her older siblings encouraged her to stay in school and her mother accepted her role as community health educator. Other participants that I interacted with in this and similar workshops corroborated Julia's story, explaining that early unions are still widely accepted, despite recent laws that establish unions or marriage with females fourteen and younger as statutory rape (Noticias Juridicas, 2013).

Marta, whom I met through a reproductive health education program, offered additional insight into the lived experiences of rural adolescent females. She laughed as she told me how she was considered an "old maid" in her community because she was sixteen and not yet married. "Older women say my boyfriend is a fool for waiting for me, that he should choose a thirteen year old because she is still innocent. They say I know too much already." Marta's family urged her to move to her boyfriend's house and make the union official, and she acquiesced a few months after sharing the "old maid" story with me. She became pregnant shortly afterwards, but continued to participate in the education program until her pregnancy showed and her mother-in-law insisted that she stay home.

Another participant, Sarah, refused to marry her boyfriend even though they had been together for over three years. She explained that she would not make the union official, because, "as long as we are not officially together I am free to pursue my education and work [as a community health educator]. I love Miguel and I like his family, but as soon as we go through a ceremony, the pressure to stay home and become pregnant starts." Sarah's self-awareness and resistance to marriage, however, are exceptional. An ongoing study by OSAR (M. Montenegro, personal communication, September 26 2014) reveals that adolescent females as young as fourteen accept pregnancy as their "destiny."

Preliminary research shows that the pressure to enter a union is more severe in poor communities (Population Council, 2013); a common justification is that "[in my husband's house] they feed me. " Personal accounts from participants in Population Council's *Abriendo Oportunidades* (Opening Opportunities) program for rural adolescent females revealed that those living in extreme poverty felt pressure to marry as early as ages twelve or thirteen (Population Council, 2012). Indeed, the role of poverty and lack of opportunity in influencing the decision to marry casts doubt on the primary significance of indigenous "culture," which is often blamed for the phenomenon in popular national discourse.

Compounding the social and environmental factors that draw adolescent females into early unions and motherhood is the lack of information for those who are interested in learning more about their bodies. Although systematic research evidence is lacking, my experiences listening to the stories of hundreds of young women in reproductive health classes reinforces that family members and community members do not discuss sexual intercourse and reproductive health with girls and adolescents. The subject is taboo, and young women are generally left to "figure it out" on their own. In 2010, the Ministries of Health and Education signed an agreement to promote sexual education and the promotion of sexual and reproductive health (Red de Jóvenes para la Incidencia Política [REDLAC], n.d.). Under the agreement, the MOH established "adolescent-friendly" spaces within public clinics, where free reproductive health information and services could be provided. However, most of these clinics were located in urban areas, limiting their relevance to rural adolescents. More importantly, the Ministry of Education delayed implementing its portion of the agreement, which was to integrate a sexuality curriculum into public schools. As of 2014, despite considerable pressure by reproductive rights groups, the curriculum has still not been deployed.

These omissions are paired with a lack of educational opportunities for adolescent females from rural communities. A study commissioned by Plan International revealed that between 2007 and 2011, the Guatemalan government invested an average of US$204.29 per year per child, well below neighboring Mexico (US$ 881.20) and Honduras (US$343.30) (Plan International, 2013). Such limited allocation of resources translates to high rates of school dropout among the poor, who also preferentially invest in sending their sons to school rather than their daughters. Indeed, only 41 percent of fifteen-year-old rural adolescent females in Guatemala are enrolled in school (United States Agency for International Development [USAID], 2014).

Finally, adolescent females also face a legal system that continues to minimize the trauma of sexual violence in favor of a focus on the virtues and benefits of maternity. Advocates I interviewed shared many anecdotes like Eladia's. For example, Judith, the director of an NGO charged with leading legal cases against perpetrators of sexual violence, related one adolescent's encounter with the judicial system: "After the judge heard the case [of rape and incest], he approached the victim, this young twelve-year old. He touched her belly and said that the child was a gift from God. That all children, despite how they were conceived, were gifts from God." Even when victims receive legal support, they are often admonished to "assume" their roles as mothers by breastfeeding and giving up their education to care full-time for their child. As Clara, an expert on gender-based violence working for an international NGO, explained:

> Many [raped adolescent] females are forced to breastfeed [their babies], something that is difficult even among adult women who chose to become pregnant. These [adolescents] are forced to become adults and behave as expected by others. They are not given a choice, even when the pregnancy resulted from rape. They are not allowed to decide over their bodies or their lives.

In these ways, the judicial sector fails to respond to its mandate to prevent adolescent pregnancy and to provide care to young victims of violence, which, by law, should include provision of appropriate shelter, medical and psychological care, competent legal representation, and sustainable strategies for reintegration to their communities. Instead, state actors and institutions enact reproductive governance by both directly and indirectly coercing adolescent females into motherhood.

ADVOCACY PERSPECTIVES ON EARLY MOTHERHOOD

Representatives of adolescents' rights advocacy organizations enumerate numerous critiques of public efforts to protect adolescents from sexual violence and to prevent pregnancies. In the past five years, as these issues have received broader media coverage, in part due to efforts of the Observatory of Reproductive Health (OSAR, 2014c), two major initiatives have emerged. First, the government campaign "*Protégeme del Embarazo*" (Protect me from Pregnancy, PROTEGEME), promoted by the United Nations Population Fund, NGOs, and civil society groups (United Nations Population Fund [UNFPA], 2013), has increased awareness of the prevalence of early pregnancies among adolescents younger than fourteen. PROTEGEME includes practical guidance for what legal route should be followed when pregnancies in females under fourteen are identified, and it spurred the Ministry of Social Development to prepare a comprehensive plan to help adolescent females plan their lives after giving birth. However, according to members of the Working Group to Prevent Early Pregnancy, this plan has not yet been implemented, meaning that there are still no government actions to ensure that adolescent mothers continue their education and acquire job skills. Second, in 2013, the government of Guatemala, with the support of PROTEGEME champions, launched the National Plan to Prevent Pregnancies among Females and Adolescents (PLANEA). This program focuses on improving the quality and accessibility of adolescent-friendly health services in municipalities with the highest rates of adolescent pregnancy. However, these services are mostly located in large municipal centers, which are out of reach for the most vulnerable populations because of the cost of transportation as well as indigenous language barriers (Office for the Defense of Indigenous Women, 2014).

Advocates also assert that the problem of forced motherhood remains unrecognized among legal institutions. Because of stigma and limited access to services and information, the majority of adolescent victims of sexual violence do not come to the attention of legal authorities until they seek obstetrical health services, usually very close to giving birth. Activists also report that relatives hesitate to seek legal help because prosecuting threatens "family stability" and may represent the loss of income to the family when the perpetrator is the sole breadwinner. In a similar vein, the legal system often attempts to quickly reintegrate victims of sexual violence and their children into their families, resulting in new potential forms of marginalization or violence. Karla, the director of an NGO dealing with adolescent rights, asserted that most judges lack a rights-based approach to legal decisions and feel that victims and their children will be "better off" with their relatives: "Current policies to ensure 'family preservation' are completely out of context when violence against females begins in the family itself. These may work well in countries like Norway, but not in Guatemala." Lastly, as described above, government employees often coerce adolescents into raising their children. In response to activists' request for clarification from the Attorney General's Office (Procuraduría General de la Nación, PGN) concerning their role in protecting pregnant adolescents, the PGN only elaborated on its responsibility towards the unborn child, emphasizing laws that criminalize abortion, and making no mention whatsoever of the rights of the adolescents (Procuraduría General de la Nación, 2014).

Frustration with the lack of sexual education curriculum in public schools is another constant topic of discussion among reproductive rights advocates and activists. Margarita, an NGO staff member remarked:

> Public entities should help to dispel myths [that reinforce early pregnancies] but many times they perpetuate them. Their contribution [to the status quo] is not always visible but by not educating the population, by not doing what they are supposed to, they become accomplices. For example, the Ministry of Education, by not providing comprehensive sexuality and reproduction lay education, are fomenting the patriarchy in this country. They transform motherhood into something sublime, something all women should want [. . .] They encourage motherhood and then don't even offer good health services during pregnancy.

Indeed, the official statements of high-ranking public officials routinely reinforce the notion that women are valuable primarily because of their reproductive role. For example, at the commemoration of the Day to Prevent Adolescent Pregnancies, on September 26, 2014, Vice-President Roxana Baldetti exhorted adolescents to "take care of your body, which is a temple, and the womb, a gift from God." In contrast, as Alicia, a journalist and reproductive rights activist, described: "What matters is what a girl wants, without pressure. You have to ask, how many are pressured [into marriage and motherhood] and how many are not? They may be conditioned more than consented. I sometimes wonder if all grandmothers were raped [by their husbands]."

Today, the National Council for Adoptions (CNA) is the only public entity that provides specific services for young women uncertain about their desire to become mothers. Social workers at the CNA offer counseling to "women conflicted about motherhood" (*mujeres en conflicto con la maternidad*), but this service is only offered to women eighteen and older. Underage adolescents can only access CNA's services if they are accompanied by a parent or tutor. Similar to the position of most judges, CNA staffers usually favor "family preservation." This means that they will often try to convince pregnant adolescents to keep and raise their child, regardless of the conditions under which the child was conceived. Alicia commented about this situation:

> There is an article in the Adoption Law that talks about conflicted motherhood, but this is element is not really addressed. If the CNA did, they would have so much work! The topic is invisible to them. In people's minds, the rights of adolescent females as women do not exist. People argue for the rights of the newborn but not for that of the mother. . . . Besides, the adoption law was created not because they saw a problem in Guatemala, but to end corruption among attorneys who were involved in human trafficking. This [form] of trafficking was often the only alternative to women forced into pregnancy.

In summary, all activists interviewed agreed that weaknesses in the public system are aggravated by social norms that perpetuate a woman's reproductive role as her sole purpose in life. Healthcare is provided to women because they are or will become mothers and not because it is seen as their own inalienable right. Activists saw themselves as a clear minority, because they opposed traditional views of women and challenged a system that explicitly and implicitly imposes motherhood upon women, advancing an alternative politics of reproductive governance to that of the state and conservative civil society interests.

THE ZERO HUNGER PACT AND THE THOUSAND DAYS INITIATIVE

On December 7, 2010, Guatemala became the fourth country in the world to join the Scaling Up Nutrition (SUN) Movement (SUN, 2014), an effort to reduce malnutrition and hunger around the world. SUN is part of a worldwide trend focusing on malnutrition as a key concept for development. Indeed, the amount of development funds for malnutrition worldwide increased 60 percent between 2008 and 2011 (Gillespie et al., 2013). In February 2012, one month after taking office, the government of President Otto Pérez Molina launched the *Pacto Hambre Cero* (Zero Hunger Pact). The *Pacto* was modeled after Brazil's Zero Hunger Campaign (Gillespie et. al., 2013). It was covered heavily by the media and enjoyed immediate public endorsement by the private business sector.

The SUN movement and Guatemala's *Pacto* rely heavily on a marketing framework known as the "Thousand Days Initiative" which was developed by a consortium of international NGOs, consulting firms, and private foundations and companies (Thousand Days, 2014). The TDI is inherently child-focused, since the "thousand days" that are referred to begin at the time of fetal conception and end with the child's second birthday. Within this malnutrition- and child-centric framework, the approach to the woman is necessary instrumentalist. She is provided with nutrition and medical care while pregnant, lactating, and rearing her infant—all in order to guarantee the health of the infant.

The principal legislative text detailing the *Pacto* exhorts all Guatemalans to confront "the immediate causes behind [malnutrition] as well as its structural roots such as poverty and the absence of development"—problems that are "fundamentally rural, indigenous and female" (Government of Guatemala [GOG], 2012, p. 8). Despite these claims, strategies to implement the *Pacto* do not substantially differ from the long-standing package of maternal-child healthcare services offered through the MOH's Program for Expansion of Coverage (PEC). As described by Maupin in this volume, through PEC, the MOH contracts NGOs to offer prenatal care, infant complementary nutrition supplements, and child vaccination in regions with otherwise low public sector healthcare coverage. Implementation and scale-up of the *Pacto* has occurred in large part through PEC NGOs operating conditional cash transfer programs, which incentivize women to access these basic services in exchange for small cash stipends. This mechanism of healthcare delivery, as critiqued by Dasgupta-Tsikinas and Wise in this volume, privileges children's welfare over that of their mothers and attends to the health needs of women only if they are mothers.

The TDI's underlying philosophy contrasts sharply with the alternative woman-centric advocacy perspectives outlined above. Mentions of women's lives beyond the Thousand Days are cursory. Indeed, the foundational *Pacto* document tucks all references to reproductive health and adolescents into the back of the document within Annex 1, under "areas of work." Reproductive health and birth spacing are subsumed under the "prevention and reduction of reproductive risk, and attention to infants" (GOG, 2012). Adolescents as a specific population are monitored and evaluated to ensure the "strengthening of basic [infant] health and nutrition services" (GOG, 2012). Education of women is included to foster "communication for development and the building of support networks" (GOG, 2012). Relegating adolescent reproductive rights and needs to an annex contradicts evidence that two of the most robust predictors of reducing malnutrition worldwide are secondary education for females and reductions in fertility (Gillespie et.al. 2013).

In this context, the launch of the *Pacto* within a TDI framework, and its heavy endorsement by private for-profit enterprise, provide an important snapshot of the current landscape of Guatemalan philanthropy. Numerous highly visible endorsements for the *Pacto* were provided both from prominent individual entrepreneurs and companies, as well as from the umbrella organization Fundación para el Desarrollo de Guatemala (FUNDESA, Foundation for the Development of Guatemala). The involvement of FUNDESA in the *Pacto* is worth detailed exploration. FUNDESA was founded in 1984 and is a trade organization comprised of some of the most powerful entrepreneurs in the country. According to its own documents, FUNDESA is "a non-profit private entity, formed by entrepreneurs. It works as a think tank to improve the development of the country in an integrated, sustainable and democratic way, in a market economy . . ." (Fundación para el Desarrollo de Guatemala [FUNDESA], 2015a, 2015b).

Shortly after the launch of the *Pacto*, FUNDESA emerged as a strong supporter, and quickly formed its own supporting initiative known as the Alliance for Nutrition, which sought to coordinate private sector responses to malnutrition (Mejoremos Guate, n.d.). Early members of the Alliance for Nutrition include some of the most powerful economic forces in Guatemala, including the foundation or CSR arms of Guatemala's most visible brands, such as the best-selling beer brand and the largest fast-food chain, as well as inputs from trade associations for the coffee, sugar, and nontraditional agricultural exports industries.[4] The Alliance was also endorsed by the Committee for the Coordination of Agricultural, Commercial, Industrial and Financial Associations (CACIF, *Comité Coordinador de Asociaciones Agrícolas, Comerciales, Industriales y Financieras*), a powerful and extremely politically conservative private sector player in recent Guatemalan political history, as well as key players from the export industry, small business associations, and megachurch and parachurch movements. Indeed, for the Alliance, malnutrition and the TDI framework became the social issue that "possessed the necessary characteristics to become the 'glue' that brings together all sectors to work together towards one goal" (Coperacha Nacional, 2012).

In its early conceptual work, the Alliance initially included among their 20 key actions a strategy for the prevention of early pregnancies, which included the promotion of adolescents' "life plans," or the establishment of educational and professional goals. However, this component did not make the final cut, and the ultimate strategy document only highlighted the TDI and the relevance of "prioritizing supplementary nutrition programs for women of fertile age" (Guatemaltecos Mejoremos Guatemala, 2012, p. 32). This omission mirrors that of the global SUN strategy itself. While the SUN's principles of engagement include a concession that interventions must "be rights-based" and "act in line with a commitment to uphold the equity and rights of all women, men and their children" (SUN, 2012), its actual strategic focus is decidedly "mother-centric" with repeated emphases on reducing low birth weight, stunting in children, and improving nutrition during pregnancy. There is no mention of improving access to other women's health services that do not directly benefit the fetus or child, such as contraception and family planning services (SUN, 2012). Indeed, a review of all the major corporate philanthropic initiatives included in the Alliance revealed that, with the exception of the Fundación Juan Bautista Gutierrez, which currently focuses on the promotion of abstinence (Fundación Juan Bautista Gutierrez, 2013), and Funcafé (Funcafé, 2014), none of the signatories of the *Alianza* are or have ever been involved in any efforts associated with reproductive rights and prevention of sexual violence and early pregnancies, nor are they partners of any of the principal actors in this movement. Additionally, the leaders of these organizations consistently oppose the implementation of sexual education curricula throughout public schools in Guatemala.

These endorsements by major private sector players succeeded in placing chronic malnutrition and, critically, these organizations' own discourse of development at the center of media attention. In this vein, one prominent Guatemalan entrepreneur organized an initiative called "I have something to give" (*Tengo algo que dar*), a weekend "awareness" field-trip activity to communities plagued by chronic malnutrition (Coperacha Nacional, 2012), for which more than 6,000 participants signed up. Similarly, an "Expo of Nutritional Solutions" was held in Guatemala City where presenters, mostly representing the Alliance's own corporate initiatives, described their existing or planned efforts to reduce malnutrition in Guatemala. At the time of this publication, none of these private sector-led efforts within the Alliance had been independently evaluated, nor had their findings been published in peer-reviewed sources, which is an important limitation identified also by Gillespie et al. (2013) in their extensive review of private sector participation in the SUN effort worldwide.

In summary, a thorough review of TDI, *Pacto*, and Alliance documents reveals a total absence of a differentiated approach to addressing pregnant adolescent females and young mothers, despite the fact that a very large proportion of the target population of the TDI are in fact adolescents (OSAR, 2014b). Just as legal and public sector efforts to address early pregnancies still struggle to incorporate the wider context of sexual violence and adolescent females' rights into their strategy, so also the TDI assumes that chronic malnutrition is a problem that can be addressed by monitoring the mother, therefore isolating the problem from its context of poverty and divorcing women from their individual rights. The TDI and the general language of the *Pacto* assume that all potential beneficiaries of the program *choose* to become mothers, which exacerbates the already established social context of forced motherhood. TDI nutritional programs continue to emphasize the role of women as good mothers, and those who do not fulfill these expectations are chastised when they come to the clinic, as Dasgupta-Tsikinas and Wise detail in this volume.

In these ways, the TDI serves as a mechanism of reproductive governance—a point not lost on NGOs and activists engaged in addressing sexual violence and adolescent pregnancy. Indeed, adolescent rights activists reacted with concern to the launching of the TDI and massive media attention that essentially framed chronic malnutrition as *the* single most important national issue. Interviewees found especially problematic the fact that the various TDI initiatives failed to account for age- and context-specific factors in the promotion of indigenous adolescent females' rights, thereby allowing powerful institutions to "normalize" pregnancy among adolescent females and perpetuate forced motherhood among rural indigenous women.

CONCLUSION

This chapter has explored the contested terrain of reproductive governance in Guatemala. Public, private, and nongovernmental institutions have competing visions of women's reproductive rights and reproduction, and due to the power imbalances between and unequal political influence of these institutions, forced motherhood is normative. The public sector, through a patriarchal legal system and under-resourced educational and health systems, has long played a dominant role in controlling reproductive behaviors in Guatemala (Carey Jr., 2014; Forster, 1999), and it continues to curtail reproductive freedoms and coerce women into motherhood today. At the same time, in the context of neoliberal economic policies emphasizing privatization of social services, the private sector has come to participate in reproductive governance in significant ways. On the one hand, a small group of nongovernmental advocacy organizations has mobilized to champion a "woman-centric" perspective promoting adolescent females' rights to safety, health, and education. On the other hand, as the SUN and TDI initiatives have captured the imagination of dominant private-sector stakeholders in Guatemala, they have reproduced a mother-centric approach to fighting chronic malnutrition. The private-public partnerships formed through corporate philanthropic initiatives related to the *Pacto* recapitulate broader trends in public health of employing women, as mothers, as the means for ensuring child health, while neglecting women's own needs (Chary, Dasgupta, Messmer, & Rohloff, 2011; Fassin, 2013; Moland & Blystad, 2009; Turshen, 1989; see also Dasgupta & Wise, this volume). Here, reproductive governance occurs through acts of omission: civil society and corporate philanthropy fail to conceptualize adolescent females beyond their reproductive roles. They maintain a traditional dichotomous approach of providing services either to (unmarried, childless) girls or to (pregnant, parenting) women. And, notably, these omissions and approaches are more powerful and have wider-reaching impacts than the laudable efforts of the relatively marginalized gender rights NGOs and activists. The mother-centric perspective dominates the healthcare landscape of Guatemala, and it enjoys both structural and financial advantages over the "woman-centric" approach, especially because the the *Pacto*/TDI has received generous financial backing from corporate philanthropy.

Fassin (2009), developing a theory of a "politics of life," or "how life and lives are treated in our world," proposes that "contemporary societies are characterized by the legitimacy they attach to life" (p. 44); certain lives are seen as more legitimate than others, and legitimacy is attributed only to certain types of suffering. In Guatemala, the suffering of adolescent females is negated and muted in favor of the suffering of chronically malnourished children, with private-sector philanthropy, in collaboration with other actors, deciding which lives are legitimate and which are not. The social development agenda is driven by whichever topics are the most palatable to a conservative elite. Indeed, the basic premises of the TDI fit well into existing corporate philanthropic policies and programs that have historically neglected reproductive rights and sexual and reproductive health education. In other words, endorsing the TDI did not require a revision of large-scale values and perceptions concerning sexual violence and rights among private sector leaders. Rather, it allowed organizations and individuals to rely on a discourse of children's rights as more morally urgent and more legitimate than those of the women that give birth to them. In an environment where advocates of adolescent females' rights are often advised to limit the use of the words sex, reproduction, and rights when promoting adolescent-centered programs—as I myself have been told to do—the TDI offered a palatable package where concern was instead shifted towards the future of unborn or young children.

Today, there are roughly one million rural adolescent females in Guatemala, and one third are currently pregnant or have at least one child (INE, 2011b). Many of these adolescents qualify for the TDI because they are poor and live in municipalities with high rates of chronic malnutrition. When a fifteen-year-old comes to a health clinic with her infant, it is easy and comfortable for healthcare staff in attendance to pay attention to the infant without recognizing that the mother herself is also a child worthy of special and individualized protection. At a bare minimum, we must ask, what would be the added benefit of providing age-specific services, tailored to the needs of this child-mother? Evidence from adolescent-centered programming and prevention programs support the feasibility of such an approach (Population Council, 2010; Population Council, 2011), and, in fact, the current Guatemalan legal framework at least on paper guarantees these age- and culturally-appropriate health services. Barriers to the effective implementation of such approaches are not only budgetary but also cultural. That is, they follow the dominant development discourse, which continues to emphasize women's reproductive roles while minimizing coercion and violence.

For the TDI, with its emphasis on chronic infant malnutrition, adolescent females are only relevant to society when they become pregnant. After dropping out of public education in early childhood, which is almost a statistical inevitability for an indigenous girl from a rural community, this child falls out of the public eye. She does not have access to educational opportunities, enrichment activities, or social outlets. Indeed, she becomes visible again, and "fundable" again, only by becoming pregnant. Focusing all societal efforts—both public and private—on pregnancy management and child malnutrition prevention, in the absence of also developing adequate sexual rights programs for young women, is akin to waiting expectantly for these adolescents to become pregnant. It is equivalent to planning for poverty.

Is it not worth asking what an alternative TDI would look like? The picture of an alternative is still incomplete due to a lack of coherent strategies that take into account the role of poverty in perpetuating the "customs" of early unions and adolescent motherhood. Mechanisms like PLANEA need to be well funded and coordinated. Decision makers at high governmental levels must be held accountable for providing access to information and services. A "thousand days" centered on adolescent females would require making secondary education, protection from violence, and compassionate health services available to this population segment. It would also mean acknowledging the right of adolescent females to choose whether and when they want to become mothers—that is, it would mean promoting "voluntary motherhood" (Lamas, 1997). The current TDI framework, on the other hand, improves the health of children through the erasure of women. In the case of adolescent mothers, this means erasing one child in favor of another.

NOTES

1. Throughout this chapter, the term "adolescent" is used to refer to adolescent females ages ten to nineteen, following the age range proposed by the World Health Organization.

2. The review and interviews were conducted with the support of two Anthropology students from Universidad del Valle de Guatemala (M. Ceballos and I. Figueroa). I am grateful for the time and interest shown by colleagues working on different aspects directly related to forced motherhood including S. Asturias, L. Caravantes, M. Chaguaceda, R. Cifuentes, S. Eiyadeh, C. Escobar-Sarti, D. Luna, M. Montenegro, N. Montoya, and O. Villalta.

3. I interacted with these adolescents and young women through my work with the Population Council from 2003–2004 and 2009–2014.

4. Some of the major signatories included the *Fundación Castillo Córdova* (CSR initiatve of the beer company *Cervecería Centroamericana)*, the Central American Beverage Company (*Cervecería Centroamericana*'s main competitor), *Funcafé* (CSR initiative of the regional coffee growers association), *Fundación Carlos F. Novella* (CSR branch of the largest cement company Cementos Progreso), *Fundación Juan Bautista Gutiérrez* (CSR branch of the fast-food chain Pollo Campero), *Fundazucar* (CSR branch of the sugar cane industry), and *Fundación Juan Francisco García Comparini* (CSR branch of the largest vegetables growing cooperative).

II

Commoditizing Care

FOUR

"This disease Is for those who can afford it"

Diabetes in Indigenous Maya Communities

David Flood and Peter Rohloff

Viviana is a fifty-three-year-old indigenous woman from Santiago Sacatepéquez, a Maya town a short bus ride west of Guatemala City. When Viviana was diagnosed with diabetes ten years ago, she first sought out care at the local government health center. However, the health center was unable to offer her a consistent supply of diabetes medicines and imposed severe dietary restrictions, including limiting her to just one half of a tortilla per meal. Viviana tried to follow this recommendation, but subsequently felt as though she were "growing weak" and "starving" as she normally ate five to six corn tortillas per meal as a dietary staple. When her health did not improve, she then visited numerous private biomedical and naturopathic clinics where she eventually spent down her cash savings. As she told us, "With a private doctor, you go just to spend money, money, money!" Viviana's diabetes continued to worsen, and her family took dramatic measures: Viviana's husband gave up his job to take care of her around the clock, and Viviana's daughter took out a large loan to sell goods in Guatemala City—only to be robbed on the bus and lose all of the merchandise. To pay off the loan, the family was forced to sell their beloved traditional Maya clothing. Although she hadn't previously considered herself poor, Viviana's search for adequate diabetes care impoverished her: "And that's how poverty came to me," Viviana summarized, "*Así me vino la pobreza.*"

This chapter explores the effects of privatization and medical pluralism in rural Guatemala on the experiences of people with diabetes like Viviana. Our perspective is informed by our work as clinicians with the non-governmental organization Wuqu' Kawoq I Maya Health Alliance, which operates a comprehensive medical program in the highlands of Guatemala. Since 2007, this program has served as a referral center for approximately 250 patients with severe diabetes and diabetes-related complications. Approximately 80 percent of our patients with diabetes are monolingual in the Mayan languages K'iche' or Kaqchikel. Using ethnographic data and our clinical experiences, we argue that the privatized, pluralistic Guatemalan healthcare landscape perpetuates the notion that medical care for people with diabetes is a luxury consumer good to be purchased *if one can afford it*. At the same time, however, the commodification of diabetes care fosters fragmentation, exploitation, and low levels of patients' biomedical understanding of diabetes to such a degree that quality treatment often cannot be purchased *even if one can afford it*.

THE GLOBAL AND LOCAL CONTEXT OF DIABETES

Diabetes is a disease defined by prolonged, abnormally high levels of blood sugar, which can cause severe health complications like heart attacks and strokes, kidney problems, blindness, and nerve damage.[1] Diabetes is a prototypical non-communicable disease (NCD) due to its long duration, slowly progressive natural history, and physiologic and behavioral risk factors such as obesity and low activity levels. The pathogenesis of diabetes is extremely complex and involves an interaction between genes and the environment.[2] NCDs, including diabetes, are the leading causes of death worldwide, and their burden is growing, especially in low- and middle-income countries (LMICs) like Guatemala (World Health Organization, 2011). Globally, four-fifths of the world's 380 million people with diabetes live in LMICs (International Diabetes Federation, 2013).

In Guatemala, studies suggest a rising diabetes prevalence rate that may exceed the prevalence in the U.S. (Barcelo et al., 2012; Danaei et al., 2011). In aggregate, the International Diabetes Federation estimates that there are 660,000 people with diabetes in Guatemala (International Diabetes Federation, 2013), a country which has a total population of approximately fifteen million. Additionally, many people with diabetes in Guatemala are undiagnosed or have uncontrolled disease (Pan American Health Organization, 2007), meaning that they have very high levels of blood sugar on a daily basis that predispose them to diabetes complications.

In rural indigenous communities, data are more limited but similarly suggest a rising diabetes burden. In our own clinical work in such communities, diabetes is one of the most common reasons for referral to our clinics (Chary, Greiner, Bowers, & Rohloff, 2012). Moreover, as Maya oral histories are an important contributory source to the historical record, the perception of our indigenous patients and colleagues that there are many more people with diabetes now than in the past merits attention. "Today, many people have diabetes," a sixty-year-old K'iche' Maya diabetic patient told us when commenting that her sisters and several neighbors also had recently been diagnosed with the disease. "Before, people were healthy. They worked hard until they were very old; they didn't have this illness."

Other lines of evidence also support the hypothesis that diabetes increasingly and disproportionately affects indigenous people in Guatemala. First, deep-rooted marginalization, high rates of poverty, and limited access to education and health resources contribute to a variety of health disparities for Maya populations (MSPAS, 2010). Second, indigenous people worldwide often have excess diabetes prevalence (Yu & Zinman, 2007) and diabetes complications (Naqshbandi, Harris, Esler, & Antwi-Nsiah, 2008) compared to corresponding non-indigenous groups. Third, studies in indigenous areas of Guatemala suggest that shifts away from traditional work patterns may be associated with higher diabetes and cardiovascular risk (Gregory, Dai, Ramirez-Zea, & Stein, 2007). Fourth, studies in the nascent field of the developmental origins of adult disease indicate a link between chronic child malnutrition—which is very common in Maya communities—and adult risk for diabetes (DeBoer et al., 2012). All these considerations lead us to conceptualize the emergence of diabetes in Guatemalan indigenous communities as a complex interaction of multiple social and biological factors, and not simply in terms of a straightforward "indigenous susceptibility" or a "thrifty gene" (Fee, 2006; Hu, 2011; Paradies, Montoya, & Fullerton, 2007).

Health system policy, practice, and privatization

Guatemala's highly privatized, fragmented, and inequitable health system, as described in this volume's introduction, significantly shapes the experiences of indigenous people with diabetes. The structure of the contemporary Guatemalan rural health system is a direct result of the 1996 Peace Accords, which ushered in the Program for Expansion of Coverage (PEC). PEC was devised to serve the specific mandate of rapid healthcare coverage expansion, and it has historically offered a "basic package" of services intended to be affordably delivered and readily scalable. PEC has largely provided preventative care for mothers and children, and importantly, does not address NCDs like diabetes despite profound shifts in the epidemiologic burden of these conditions.

On paper, the Guatemalan Ministry of Health (MOH) has developed a chronic disease action plan (MSPAS, n.d.-a) and clinical guidelines

(MSPAS, 2011) aimed at preventing and treating common NCDs in public facilities. However, on the ground, we have observed that quality public sector diabetes care in rural Guatemala is effectively unavailable. The majority of the MOH guidelines are not feasible due to minimal competencies of health providers and severe resource constraints. Typically, MOH facilities offer some free diabetes care, which consists of glucose monitoring and distribution of oral diabetes medicines. However, patients who live in outlying villages must travel to the health center in the municipal seat to access services. In addition, at MOH health centers, there tend to be long wait times, significant cultural and linguistic barriers, and frequent medicine and supply stock-outs. Other services recommended in MOH guidelines, such as measuring glycosylated hemoglobin,[3] screening for common diabetes complications, and treatment with insulin are usually only available in urban, tertiary-level hospitals.[4]

In the context of a structurally limited public-sector health system overwhelmed by the rapidly increasing diabetes burden, the majority of individuals in Guatemala seek diabetes care in the private sector. As described in this volume's introduction, the private health sector refers to the system of private biomedical clinics (for profit or not-for-profit), pharmaceutical manufacturing and sales, and non-biomedical care that has proliferated in Guatemala in recent years. We argue that this privatized health sector effectively serves as *the* healthcare system for indigenous people with diabetes rural Guatemala. To be clear, this is not a case of market-based healthcare supplanting an eroding public sector. Rather, the public sector has never provided meaningful chronic disease care in rural Guatemala, so prior to the emergence of the private sector, the only realistic option for diabetes care was, in fact, *no diabetes care at all.*

DIABETES CARE IN AN ERA OF PRIVATIZATION AND MEDICAL PLURALISM

We now turn to how the inadequacies of the public health system, the diversity of private providers, and the availability of a wide array of medicines figure into the experiences of people with diabetes in rural Guatemala. We begin by presenting the trajectories of four Maya individuals with diabetes.[5]

Paulina: Private providers and poly-pills

Paulina is a fifty-five-year-old indigenous woman from Tecpán, a bustling Kaqchikel Maya town in central Guatemala. She, her two daughters, and several extended family members operate a small home business selling tortillas and snacks along one of Tecpán's busiest roads. Paulina and her daughters self-identify as indigenous, wear indigenous clothing, and speak Kaqchikel fluently.

Paulina was diagnosed with diabetes in the mid-1980s. Like many rural Guatemalans, she attributes her illness to *susto*, or "fright," caused by severe trauma and violence experienced during the Guatemalan Civil War: "It was tremendous the fright that we had because of the war, and now with diabetes we are suffering the consequences." In the early 1980s, caught in the conflict between guerrillas and the military, Paulina's father was kidnapped and disappeared. Seeking safety, she and her family fled to Guatemala City as it was "no longer possible to live in Tecpán."

After moving back to Tecpán in the mid-1980s, Paulina developed frequent urination, dry mouth, and severe weight loss—classic symptoms of diabetes—which greatly impacted her ability to work and her quality of life. She visited a local practitioner, whom she characterizes as "like a *curandero*" (traditional healer), who tested her urine, diagnosed her with diabetes, and treated her with pharmaceuticals. Over several years, her sugar levels remained very high. She tried a few private and public clinics in Chimaltenango, but was dissatisfied with the quality of care and the cleanliness of the facilities. She reserved her harshest judgment for the local government health center. "They don't have anything; you just die there," she said. "I'm not interested in going there to waste my time and get angry for nothing."

It was at this point that Paulina learned about a diabetes program based at a public hospital near Antigua, a tourist hub about two hours away by bus. Over the next twenty years, she primarily sought care at this hospital, although she sometimes visited other providers whenever she "became desperate." For example, on two occasions she paid large sums of money to naturopathic providers who promised to cure her diabetes with "natural medicines." They threatened that the "chemical medicine" she was taking—referring to biomedical pharmaceuticals—would kill her. Later, when her diabetes worsened, she felt that "they had robbed my money."

Paulina was relatively satisfied with her care at the hospital in Antigua. The doctors were respectful, the consultations were free and lasted more than just a few minutes, and the clinic also offered visits with a nutritionist. However, she was prescribed medicines that were not freely dispensed at the hospital, and the costs were burdensome to her. She tried to make ends meet by selling more goods in her store, but she felt as though "the pharmacy was always taking the money from my pockets."

In 2013, Paulina's health acutely deteriorated when she suffered a stroke. Although she mostly recovered in the subsequent months, her diabetes continued to worsen and she was told she needed to purchase insulin, an expensive medication that further taxed her limited resources. Over the course of this diabetes exacerbation, Paulina sought out new biomedical providers and medications. One private physician suggested that to reduce her risk of having another stroke, she should purchase a boutique, brand-name combination pill that contained three individual components for treatment of blood pressure, blood clotting, and cholesterol. Paulina paid thirty USD each month for this medicine. She was unaware that the three individual components were generic and could be purchased separately for a total of approximately seven USD per month.

Although Paulina's diabetes treatment had always been very expensive, the total costs skyrocketed after her stroke. Each month, Paulina spent at least seventy-five USD out of pocket per month on consultations, insulin, medicines, and syringes.[6] She also accrued many indirect costs, spending several full days on buses and in waiting lines during trips out of town for diabetes consultations, specialty appointments, and pharmacy visits. A friend who often accompanied Paulina to appointments once joked, "Señora, this disease is *de lujo* (for those who can afford it)!"

In January 2014, Paulina heard about our diabetes clinic in Tecpán and paid us a visit. She told us that she had liquidated her store's inventory to pay for the costs of her treatments but could no longer afford to purchase medications or travel to her clinic appointments in Antigua. Her intake blood work with us indicated that her sugar was dangerously high. Moreover, although Paulina reported receiving formal biomedical instruction about diabetes from numerous providers and even had met with a nutritionist on several occasions over the many years, on our initial questioning, she had limited understanding of diabetes-related biomedical concepts such as the types of foods that would raise her blood sugar or the symptoms of low versus high blood sugar.

Juan: "In the consultations you pass rapidito*"*

Juan is a forty-three-year-old Kaqchikel-speaking man with diabetes. He lives in a rural settlement near Comalapa, a highland town, with his four young children and wife Cindy. Before he became very ill and could no longer work, Juan was a construction contractor. He and his family do not have any agricultural land holdings, so they need cash earnings to purchase food, pay for firewood, and meet other household needs. The family relies on small gifts from the local Catholic Church to make ends meet, and, when Cindy is not taking care of Juan, she tries to make money by washing clothing.

Juan remembers first having symptoms of abdominal pain and thirst at age thirty-five. Three years later, a private physician in Comalapa diagnosed him with diabetes. This physician prescribed metformin, an oral diabetes medication, and insisted that Juan purchase the medicine from his private pharmacy. The consultations and medicines were expensive, and, as Cindy remembers, "It became impossible because we could no longer pay the doctor and [buy] the medicine." Juan sought out lower drug prices at other private pharmacies in town, but due to financial constraints, he frequently went for long stretches without taking his medicines.

With only intermittent treatment, Juan experienced an acute diabetes crisis, likely diabetic coma, in which his sugar rose to such high levels that he became unconscious and was hospitalized for two weeks at a regional public hospital. There, Juan's family was required to care for him around the clock and pay for various items, including lab tests only available at an outside private laboratory. Juan was stabilized on insulin while in the hospital, but he still could not afford the prescribed diabetes medicines upon discharge.

Juan and Cindy attempted to engage with the government health center in Comalapa, but they encountered various barriers. On the few diabetes clinic days per month, patients needed to arrive by 4:00 a.m. to stand in a long line of patients waiting to be seen by a physician when the health center opened. Each consultation only lasted a few minutes. Diabetes medicines were free up to a limited quantity, but patients did not receive enough pills to last the month. For these reasons, Juan and his wife preferred intermittent appointments with a private doctor.

Subsequently, Juan developed cataracts and lost his vision. He traveled to Hospital San Rafael, a private charity hospital in Antigua, where he visited an ophthalmologist who insisted that Juan improve his diabetes control before performing cataract surgery. The ophthalmologist made an obligatory referral to a private clinic in Antigua, telling Juan that if he did not obtain care there, he could not continue seeking care at Hospital San Rafael. After several expensive consultations at the private clinic, the family was at the point of bankruptcy and decided to abandon this course of treatment. The following year, they heard of a large public hospital in Guatemala City where eye care was reportedly free. Over the next several months, they made approximately fifteen separate visits to the hospital from their home in rural Comalapa and paid for numerous tests out of pocket. Since Juan had developed severe diabetic nerve problems, he needed significant help from his wife, who told us: "He couldn't walk. What could I do? With effort, I could carry him." Despite these challenges, Juan eventually succeeded in getting cataract surgery.

Although Juan frequently visited multiple providers, he never received any formal education about diabetes. "Sometimes the doctors would say 'you can't eat this' or 'you can't eat that,'" Juan's wife relayed. "But in the consultations you pass *rapidito* (very quickly), so there isn't much time. They talk about the medicines and that's it." When diabetes education was offered during consultations, it was often rigid and impractical. For example, at the beginning of Juan's illness when he was still working in construction, one doctor told him that he could never eat more than two tortillas per meal. Juan found this advice impossible to follow and did not know what other foods to substitute. Additionally, when Juan and Cindy attempted to discuss biomedical issues about diabetes with their providers, such as whether diabetes was inherited, they felt no one ever took the time to answer their questions.

By the end of 2012, Juan and his family could no longer afford any biomedical care. Juan could barely eat, as his teeth had become eroded from dental infections. He could not get out of bed or use the bathroom without assistance. When he presented to our clinic, he had not been taking any diabetes medicine for over six months and weighed only seventy pounds.

Maria: Between the doctor and the naturopath

Maria is a sixty-year-old Kaqchikel-speaking woman from Comalapa who has had diabetes for almost twenty years. She says that when she was growing up, there wasn't much diabetes in Comalapa. "We had heard of it, but it's because of *susto* from the violence and the earthquake that there's so much more diabetes now."[7] For many years before coming to our clinic, Maria sought medical attention at pharmacies, where she would ask pharmacy staff for treatment recommendations. However, she did not consistently take medicines, both because she was unaware that the medications were meant to be taken daily, rather than just when she was feeling poorly, and because she at times could not afford them. Maria's intermittent diabetes treatment, driven by periodic interactions with pharmacy staff, sometimes had quite dangerous implications. For example, at one point, a pharmacist sold a vial of insulin to Maria's sister Telma, who is not a medical professional. Without any clear directions on proper insulin dosing, Telma injected Maria with a large quantity. Almost immediately, Maria developed the symptoms of severely low blood sugar—sweating, heart palpitations, and feeling as if she were going to die. Although Maria survived this insulin overdose, as a result of this experience she adamantly has resisted our recommendation to initiate insulin therapy under biomedical supervision.

Despite her hesitance to use insulin, Maria's diabetes control has significantly improved in our program with oral diabetes medicines and frequent home education visits. Home visits were particularly important as Maria initially told us that she did not understand what foods were best for her and that she received minimal social support from her family. Now, after home- and family-based educational sessions, Maria says that her two daughters remind her to take her medicines each day and help prepare meals more in line with her recommended diabetic diet.

Recently, at the urging of her husband and son, Maria informed us that in addition to seeing us, she had also visited a *naturista,* or naturopath, in Guatemala City. She was attracted to the idea of natural medicines due to concern that the "chemical medicines" (glibenclamide & metformin) that we had prescribed as biomedical practitioners caused many side effects, such as stomach upset. Additionally, Maria told us that she trusted naturopaths because natural medicines had helped her pass a kidney stone even when several biomedical providers told her that she had needed surgery.

The naturopath in Guatemala City advertised that he could cure diabetes with natural medicines. At the visit, he also warned Maria that she was taking a dangerously high dose of chemical medicine, and instead, he recommended six natural therapies that would not only "cure her diabetes" but also treat other ailments, including gastritis and high blood pressure, although Maria does not have either. These medicines were advertised as plant-based, but they were branded (*Diainella, Ginfer, Prolem, Dirbellida, Gastroprall,* and *Alegridad)* and were sold in capsule form. The total cost was fifty USD for a one-month supply, which the family paid using cash savings. Maria subsequently stopped taking her oral diabetes medicines. "You can't mix chemical medicine and natural medicine," she told us.

Six weeks later, Maria returned to our clinic and requested to be put back on metformin and glibenclamide because she could no longer afford her natural capsules. At this return visit, her blood sugar was much higher than it had been in the prior six months, suggesting that her diabetes had worsened significantly. Maria's interpretation was different from ours, however. She told us that she felt better after taking the natural medicines and that she was overall very content with the care received from the naturopath. Aware that we, as her biomedical providers, and the naturopath, have made contradictory statements about curability and treatment, Maria tells us that she does not know whom to believe: "The natural doctor says one thing; you say another thing." Maria states that she will most likely visit the naturopath again in the future, but, in the meantime, she continues to visit our clinic "because we're free."

Viviana: The diabetic Maya in the mall

Let us return to Viviana, the diabetes patient from Santiago Sacatepéquez whose case we introduced at the beginning of this chapter. Viviana first came to our diabetes clinic in 2008 after becoming impoverished while seeking diabetes treatment from multiple biomedical and natural providers. By 2011, after several years of regular medical care with our organization, Viviana's blood sugar, blood pressure, and kidney function all had stabilized for the first time since her diagnosis. However, at this point, she developed an infected foot ulcer, a common complication of longstanding diabetes, which required hospitalization for the initial treatment course. While admitted to a large public hospital, Viviana was recruited by her physician to complete her post-discharge follow-up care in his private diabetes clinic, located inside of one of Guatemala City's largest, most upscale shopping malls. Soon, Viviana's family was taking her to appointments every two weeks in this clinic where they paid roughly thirty-five USD for each consultation. Viviana's new physician immediately decided to convert all of her generic diabetes prescriptions to brand-name alternatives at an additional out-of-pocket cost of 150 USD per month.

When we saw Viviana again, several weeks after her hospital discharge, she told us that her daughter had mortgaged a piece of land in order to pay for these new medications and consultation costs. We asked her why she had not simply returned to our clinic after hospital discharge where she would have received—in our estimation—the same quality of biomedical care at no cost to her. She smiled and began to regale us with enthusiastic descriptions of the private clinic's marble floors, hot water and toilet installations, and marvelous high-rise views overlooking Guatemala City. Two months later, when the family ran out of cash, Viviana resumed her care at our clinic where we re-prescribed her generic medications. She did, however, express anxiety that her diabetes would worsen under our care since she doubted that medication that was "so cheap" could possibly be as good for her as the expensive, brand-name versions she had consumed for two months.[8]

DIABETES AND THE "NEW" MEDICAL PLURALISM

Paulina, Juan, Maria, and Viviana are victims and beneficiaries of what this volume refers to as the "new" medical pluralism in Guatemala. As we argue below, two distinctive features make the healthcare resources and health-seeking behaviors for diabetes "new." First, as a chronic and progressive disease, diabetes requires new forms of patient engagement with the healthcare system. These include longitudinal patient-provider relationships, an emphasis on prevention, and the centrality of behavioral risk factors. Such features are paradigmatic of the transition away from the "old" system of acute, episodic disease management, which still represents the primary disease management strategy of the public system. Second, the convergence of rising out-of-pocket health spending and novel health resources (both biomedical and non-biomedical) creates a vibrant yet uncharted private healthcare market where people with diabetes seek to purchase good health. The structural particularities of this diabetes market and the chronic, progressive nature of diabetes have profound effects on the trajectories of individuals seeking care. The themes of high costs, naturopathic consultations, fragmentation, and limited patient education that arise from these vignettes help underscore how privatization and medical pluralism are rapidly changing the nature of diabetes care in rural Guatemala.

Costs

Indigenous people in Guatemala with diabetes seek out certain treatments and eschew others in part due to the high cost of diabetes care, which include both direct as well as indirect costs (Barcelo, Aedo, Rajpathak, & Robles, 2003). For families dealing with diabetes, direct costs for biomedical and naturopathic consultations, treatments, and laboratory studies make up a considerable portion of household expenses. As Juan's case illustrates, indirect costs also can be consuming: Juan's inability to work, his wife's evolution into a primary (and unpaid) caregiver, and the family's foregone income are absolutely central to the experience of diabetes. Juan's hospitalization also demonstrates that the cost of treating a disease exacerbation can be especially catastrophic. Health insurance is not widely available in rural Guatemala, so catastrophic healthcare spending usually occurs out of pocket. One recent general health study estimated that 60 percent of poor Guatemalan households are exposed to catastrophic health expenditures each year (Bowser & Mahal, 2011). Viviana's experiences also indicate that a healthcare catastrophe can introduce elements of therapeutic uncertainty, where encounters with new care environments or providers can lead individuals and families to assume even higher costs once an acute episode is complete.

Any discussion of the cost of diabetes care in rural Guatemala must also address the issue of availability and affordability of diabetes pharmaceuticals on the private market. Essential biomedicines, including diabetes medicines, are unavailable or unaffordable in Guatemala and other LMICs (Anson, Ramay, Ruiz de Esparza, & Bero, 2012; Mendis et al., 2007), and our patients frequently tell us that the cost of biomedicines leads them to ration their own care (Chary et al., 2012). On a national level, overall expenditures on biomedicines are growing rapidly in Guatemala (U.S. Agency for International Development [USAID], 2008). Some individuals with diabetes that we have interacted with over the years question the very purpose of seeking biomedical clinical attention when the resulting medication prescriptions are prohibitively expensive. In many other settings, ethnographic inquiries have similarly highlighted unaffordable diabetes biomedicines as a problem frequently experienced by poor people (Awah, Unwin, & Phillimore, 2008; de-Graft Aikins, 2005; Whyte, 2014a). As an informant in a study in Tanzania summarized, "For someone who's rich, it's not a problem" (Kolling, Winkley, & von Deden, 2010). In Cambodia, supply-side barriers including limited access to treatments lead some people with diabetes to "wish they had AIDS," for which treatments are available through internationally-subsidized programs, instead of diabetes (Men, Meessen, van Pelt, Van Damme, & Lucas, 2012).

In our clinical roles teasing out medication histories from patients with diabetes, we have observed a conspicuous underutilization of low-cost generic medicines. In general, there is a dearth of publicly available information about the pharmaceutical sector in Guatemala. Guatemalan law enthusiastically protects the intellectual property of brand-name pharmaceuticals, thus limiting access to generics relative to neighboring countries (Godoy & Cerón, 2011). In fact, for some branded drugs like the long-acting insulin Lantus (insulin glargine), Guatemalan law will prohibit a generic version from entering the market even after the U.S. patent expires (Shaffer & Brenner, 2009). Even when generics are legally and readily available, questions arise about the competitiveness of the Guatemalan pharmaceutical market in bringing down prices, the quality of low-cost generic drugs, and the use of aggressive marketing strategies that encourage loyalty to "branded generics"[9] (Godoy, 2013). Recent accounts point to the ways in which business elites manipulate pharmaceutical industries to raise medicine prices, and the non-transparency of the government pharmaceutical acquisitions process that also may ultimately affect generic affordability and availability (Hernández, 2013; Hernández, 2014; Orozco & Rojas, 2013). Moreover, the intensity of activism for pro-generic government policies waned after the country's ratification of CAFTA in 2005. Since that time, as Angelina Snodgrass Godoy (2013) describes, much of the discourse on access to medicines has centered on individual patient petitions for high-cost, branded drugs within the social security health system, rather than on population-level access to off-patent essential medicines.

As Paulina's and Viviana's use of expensive branded medications illustrate, individuals are steered to higher-cost, non-generic drugs. In Viviana's case, as her biomedical providers, we believed that prescribing expensive, branded medicines added no therapeutic benefit above cheaper generic alternatives, but she wasn't so sure. The reluctance of Viviana and many other patients in our clinical program to take low-cost generic medicines suggests to us that the commodification of diabetes care leads to the assumption that higher-cost, branded products are, in fact, higher quality products. This notion of cost as a proxy for quality is also a prominent theme in Hall-Clifford's discussion of oral rehydration therapy (ORT) in this volume. As one of her informants eloquently summarizes, "Everyone wants them [expensive products] because not everyone can get them."

Naturopaths and Non-traditional Parapharmaceutical Products

Maria's case illustrates another important consideration regarding the care-seeking behaviors of indigenous people with diabetes. Although not well captured in official nationwide surveys, the non-biomedical health sector is vibrant in rural Guatemala and accessed very frequently. We use the term "non-biomedical" to refer a wide spectrum of healing modalities deemed "natural," in contrast to the pharmaceuticals commonly referenced by our patients as *medicina química* (chemical medicine). Within this spectrum, we have especially noted rising use of non-traditional parapharmaceutical products. An understudied topic in Guatemala, these products are distinct from traditional Maya ethnomedicinal practice as they tend to be nonlocal, highly processed, and aggressively marketed by a new class of professional or itinerant naturopaths. Sold on buses, at markets, and in health fairs or clinics, parapharmaceutical products are now ubiquitous in rural Guatemala. This finding has also been reported in Uganda's diabetes "therapeutic marketplace" (Whyte, 2014a).

Without more detailed ethnographic inquiry, we hesitate to offer a definitive analysis on the different factors that draw Maya people with diabetes to parapharmaceuticals. In clinical encounters, patients frequently tell us that they grow tired taking daily pharmaceuticals that have side effects and that they seek natural cures, a common theme in the cross-cultural diabetes literature (de-Graft Aikins, 2005; Kolling et al., 2010; Men et al., 2012; Rutebemberwa et al., 2013). It is possible that non-biomedical products appeal to a traditional heritage in the face of a "modern" disease like diabetes, as Ferzacca (2001) has written in his study of medical pluralism in Java. Studies in other countries have shown that people with diabetes seek non-biomedical treatments in part due to lower costs (Awah et al., 2008; Kolling et al., 2010; Rutebemberwa et al., 2013). In Guatemala, however, such products frequently cost more than biomedical treatments (Chary et al., 2012; Harvey, 2011; Nelson, 2013), although, as we describe above, these high prices may paradoxically increase their appeal. In our clinical roles, we have grown concerned that the parapharmaceutical industry takes advantage of indigenous health seekers like Maria.

Maria's case is not unique; many diabetes patients in our clinical programs use plant-based remedies dispensed by naturopaths. These practitioners do not offer herbal remedies in the same way that midwives, local healers (*curanderos*), or Maya spiritual leaders have traditionally prescribed teas and baths of locally available plants. Rather, most of the items we have seen are highly processed plant or animal extracts—such as St. John's wort, ginseng, ginkgo biloba, and royal bee jelly—usually packaged as capsules. Some of these products are manufactured in Guatemala, but many are imported from international markets, especially China and India. In towns where we manage diabetes patients, several well-established naturopathic practitioners operate their own clinics. Similar to Maria, many of our patients who also seek naturopathic care describe that their naturopaths have informed them that taking chemical medicine for long periods of time will eventually harm their body and will never cure their disease. Instead, the naturopaths encourage them to "stop taking chemicals" and switch to alternative products, which will "cure" them of their diabetes and are vended on the spot.

Fragmentation

Paulina, Juan, Maria, and Viviana's care has spanned a multitude of providers, including traditional and non-traditional naturopathic healers, private clinics, public health centers, charity hospitals, regional and national hospitals, religious groups, and private pharmacies. Their trajectories are disjointed and non-linear; they often have visited more than one provider at the same time, but, at other intervals, they have gone without any care at all. For the most part, none of their various competing providers ever spoke with one another. In this chapter, we use "fragmentation" to refer to this lack of coordination, communication, and unified decision making by those providers who care for a given person with diabetes. Fragmentation is particularly important in the context of chronic diseases like diabetes because quality biomedical care requires longitudinal interactions with multiple practitioners to assess clinical status, screen for and treat complications, provide education on behavioral and dietary risk factors, and monitor the effects of treatment.

Many prior studies of health-seeking behavior have described how medical pluralism and resource shopping are common among Maya people with various acute medical conditions such as diarrhea, respiratory infections, and obstetrical emergencies (see, for example, Berry, 2006; Cosminsky & Scrimshaw, 1980; Goldman & Heuveline, 2010). In the case of diabetes, Maya people similarly resource shop across multiple dimensions: among naturopathic and biomedical providers; within the biomedical sphere among health promoters, pharmacies, and physicians; and especially among physicians themselves, be they local or distant, public or private, or for profit or nonprofit (see also Chary, this volume). In general, we agree that the rural poor are particularly attracted to the "packaging that [biomedical] private care has to offer" (Molina & Palazuelos, 2014), which refers not only to claims of responsiveness, but also to the social status of receiving private care. However, such packaging generates vulnerability and fragmentation as it also supposes quality care is a good to be purchased, if it can be afforded.

While patients like Paulina, Juan, Maria, and Viviana superficially have many choices about where and with whom to seek care, they are restricted by many barriers including limitations in the expertise (Corral, Arnold, Argueta, Ganju, & Barnoya, 2012), affordability, and availability of providers. The significant disparity in the distribution of physicians in Guatemala—from between 1–3 per 10,000 people in most rural departments to 30 per 10,000 in Guatemala City (Universidad Rafael Landívar & Pan American Health Organization, 2009)—entails that only 16 percent of the poorest quintile of Guatemalans seek care from a physician or dentist during a given illness episode (Garcés de Marcilla del Valle & Garcés de Marcilla del Valle, 2008). As illustrated by Maria, many indigenous people with diabetes seek medical consultations at private pharmacies, where consultations are technically free though of poor quality (Kroeger et al., 2001).

Fragmentation emerges as a direct consequence of a privatized, patchwork diabetes market whose indigenous patients are poor, sick, and desperate. Nevertheless, facing many constraints to quality care, patients like Paulina and Juan display relentlessness and entrepreneurialism. They actively mold an imperfect, fragmented, and sometimes predatory health system into one that meets their vision and desire for quality chronic disease care.

Health education and market-driven diabetes care

A final dynamic that surfaces in our ethnographic data and clinical experience is the way that thoroughly commoditized diabetes care perpetuates low levels of disease-related biomedical understanding among indigenous people with diabetes. Patient education is a central component in the biomedical treatment of diabetes, particularly as it relates to encouraging behaviors that improve dietary intakes, increase physical activity, and promote adherence with medication regimens. However, despite the proliferation of biomedical services for diabetes in Guatemala, very few patients we encounter have received even the most minimal instruction from their providers about biomedical concepts of diabetes etiology and treatment strategies. Paulina, for example, was not aware of basic elements of a diabetic diet despite encounters with dozens of providers over a period of nearly thirty years. Her experience reflects broader trends about biomedical disease education among indigenous people with diabetes in Guatemala. As we've documented elsewhere, very few Maya with diabetes demonstrate understanding of long-term diabetes complications, disease chronicity, the hereditary component of diabetes, or the recommended diabetic diet (Chary et al., 2012).

At the most basic level, this means that biomedical diabetes care in Guatemala fails to establish a shared vocabulary or conception of disease that can unite providers and indigenous care seekers. Our observations echo experiences in other settings where the absence of culturally and linguistically sensitive biomedical care hinders health-seekers' adoption of biomedical paradigms of diabetes understanding and self-care behaviors (Bird, Wiles, Okalik, Kilabuk, & Egeland, 2008; de-Graft Aikins, Awuah, Pera, Mendez, & Ogedegbe, 2014; Hjelm & Mufunda, 2010; Tessaro, Smith, & Rye, 2005).

In Guatemala, we further hypothesize that with the rapid commodification and marketization ("buy this pill"; "pay this consult fee") of diabetes pharmaceuticals, there is no financial incentive to engage in education. Resource shopping, fragmentation, and the high cost of diabetes treatments exacerbate the problem. Individuals like Paulina rarely get to know a single provider well enough to engage in longer-term health discussions as they drop in and out of the care market as their finances allow. Such commodification is noticeable even in the naturopathic market in Guatemala. Although one might anticipate that naturopathic practitioners would be more focused on lifestyle, diet, and holistic wellbeing, they appear primarily concerned with positioning themselves in opposition to biomedicine while at the same time engaging in mimicry of the stereotypical biomedical "cure" through "natural" pills.

In some circumstances, however, opportunities for the formation of more durable alliances and the development of shared therapeutic language can emerge. In our own clinical programming, we have implemented an education initiative for all diabetes patients. A fluent Kaqchikel-speaking nurse educator carries out regular home visits to teach about diabetes using a biomedical curriculum we have specifically designed for highland Kaqchikel communities. Family members are encouraged to participate along with patients in these visits since they play a critical role in supporting self-care and coping behaviors. These strategies can be very effective in catalyzing new family dynamics. Paulina, for example, reminds her daughters, who have both developed diabetes and subsequently have entered our clinical program, about taking their diabetes pills each day. In turn, both daughters encourage Paulina to wake up earlier each morning to accompany them on a long walk.

CONCLUSION

The issue of diabetes in indigenous communities falls at the intersection of two critical transitions currently taking place in Guatemala: one epidemiologic—the inexorable rise in the burden of NCDs—and the other socio-political—rapidly increasing health system privatization. Our analysis begins with the observation that comprehensive, sustained biomedical care for diabetes is effectively unavailable for rural, indigenous populations. We argue that this situation is not straightforwardly a problem of attenuation and privatization of the public sector; quality NCD care in rural areas has *never* existed in the public sector. In this void, the privatized diabetes market has become the default healthcare system for indigenous people with diabetes, but not without consequences. The market-based system commodifies diabetes care into a consumer good to be purchased if one can pay for it, and generates distortions like fragmentation, exploitation, and limited biomedical understanding that inhibit quality outcomes even for those with resources.

Given the historical and political context in Guatemala and the stasis of government health budgets relative to gross domestic product (MSPAS, n.d.-b), we think it unlikely that the public sector will radically strengthen its rural NCD care in the coming years. Yet, diabetes already presents a public health emergency in Guatemala, and its burden will only continue to rise. Therefore, discussing the future of diabetes care for indigenous populations necessitates discussing the future of the private sector and working through the challenges that rural Maya people with diabetes encounter there. As we have shown, the consequences of increasing privatization and medical pluralism are not universally negative for indigenous patients seeking care for diabetes. Private providers may be less limited by unpredictable budget outlays and supply shortages that permanently cripple public health facilities. In the absence of sustained public-sector diabetes programming in rural areas, private care—despite its abundant shortcomings—is frequently the only healthcare option available.

How do such benefits of privatized diabetes care weigh against its trade-offs—heightened costs, care fragmentation and commoditization, and loss of a public health orientation toward prevention and behavior change? Privatization and pluralism require providers to compete along axes like responsiveness, friendliness, and professionalism—all features notably absent from the public health system. However, our ethnographic data and clinical experiences make us skeptical that these characteristics are adequate proxies for quality. Most alarmingly, as in the case of the underutilization of low-cost medicines, the private diabetes market opens up the possibility that higher cost will be perceived by patients as a major determinant of quality. Finally, although privatization and pluralism empower indigenous patients to seek care outside a failing public system, power gradients and information asymmetries make them vulnerable to predatory private providers, both biomedical and naturopathic. These are all urgent topics which future research and health advocacy work must address.

NOTES

1. Throughout this chapter, we use the term *diabetes* to refer to adult type II diabetes mellitus, which is the most common type of diabetes in rural Guatemala and around the world. Type 1 diabetes presents its own important challenges but will not be addressed here.

2. The biomedical literature often refers to Western "lifestyles" of high-calorie diets and reduced physical activity levels as shorthand for environmental risk factors. However, a vast literature implicates broad structural and social variables in increasing the risk of diabetes in indigenous populations. As an example, Wiedman's (2012) concept of "structural chronicities" emphasizes the historic forces giving rise to the diabetes epidemic on Native American reservations in Oklahoma.

3. Glycosylated hemoglobin, or hemoglobin A1C, is a blood test that indicates the average blood sugar of a diabetic over the most recent three months. This test is essential for high-quality clinical management of diabetes.

4. Diabetes care exists in other parallel government health systems in Guatemala, including the Guatemalan Social Security Institute (IGSS). However, these systems are not available to the vast majority of the rural population.

5. From Wuqu' Kawoq's larger cohort of approximately 250 patients with diabetes, we chose to interview these four people as their experiences illustrate many of

the themes we have repeatedly observed in our clinical roles. We have interacted with each of these patients and their families in dozens of encounters over multiple years. Verbal consent was obtained in each case.

6. In comparison, according to our patients, the average income for a non-professional, indigenous woman like Paulina working in the informal sector in her town is less than five USD per day.

7. In 1976, a massive earthquake struck Guatemala, leveling many highland towns and killing more than 20,000 people.

8. Viviana continues well in our clinic to this day.

9. "Branded generics" refer to bioequivalent generic medicines marketed with branding strategies.

FIVE

Capitalizing on Care

Marketplace Quasi-pharmaceuticals in the Guatemalan Health-seeking Landscape

Rachel Hall-Clifford

The move toward decentralization of government healthcare in Guatemala, as in other low and middle-income countries, has encouraged the growth of private-sector health services and commodities in the interstitial spaces created by an inadequate formal health system. This chapter analyzes the explosion of pharmaceuticals and manufactured remedies, focusing on treatments for diarrhea, a seemingly mundane but far too frequently lethal childhood experience in Guatemala, and a quasi-pharmaceutical pyramid scheme popular throughout Latin America. The rural indigenous poor are doubly affected by these schemes that both recruit them as low-level vendor-investors with promises of huge profits and simultaneously misinform them as consumers of the products. Social obligations and aspirations encourage the purchase of expensive "miracle" products whose shifting indications seem to always match customers' symptoms. This chapter considers the motivations of the vendors and purchasers of these pharmaceutical remedies as they endeavor to offer and seek healthcare on their own terms through prioritizing costly, private-sector services.

I became interested in the role of pharmaceuticals and "quasi-pharmaceuticals," or health supplements, during a study of treatments for childhood diarrhea in the Chimaltenango Department of the central highlands. While I was primarily concerned with the health-seeking pathways of individuals through the tiers of the government health system and the top-down penetration of long-term public health programming on diarrheal prevention and treatment to the community level, it quickly became impossible to ignore the important role of independently purchased pharmaceuticals for families seeking care for ill children. Also, like many ethnographers before me, I was interested in how adherence to traditional healing practices impacts the adoption of public health behavior change messages and utilization of the government health system. I was soon disabused of the romanticized notion that it was traditional healers who were preventing families from fully adopting oral rehydration therapy (ORT), the biomedically recommended first-line defense against dehydration from diarrhea in children that was the focus of my study. While traditional healing continues to have a place in the treatment of childhood illnesses, it was, rather, the pharmaceutical sector that formed a parallel and often competing health-seeking structure to the formal biomedical system. The pharmaceutical sector encompasses private pharmacies, non-specialist shops selling packaged pharmaceuticals, both biomedical and non-biomedical, ambulatory vendors, health promoters with supplies of medicines, and individual vendors of branded nutritional and health supplements, all of which provide pharmaceutical-based alternatives to accessing traditional biomedical institutions—clinics and hospitals—and ethnomedical healers in times of illness.

During this longitudinal ethnographic study, I conducted research and lived in the departmental capital of Chimaltenango, one predominately indigenous town, one town of mixed European and indigenous ancestry, and one indigenous village for a period of one year with ongoing follow-up visits.[1] In addition to conducting observations, surveys, and in-depth interviews at every tier of the government health system, I observed client-vendor interactions at pharmacies and marketplace drug stalls. I also investigated a quasi-pharmaceutical pyramid scheme by conducting in-depth interviews with vendors and consumers of its products, interviews with the Guatemalan marketing director and sales coordinator, and observations of vendor training sessions by becoming a licensed vendor. Indigenous Maya populations in Guatemala face stark social, economic, and health disparities in comparison to the nonindigenous population, whose cultural patterns have forged the hegemonic norms of Guatemalan society since the time of conquest and who continue to control national governance and economic structures. The disparities between indigenous and nonindigenous correspond to disparities between rural and urban areas, with nonindigenous populations largely clustered in urban centers better served by public services and infrastructure and indigenous populations in marginalized rural areas (Maupin, 2009).

The multi-sited approach of this research tracing the tiers of formal healthcare services enabled a "view from below" of the many top-down health system reforms enacted in Guatemala following the 1996 Peace Accords (see this volume's introduction; Maupin, 2009) and the sequelae of these reforms across the public, private, and non-profit sectors. In contemporary Guatemala, families must forge health-seeking pathways through a confusing jumble of public, private, and NGO services. Because of this, many rural Guatemalans believe health and the ability to seek healthcare are the provinces of the wealthy alone—and that health must be purchased. Amid the nods and words of agreement of her neighbors, one focus group participant in the village of Miravel[2] matter-of-factly explained, "We are poor and cannot take our children to the doctor often. We do not take our children to the doctor until they are seriously ill. Unlike rich people, who take their children to the doctor to be examined even if they are not sick. Imagine, even if they are not sick!" Indeed, as we talked in the small dirt yard outside the home of a group member with a view down the dusty road where no vehicle would pass until the weekly market day, the idea of taking all sick children to a healthcare provider, let alone the healthy ones, seemed the stuff of pure fantasy. Despite their economic limitations, women like this focus group participant actively seek to do the best for their children in times of illness. This chapter argues that what is "best" in terms of health-seeking is defined within the social nexus of community life. Favored health-seeking solutions typically mean reliance on the emergent pharmaceutical sector for the care of acute diarrhea episodes and other similar illness, rather than interaction with biomedical healthcare providers.

PHARMACEUTICALS AND CHILDHOOD DIARRHEAL ILLNESS

Pharmacies are a critical source of treatment for sickness in Guatemala, including childhood diarrhea. A study of health-seeking for children in Guatemala found that 30 percent of ill children were seen by a pharmacist (Heuveline & Goldman, 2000). In my survey data of both indigenous and nonindigenous mothers from Chimaltenango, 64 percent (n=236) reported that they seek treatment for their child's diarrhea in a government health post or clinic, 18 percent from a health promoter, and 12 percent from a pharmacy (Hall-Clifford, 2009). These data, based on my long-term ethnographic observations, likely under-represent the reliance on pharmaceuticals and packaged remedies by Guatemalans in their routine health-seeking behaviors. In the absence of comprehensive and accessible primary care services, families frequently prioritize the purchase of pharmaceuticals that are available in local communities and market towns.

The term "pharmacy" spans a wide gamut of establishments. Government pharmacies are typically connected to a clinic or a Drug Access Program (PROAM, *Programa de Accesibilidad de Medicamentos*) facility, as described below. In the case of oral rehydration salts (ORS) solutions, the fluid used in administering ORT, government pharmacies typically offer low-cost powdered ORS to be mixed with water at home. Private pharmacies can range from a large chain store to stock held in private doctors' offices to non-specialist storefronts in proprietors' homes, where ORS is frequently sold amidst a colorful array of sodas, chips, and paper goods. Individual vendors also sell pharmaceuticals in market stands and on public transportation, calling out the available products and their virtues. The type of ORS available across private pharmaceutical outlets varies widely from high-cost brightly colored and flavored bottles of pre-mixed solution to dry packets similar to government ORS packets, depending on the target market and their ability to pay.

While a trained pharmacist must legally be listed on the permit for a physical pharmacy establishment, these standards are not enforced, and even formal pharmacies are typically staffed by untrained personnel (Amorim, 2012). With the exception of narcotics, medications are not controlled by prescription requirements in Guatemala (Ministerio de Salud Publica y Asistencia Social [MSPAS], 2006). One study of drug advice given in pharmacies in Mexico and Guatemala found that more than 80 percent of treatments recommended for diarrhea and acute respiratory infections included unnecessary or dangerous medicines. Advice in pharmacies was unsurprisingly found to be of poorer quality than advice from physicians, but shockingly also of poorer quality than advice from family members (Kroeger et al., 2001). Individuals rely heavily on trusted social networks and previous experiences in health seeking and decision making on pharmaceutical purchases.

Formal Pharmacies

In 1998, the government opened a network of pharmacies as part of the Drug Access Program (PROAM) (Anson, Ramay, Ruiz de Esparza, & Bero, 2012). The aim of the program is to make pharmaceuticals accessible and affordable to everyone in Guatemala, and it includes pharmacies at the departmental and municipal levels as well as the stocks of drugs used by health centers, health posts, and health promoters. The government negotiates group contract pricing for the basic drug list available within the PROAM network (Pan American Health Organization [PAHO], 2012). Their pricing is competitive but not considerably lower than private pharmacies for basic medicines, including ORS powder sachets or bottled solution. Since diarrhea is the second leading cause of mortality of children under five in Guatemala (PAHO, 2012), ORS and other diarrheal treatments are among those most commonly sought for children across pharmaceutical sectors. When surveyed during my research in 2006-2007, the main PROAM pharmacy in Chimaltenango had no ORS available, while a municipal PROAM location only had bottled solution (at 14–19.50 quetzales or 1.82-2.54 USD) and another had sachets (1.5 quetzales or 0.20 USD) (Hall-Clifford, 2009). A more recent availability study found that some form of ORS could be found in 75 percent or more of PROAM and private pharmacies (Anson et al., 2012), which indicates both an increase in availability as well as a demand for manufactured pharmaceutical products.

So great is the reliance on pharmaceuticals that staff in both PROAM and private pharmacies uniformly suggested antibiotics or antiparasitic medications when asked about recommended treatments for children with diarrhea, despite the fact that ORT should be the first treatment in all cases of childhood diarrhea where no blood is present in the stools. At only one private pharmacy of thirteen surveyed did the salesperson recommend that an ORS solution be used in conjunction with the medication suggested (Hall-Clifford, 2009). The high cost of antibiotics and antiparasitics in comparison to ORS packets may motivate pharmacists and drug sellers to more actively promote these medicines. Beneath this facile explanation of profit margin, however, lies a more startling and widespread trend in health-seeking in Guatemala: packaged medicines are seen as powerful, and the more expensive they are, the more effective they are perceived to be. For example, although effective ORS solutions can be made using common household ingredients, only 1 percent of survey respondents in Chimaltenango (n=236) reported ever having used homemade ORS (Hall-Clifford, 2009). When directly asked whether homemade solutions or manufactured ORS packets are better, one focus group respondent said, "The ones in the packets are better because they are *actually from the doctor*. They work better." Further, the commercial bottled solutions of ORS lining the shelves of private pharmacies and local shops are by far the most popular form of ORS solution, and they are also by far the most expensive.

If families undertake health-seeking steps for their children, they rationally desire a treatment perceived as strong and effective for their efforts. Homemade ORT is not such a treatment, and more interventionist treatments like antibiotics and IV fluids are highly valued. Dr. Katu of a government ambulatory health team in the Department of Chimaltenango remarked, "People here don't accept ORT very well. They want something more heroic, such as an injection or more expensive pills, like antibiotics. They don't like the little envelopes much. We are always talking with them to change their minds." This underscores not just a preference for visible, "heroic" treatments but also the idea that health can be bought through such treatments—and that individuals can exert agency through their decision-making power in the marketplace. However, as Mulligan (2014) has observed in Puerto Rico, the transition of healthcare from public good to marketplace commodity positions parents of sick children as consumers who are financially and even morally responsible for their family's care.

Marketplace Pharmaceuticals

Despite the popularity of pharmaceuticals, availability of essential medicines throughout the Guatemalan pharmaceutical sector is a significant problem; average availability of World Health Organization essential medicines was found to be 25 percent in PROAM pharmacies and 35 percent in private pharmacies (Anson et al., 2012). When formal pharmaceutical channels are not accessible, financially or geographically, or when they do not have desired medicines in stock, treatment-seekers look to informal drug sellers. As in many parts of the developing world where pharmaceutical sales are not controlled by prescription (van der Geest, 1991), an ever-changing variety of pharmaceuticals abound in local markets. Laid out on blankets and tables amongst vegetables, laundry detergent, and hair gel, medicines—most often antibiotics—are a typical and expected part of the marketplace landscape. While marketplace drug sellers have no knowledge of pharmaceuticals other than anecdotal evidence gleaned from personal experience, their stocks seem to magically contain a remedy for any condition that presents itself. Van der Geest (1991) has elaborated on this phenomenon:

> The instant production of popular medical knowledge during market transactions comes close to what more than thirty years ago Festinger called "reduction of cognitive dissonance." From such a perspective knowledge can be viewed as a cultural device to assuage or avoid the pain of any discrepancy between what is and what ought to be. The Ebolowa market [in Cameroon] shows us in miniature how culture 'works' all the time, smoothing over, alleviating irreconcilable differences. For the poor customer this means he manages to believe in the efficacy of the few medicines he can buy. (p. 80)

Purchasers of pharmaceuticals in the marketplace are reliant on vendors for advice and are willing to believe that the quantity of medicine they can afford will be sufficient to restore health. They also look to the recommendations and experiences of family and neighbors in their self-medication processes (van der Geest & Hardon, 1990).

The many market vendors and shops selling "natural" remedies are an additional element of the market-driven pharmaceutical scene. Sellers of these products often told me that their most popular remedies are for gastrointestinal health and male sexual "vitality." Pricing for these products vary: some are cheaper than biomedical pharmaceuticals, and others cost more. In many contexts in the Global North, naturopathy and traditional natural remedies may hold secondary status relative to biomedical care (Baer, 2012), but in low and middle-income countries such as Guatemala, they can be viewed as desirable alternatives to biomedical institutions. As Harvey (2011) notes, sales pitches and demonstrations by indigenous community members on buses and in public markets are pervasive and frequently poised in resistance to biomedical pharmaceuticals. A pharmaceutical purchase enacts individual autonomy and power, demonstrating to the individual that they can make choices in health-seeking, whether in opposition to government biomedical structures or not, and to their community that they have the money to do so.

Traditional Healers and Pharmaceutical Syncretism

In addition to community health promoters and pharmaceuticals vendors, traditional healers are another group embedded within community structures that influence health-seeking decisions; however, their prevalence and popularity should not be inflated. Even in the early 1970s, H. K. Heggenhougen (1976) found that there were few practicing shamans or *curanderos* (traditional healer, typically utilizing plant remedies) in the Chimaltenango Department. The importance of traditional healers in health-seeking patterns in Guatemala has recently been debated, with one study of childhood illness showing virtually no use of healers (Heuveline & Goldman, 2000) and another arguing that local healers continue to play a key role in treatment-seeking for Guatemalan Maya (Eder & García Pú, 2003). Many indigenous communities do still have a healer, typically an older woman, who is seen as knowledgeable about plant and home remedies and skilled in healing common ailments, though consultation with traditional healers does not necessarily affect use of biomedical treatments in general or pharmaceuticals in particular. Traditional healers readily draw on traditional, biomedical, and popular understandings of illness and treatment through syncretism (Helman, 2014), dynamically maintaining their relevance in shifting healthcare environments.

Lety is a 66 year-old Kaqchikel healer who lives in an indigenous market town with three of her daughters, two of whom are married and have children of their own. Lety's mother was a renowned healer, and her daughters have learned the remedies as well, although they do not practice as healers. Lety typically sees between two and five patients a day, most of whom are neighborhood children brought by their mothers. She charges 5 quetzales (0.65 USD) for adults and 3 quetzales (0.39 USD) for children, which she sometimes accepts in the equivalent value of eggs, dried beans, or other staples.

Lety is frequently consulted for cases of persistent diarrhea in children, and most of her treatments involve a combination of herbs, packaged pharmaceuticals, and Catholic prayer. Lety, like many other practicing "traditional" healers (see also King, Chary, & Rohloff, this volume), incorporates elements of traditional healing and popular biomedically-influenced home remedies, and she sees no conflict in combining across these sectors. Indeed, she would not herself construct the categories of "traditional," "religious," and "biomedical" remedies but rather picks and chooses from the treatments known to her based on personal experiences of efficacy. She frequently recommends that mothers buy a particular packaged medicine, such as Alka-Seltzer or acetaminophen, to use in conjunction with herbal treatments for their children. Lety says she frequently recommends that her child patients be taken to the health center if she perceives that the sickness is severe or that she will not be able to treat it successfully. In the same vein, she reports that she also has patients who come to her after an unsatisfactory visit to the health center.

Although I have never heard Lety recommend purchasing ORS to a mother, she told me that she thinks ORT is very useful for children with diarrhea. She said, "*Suero oral* [ORS] is good because it keeps the kids hydrated, their eyes moist. It is good for diarrhea." I asked her on multiple occasions how she would differentiate the types of diarrhea for which ORS would be useful, and she consistently answered that ORS is good for all types of diarrhea. I asked specifically about her distinctions between treatments for hot, cold, and worm-induced diarrheas, and she held fast to her assertion that ORS would be useful in each of these traditional categories of diarrhea. This contradicts previous research that found traditional humoral systems in Latin America would prevent the use of ORS for some categories of diarrhea (Kendall, Foote, & Martorell, 1998), indicating that, at least for Lety, biomedicine (and its remedies) does not stand in conflict with contemporary ethnomedical practices. The syncretic practices of traditional healers in contemporary Guatemala may partially obscure their continued presence and influence on health-seeking behaviors, particularly in the encouragement of the use of manufactured products and remedies.

ORAL REHYDRATION, QUASI-PHARMACEUTICALS, AND THE OMNILIFE PYRAMID

The Business Model

Omnilife is a multinational corporation that sells vitamins and other health supplements and remedies, including products claimed to be useful for ORT. Omnilife follows a direct sales model by selling its products to customers through licensed vendors, who earn money by selling the products at a set rate of profit mark-up and by recruiting other vendors. Founded in Mexico in 1991, the majority of Omnilife's distribution centers and vendors continue to be in Mexico and Central America; however, Omnilife is a registered company in eighteen countries worldwide, including the U.S., Russia, and India (Omnilife, 2015). Omnilife has a strong presence in Guatemala: it has now been operating in the country for thirteen years and grosses approximately twelve million U.S. dollars annually (Hall-Clifford, 2009). Direct sales and multilevel marketing have become popular strategies in developing countries, with the rise of Omnilife (Cahn, 2006) alongside other multinationals such as Amway (Sethi, 2014).

Multilevel marketing strategies rely on large numbers of small-scale investors and on the continuous recruitment of new investors and customers to fund payments to existing investors; across multilevel marketing strategies, or pyramid schemes, 90 percent of investors do not have their expectations for returns on investment met (Akinladejo, Clarke, & Akinladejo, 2013). A Harvard Business School brief states that the economic environment of developing countries favors direct selling, in contrast to developed economies where strong infrastructure supports primarily online and retail location sales. The report finds, "When the formal retail environment is weak and paid employment well under 5 percent of the population, direct selling fills the distribution gap while offering substantial employment opportunity" (Chu & Segre, 2010). The aspirational message of high potential earnings for vendors with few economic opportunities as well as a consumer-base desirous of "strong" packaged remedies make Guatemala a location ripe for Omnilife's multilevel marketing and direct sales strategies. The packaged nature of Omnilife's health supplement and quasi-pharmaceutical products makes them appealing in the same way as, and for some indistinguishable from, pharmaceuticals.

Selling Wellbeing: Omnilife Vendors

I first met Felix at a Guatemalan fast-food chain restaurant on the edge of the central park in Chimaltenango. I had been referred to him by the national offices of the Omnilife Corporation in Guatemala City as the leading seller and most knowledgeable sales representative in Chimaltenango. That afternoon, Felix and his fellow Omnilife vendor Jorge were the picture of upwardly-mobile ambition: dressed in knit polo shirts and carrying branded Omnilife attaché bags, they looked the part of businessmen ready for a sales pitch to a new client. They seemed excited and a little nervous to have the chance to talk about Omnilife to a foreigner. Although I had explained over the telephone and again when we met that I was a researcher interested in Omnilife and not a prospective vendor, I could not sway Felix from his recruitment sales pitch that afternoon. As we ate our Guatemalan fast-food, Felix extolled the virtues of a multinational company.

Over phone calls and meetings across several months, I learned that Felix used to live in a dirt-floored, badly built house in his hometown and always worried about putting the next meal on the table. Since he began working as an Omnilife vendor four years earlier, Felix's standard of living improved immensely. He bought a used car, has traveled to Omnilife conventions at resorts in Central America and the Caribbean as rewards for high sales, and even had a new two-story "mansion" under construction. Felix reports that he makes about 20,000 USD per year from his own product sales and an additional 4,000 USD in annual bonuses for his recruitment of new vendors and their product sales, which he proudly reminded me is a very high wage for Guatemala. In this respect, Felix is not representative of other Omnilife vendors, who typically sell a far lesser volume of products and earn less. Most vendors in my observations in Guatemala and those included in studies of Omnilife in Mexico (Aguilar, 2005; Cahn, 2006) and Ecuador (Stracuzzi Ramirez, 2009) do not actively sell products or meet intended profit levels from their initial investment. Felix told me of his positive experience as a vendor, "Working in the fields is hard. Omnilife has made my life so much better. My grandparents are poor, my parents are poor, but I am not poor. I think everyone should do it. *There's no reason to be poor.*"

During my initial meeting with Felix and at all subsequent Omnilife vendor events I attended, the products themselves were eclipsed by discussions of the lifestyle aspects of the company. Felix brought samples of some of the products for me to try. He insisted that he could taste the difference between an Omnilife "extra pure" bottle of water that sells for 6.25 quetzales (0.81 USD) and the regular bottles of water (3 quetzales or 0.39 USD) we had ordered from the restaurant, and he was a little disappointed that I could not make the same fine distinction. Many of Omnilife's products are vitamin powders that you mix with water. One such powder, called *Biocros,* is touted as good for digestive health (Omnilife, 2006), and Felix told me that this powder had cured his wife's painful ovarian cysts and kept her from dying. Omnilife bills its products as healthy and all natural, although many products have sucrose/fructose as their first ingredient and also have fairly extensive lists of chemical ingredients.

Vendor knowledge about the products they are selling is limited, and the indications for the individual products are ambiguous. Felix told me that everyone has to choose the products that are right for them, adding that you could mix four or five different powders in one drink and "nothing [bad] would happen." When I questioned how this would affect the efficacy of individual products, he said that more is always better and that you would see results more quickly the more you took. This is an effective sales strategy, as his customers could only benefit by purchasing greater quantities of products, but it does not say much for the efficacy of the individual products themselves. While Felix is very focused on making sales, I never felt that he was operating from a position of deception: he truly believes in the life-changing power of Omnilife and its products.

Vendor Recruitment and Training

After attending a few of the sporadic meetings of Omnilife vendors in Chimaltenango, Felix invited me to accompany him to a "top vendors" meeting in Guatemala City, where, he said, the vendors learned about the properties of and uses for the products. I had to become an authorized vendor in order to attend the meeting, so I became one of Felix's recruits and paid the 170 quetzales (22.1 USD) initiation fee.[3] I thought this would finally be my chance to learn about exactly what the products are good for and how some of them are conceptualized as ORT, which I had heard from community members. Maybe it made sense that the local Chimaltenango meetings were all about sales, but I felt sure that the Guatemala City meeting would be where actual product education took place.

In a meeting hall of a small, mid-range hotel in Guatemala City, the vendors gathered for their afternoon meeting. The crowd of about 200 vendors was a mix of largely indigenous men and some indigenous women. Loud music blared through oversized speakers, and Omnilife beverages were sold at the door, where an entry fee of 15 quetzales (1.95 USD) was charged. Amid much fanfare and applause, the meeting's leader ran to the front of the room and began an impassioned testimonial about the multitudinous ways that Omnilife has improved his life. Attendees clapped and shouted words of affirmation as one might at a charismatic religious meeting. Indeed, Omnilife draws on charismatic leadership and faith-based models of group-building, such as call and response activities (Cahn, 2006). God was directly called upon to help us in our sales during the meeting. As the afternoon wore on, we heard testimonials from other vendors and repeated explanations of how the Omnilife vendor system operates. Depending on your volume of sales, you can buy the products at increasingly reduced wholesale prices for a larger profit margin; you cannot vend the products from a store; and you receive a bonus plus profit shares from the sales of three generations of your recruits. A marker board was used to carefully explain this process and to draw out the pyramid structure of profit, lest there be any doubt that it is indeed a pyramid scheme.

Throughout the afternoon, I wondered if the vendor-attendees would not already be well aware of the information being presented, yet the responsive crowd was far from bored. Towards the end of the three-hour meeting, there was a "product education" segment during which vendors were reminded to push sales of two different products: one powdered vitamin supplement for "vitality" and a liquid syrup for "digestive health." Nothing more specific than these vague uses was given; discussion centered on how "good" the products were and the possibilities for profit margins. Essentially, the meeting served as a pep rally for the vendors, re-igniting their interest in and commitment to the Omnilife way of life rather than providing them with product knowledge that would help them select the best products for particular conditions that customers may face. On the drive back to Chimaltenango, Felix talked animatedly about the meeting and about his future plans for increased sales. He said he planned to buy a trunk-load of products and drive them out to the rural markets on a more regular basis. He has had some success with this sales strategy in the past. "The rural people," he said, "are *hungry for health*. They will buy these products that they need."

When I pressed Felix and other Omnilife vendors on how they decided which products to recommend for patients with particular conditions, they said they relied on firsthand knowledge of and experience with the products themselves. Felix said he also reads Omnilife publications, including the *OM* company magazine, to learn more about the products, though my own perusal of these publications again revealed an emphasis on testimonials and sales techniques. However, Felix and other Omnilife vendors repeatedly reiterated to me that Omnilife is exceedingly "equal opportunity" in that you do not have to be able to read or even speak Spanish well to be able to be a good vendor. This means that written promotional and educational materials are not accessible to less-literate vendors, let alone their rural, indigenous customers. Furthermore, the vast majority of vendors and clients alike do not have the education and experience necessary to be critical of the promises of a multinational corporation like Omnilife and its methods of operation. As I talked with more vendors and customers, it became increasingly clear to me that product education is not a priority of Omnilife. Rather, there is an emphasis on users individually experimenting to find the combinations of products that work for them.

OMNIPRESENCE: OMNILIFE AND ORS

Popular Demand: Omnilife in the Community

My specific interest in understanding Omnilife's promotional and sales processes focused on the use of some of the products as ORS solutions. Although vendors all agreed that their products made more effective ORS solutions for children than the free or low cost packets given out at health posts, they invariably recommended a different selection of products for this purpose. Felix was extremely opinionated on the topic, saying that rural parents did not know any better and gave their children unhealthy drinks like sodas when they have diarrhea. He urged that they should be using healthier solutions, like any of the wide variety of drinks and powders offered by Omnilife. When I pointed out that some form of sugar was the first ingredient in several of these products, Felix defended them by noting that the benefits of the vitamin content are what sets Omnilife apart from all other ORS solutions. It also became clear through our discussions that he did not realize that ingredients like sucrose and fructose are chemical names for sugar on the lists of ingredients found on Omnilife product packaging.

The costs of Omnilife products that would be used for ORT purposes are far higher than the government packets or even other commercial products available at private pharmacies. Depending on the specific product recommended, Omnilife "digestive" remedies utilized for ORT can range in price from 3 quetzales (0.39 USD) per packet to 12 quetzales (1.56 USD) for a bottle of vitamin water to as high as 72 quetzales (9.36 USD) for a bottle of syrup. A sort of attainable, or perhaps aspirational, elitism seems to be the modus operandi of many Omnilife vendors with whom I spoke and who sell products in rural areas. As one vendor in an indigenous market town put it, "The thing about Omnilife products is that everyone wants them because not everyone can get them." An upwardly mobile indigenous man himself, he added, "The peasants come into town each week to the market, and they see and hear how good our products are. These people are poor and often can't afford them [Omnilife products] right away, but it makes them want to afford them." Again, the concept that health is for those who can pay comes to the forefront: health is something that must be paid for like any other market good.

By building social caché around the purchase of Omnilife brand ORT products, Omnilife vendors hope to create a market where people eschew cheaper products in favor of their own, supposedly superior products. Vendors are often friends or at least a fellow indigenous neighbor with whom rural customers can identify. Omnilife sales rely on the trust relationships present within rural communities to sell products and to convince people that no other brand is worth purchasing. It is socially desirable to be seen with Omnilife products touted as ORS, even if you cannot afford enough to give your sick child a dosage that would be effective. I have seen unopened or slightly used bottles of Omnilife products sitting in windowsills and on shelves in many low-income households, suggesting that the products are being hoarded for later use because of their cost or simply kept as status symbols. The social caché of using expensive packaged treatments paradoxically means that more cases of childhood diarrhea go untreated.

Prescription for Omnilife: Leakage into the Public Health Sector

One morning I made the forty-five-minute walk with my indigenous neighbor Juana from the village of Miravel to the nearest health post, which serves as the primary level of healthcare for the area. It is staffed monthly by a government ambulatory health team of a doctor and two nurses, and a local community health promoter is responsible for opening the post a few mornings a week to triage patients and vend basic medicines at the government pharmacy prices. However, the community health promoter at this post, Carlos, is lax about the hours the post is open, so much so that I heard women in Miravel discussing their frustration on having made the long walk to the post only to find it closed. As

Juana and I approached the one-room health post, she expressed optimism about the service she would receive, taking it as a good omen that the door was open. I listened as Juana described the cough and mild diarrhea that her 18 month-old had been having over the previous week. Carlos listened and periodically asked questions, his self-bestowed white coat lending him an air of medical authority. When Juana's brief narrative ended, I watched as Carlos's eyes shifted smoothly from her care-worn face, lined with dust and sweat after our long walk, to two shelves of Omnilife products *inside the health post*. Without missing a beat, he said that for a child with diarrhea, he recommended one of the Omnilife bottles of vitamin water as an ORS solution, which would "restore vitality and fluids." Juana could not afford the high cost of the proffered Omnilife product, and, after making eye contact with me in an unspoken request for help that I pretended not to understand, she asked for one of the government ORS packets. Carlos said he was out, and we left the health post empty-handed.[4]

After a couple of attempted follow-up visits, I finally found Carlos in his health post again one afternoon. I asked him my usual questions about what kinds of problems he sees most frequently and which medications he is able to offer. I then turned to questions about the Omnilife products, and Carlos said he had them in the post as a service to the customers and that many preferred them to the government products. He related that if a mother cannot pay for Omnilife products, he will sell her a government ORS packet if he has any left. He pointed to the frequent stock-outs of medicines in the government system as the rationale behind his entrepreneurial turn. Although community health promoters are intended to be volunteers for their communities who are only compensated for the time they spend away from other income-generating activities, Carlos has found a way to increase revenue through the health post. There is very little time and money for oversight of the health promoters, so it is unsurprising that some promoters chose to add other money-making ventures onto their official activities. Carlos's power to do as he wishes with the health post goes unchecked and unquestioned within the community, and he is able to increase his own social status by earning more money. Indeed, Flood & Rohloff and Pezzia in this volume describe similar dynamics among government healthcare workers who use public health facilities as a means for promoting private sector health services.

I saw Omnilife products in only one other health post in Chimaltenango Department, though a majority of my visits were with announced trips of the ambulatory health teams. While Omnilife rules prohibit sales from a store, they do not explicitly ban sales from health posts, which are technically not run as for-profit businesses, creating a gray area for community health promoters to take advantage of their position and earn extra money as Omnilife vendors. The Omnilife vendor's manual also states that Omnilife products are not medications and should not be made part of a medical prescription. This distancing from formal biomedical practice, which for most of the poor, rural indigenous populations is experienced through the government system, only seems to bolster attitudes that government health services are of inferior quality and that greater health can be purchased with a greater expenditure of money.

CONCLUSION

Poor, indigenous Guatemalans recognize all too clearly that the wealthy have access to superior healthcare, generating the perception that health requires wealth. The high visibility of (quasi-)pharmaceuticals across the health-seeking landscape and their accompanying promises of good health through consumption positions health as a (luxury) commodity to be purchased. The distinctive Omnilife branding on products is widely recognized, and trust in their effectiveness is bolstered by the social networks through which they are sold. The same feelings of trust and solidarity in vendors and products are not widely experienced through encounters with the government health system. Rather than being put off by the high cost of Omnilife products, potential customers aspire to purchase them *because* of the high cost. Indeed, Omnilife is an extreme example of more general phenomena: the out-of-pocket purchase of medicines across the private pharmaceutical sector and the growing preference for more expensive products in lieu of often therapeutically similar low-cost ones (see also Flood & Rohloff, this volume). In particular, public sector products are seen as representing an inferior level of care and, as such, are sometimes rejected by the populations for whom they are intended.

It is tempting to view the preference of the poor for costly pharmaceuticals as irrational, particularly through the lens of neoliberal economic rationality, with its assumption that individuals will seek to maximize surplus cash reserves in a privatized marketplace. Yet, as Salmaan Keshavjee (2014) argues, "In neoliberal terms, individual choices about purchasing goods and services in the private market without so-called government interference constitute 'freedom'" (p. 122). A health systems-level focus on structures and top-down health policies can lead us to forget that individuals and communities are not passive recipients of health-seeking messages and that a desire to exert agency is itself rational, particularly for a population who has faced repression and control of historic proportions (Hale, 2006; Sanford, 2003). The indigenous poor in Guatemala have faced decades of brutal exclusion from social, economic, and political participation and centuries of marginalization. In this light, the small doses of freedom bought in the (quasi-)pharmaceutical marketplace becomes a rational way to escape the impositions of the government and its health system. At the same time, this creates a dynamic in which such freedom is only available to those who can afford it.

Individuals—even poor ones—have their own desires and social objectives, and as Deborah Lupton (1995) states, "There is a symbiotic relationship between the social and the individual; the subject is constituted in and through social processes, and subjects, in turn, influence the character of the social" (p. 48). The popularity of Omnilife demonstrates a desire to resist the entrenched macroeconomic and class structures that perpetuate vast inequalities as well as an attempt to carve out new pathways for economic participation and mobility. Some vendors and their families associate Omnilife with modernity itself, seeing association with the company as a sign not just of economic gain but of their status as a participant in a globalized neoliberal economy (Nelson, 2013). A desire to participate in the wider globalized economy has been an important shift seen among indigenous Guatemalans in the postwar era, particularly through engaging in factory labor and cash cropping (Fischer & Benson, 2006; Goldín, 2011). This trend has occurred in tandem with large-scale conversion to Prostestantism in Guatemala, and shifts in values among the indigenous population commensurate with the Protestant work ethic of social and economic mobility through hard work (Berger, 2010) may also help to explain the allure of Omnilife.

The gains wrought through participation in the neoliberal economy are unequally distributed, however, and in the case of (quasi-) pharmaceuticals, not everyone can access Omnilife as a vendor or purchaser (Nelson, 2013). In part, it is this exclusivity that makes Omnilife and its products desirable. Another is hope. The "rhetoric of spiritual uplift" is consistent through all of Omnilife's corporate messages (Cahn, 2006), and these messages fall on the eager Guatemalan ears of potential vendors who feel hopeless in their poverty. Omnilife offers hope—to the sick through their products and to the poor through their sales model. The Omnilife model also offers the hope of becoming someone "important" through financial gain; it is an individualized plan for economic development rather than a community one. Omnilife's training and promotional materials lift up successful examples of vendors like Felix, whose lives have changed as a result of their sales activities, though such life-altering economic benefits are rare. Against a background of the Protestant work ethic, failure to succeed as a vendor can easily be seen as due to lack of individual effort and skill (Cahn, 2006) rather than a failure of community or national-level economic strategy. Engagement with Omnilife as either a vendor or consumer is positioned by the company as the choice of upwardly mobile, healthy, and hardworking individuals. Widely advertised, but rarely achieved, narratives of success obscure systemic inequalities in access to essential social goods and services, such as healthcare and meaningful occupation. While the Omnilife strategy can benefit some individuals, it also exacerbates existing inequalities from the community level to a global one; certainly, the apex of the multinational Omnilife pyramid does not reside in a Guatemalan village or even Guatemala at all.

Heggenhougen remarked of the healthcare situation in rural Guatemala in the 1970s, "The Cakchiqueles were faced with the classic double dilemma of having been influenced enough by the [nonindigenous] world to doubt the powers of traditional curing practices and of finding western medicine inaccessible" (Heggenhougen, 1976). In the intervening years that have seen post-conflict privatization of the health system, the double dilemma that poor Guatemalans face is no longer one of traditional healing versus biomedicine but one of public health services versus private ones perceived to be both of higher quality and more socially desirable as markers of economic success (see Flood & Rohloff, this volume; see further Whyte, 2014a). The medical pluralism with which contemporary rural populations in Guatemala grapple, as elsewhere in low and middle-income contexts, spans the public and private sectors of biomedicine, creating a medical environment where health-seekers must undertake complex reckonings of affordability, accessibility, and quality in order to maximize health outcomes with limited resources (see introduction, this volume). The biomedical sectors of this "new" (bio)medical pluralism are bridged with a complex array of (quasi-)pharmaceutical products available in the marketplace—a bridge that buckles and gives way each time a person has no money. The now widespread execution of decision-making autonomy through the purchase of these products is encouraging in some ways: individual empowerment, social enterprise, and local profit sharing to name a few. However, with each purchase made, individuals assume a burden, perhaps construed as choice, for provisioning their own healthcare and shouldering the risks alone.

NOTES

1. This research was approved by the Institutional Review Board of Boston University and supported by Boston University and the Whiting Foundation.

2. Names of some local communities and individuals have been changed to protect the anonymity of study participants.

3. Though a great disappointment to Felix, whose visions of profit shares from a U.S. recruit loomed large, I never ordered or sold any Omnilife products.

4. I did assist Juana in purchasing a packet of ORS from a private pharmacy at low cost.

III

Navigating Resources

SIX

Engaging Mental Healthcare in a Disengaged System

Carla Pezzia

Magda,[1] a thirty-five year-old Kaqchikel woman living in Panajachel, often wonders if there is "something wrong with [her] mind." Five years ago, a man attacked her while she was walking home late at night. She escaped physically unharmed, but now anytime she walks down a dark street alone, her heart starts to race and she feels short of breath. She thinks she is suffering from "*nervios*" (nerves). A few years back, she went to a local healer who prescribed her herbal remedies. She took them daily, but still found herself feeling anxious anytime she was walking alone and decided to visit the local government health clinic for help. To her luck, a visiting psychology student from Guatemala City just happened to be at the clinic that day, completing requirements for a short-term rotation.

"I liked speaking with the psychologist," Magda told me. It helped her feel more relaxed and confident. However, Magda was only able to speak with the psychologist once. When she returned to the clinic, hoping for another session, the psychologist was no longer there. The clinic doctors suggested Magda visit another public health facility in a neighboring town to see a psychiatrist, but Magda was never able to take the time off from work to secure an appointment. One day, when Magda got very sick with a cold, she went to a private clinic with sliding scale fees and extended hours. After consulting with a general practice physician about her cold symptoms, she took the opportunity to ask him about her anxiety. The doctor wrote Magda a prescription for her anxiety, but Magda never filled it. She felt uncertain about the doctor's recommendation and did not have the money to buy the pills.

Magda's story highlights two themes that typify mental healthcare seeking in Guatemala. First, what Magda perceives to be a mental health problem is closely associated with an experience of violence. While not all mental illness can be directly connected to violence, Guatemala's historical and contemporary notoriety as a violent country has impacted the mental health of its citizens. Many individuals trace the root cause of their mental health issues to experiences of torture, assassination, or other forms of violence experienced by themselves, family members, or friends during the thirty-six-year long civil war, during which the Guatemalan government targeted indigenous peoples for murder (Godoy-Paiz, 2005; Herrera, de Jesus Mari, & Ferraz, 2005). Several clinical investigations of victims and witnesses of this political violence have documented high rates of post-traumatic stress disorder, anxiety, and depression (Herrera, de Jesus Mari, Andreoli, Quitana, & Ferraz, 2008; Sabin, Lopes Cardozo, Nackerud, Kaiser, & Varese, 2003), as well as concomitant substance use disorders, especially alcoholism (Branas et al., 2013; Petrakis, Gonzales, Rosenheck, & Krystal, 2002). Although the civil war ended in 1996, the subsequent explosion of gang activity and narco-trafficking, as well as the ongoing suppression of activist and community leaders of various environmental and human rights causes, has kept the idiom of violence alive for many Guatemala citizens. Indeed, since the Peace Accords, scholars have noted that yearly murder rates nationwide have surpassed the death tolls of some of the most destructive years of the civil war (O'Neill & Thomas, 2011).

Second, Magda's experience also indexes the fact that more and more Guatemalans are seeking biomedical resources for mental healthcare through multiple, diverse avenues. Although Magda initially visited a local ethnomedical healer for her symptoms, she subsequently sought care at both a public-sector health center and a private clinic. Both of these efforts were of limited therapeutic utility, however: the provider who helped her at the public clinic stopped working there soon after their initial consultation; the private physician wrote her an expensive prescription she was unable to fill. Magda continues with a generalized, disabling feeling of anxiety in her daily life. Her continued psychological distress underscores the question: while both public and especially private biomedical resources for mental health have proliferated in the postwar years—seemingly providing more options and points of access to care—why do individuals like Magda continue to suffer from such poor mental healthcare access?

This chapter examines patient engagement with a fragmented array of biomedical services for mental healthcare, using ethnographic data from the highland town of Panajachel. I highlight two key characteristics that underlie mental healthcare seeking in the context of the "new" medical pluralism of multiple biomedical systems and sectors this volume proposes: slippage and serendipity. "Slippage" refers to the increasing tendency for patients to be systematically diverted to the private sector for care when the public healthcare system predictably does not meet their needs. This was the case when Magda sought care in the private clinic when the public clinic no longer provided specialized mental health services. While slippage may occur inadvertently as a side effect of public health systemic shortcomings, it can also happen more deliberately, when healthcare providers use the public health system as a pipeline to recruit patients into their private practices, thereby contributing to the commoditization of mental healthcare.

"Serendipity" refers to my finding that access to mental healthcare often occurs through chance encounters or sheer luck. In some ways, serendipity overlaps with the phenomenon of "contingency" described by Whyte (2014b) for care-seeking among individuals living with AIDS in Uganda, where chance encounters with other individuals can help to point them in the right direction to receive appropriate care. For Whyte, contingency is deeply tied to sociality, the strategic use of social networks to become informed about and access various AIDS care programs. Whyte's analysis importantly details the ways in which individuals interact creatively and resourcefully with complex and chaotic social networks in order to get the care they need. While individuals in Panajachel exhibit a similar degree of resourcefulness in exploring healthcare options provided through social networks, I use the term "serendipity" to foreground the ways in which personalistic, arbitrary aspects of both institutional cultures and health provider engagements influence mental healthcare options. The phenomenon of transient and constantly shifting healthcare offerings is quintessential of the emerging privatized and aid-oriented healthcare sector in Guatemala. Magda, for example, went to a local public health center primarily because it was affordable to her. She was able to obtain psychiatric care because, by chance, on the day that she visited the center, a psychology student *just happened to be* completing a rotating internship. The health center had no formal psychiatric programming, so when the student completed her internship, Magda was disappointed to find that the clinic's psychiatric resources had disappeared as quickly and as unexpectedly as they had materialized.

MENTAL HEALTH AND HEALTHCARE: GLOBALLY, REGIONALLY, AND NATIONALLY

Mental and behavioral disorders are primary contributors to disability-adjusted life years globally, and they are especially on the rise in low- and middle-income countries (LMICs) (Murray et al., 2012). Critically, this rise in mental health morbidity places further strain on already overtaxed LMICs' healthcare systems, where care for many chronic illnesses—including mental health disorders—is often minimal. Other factors contributing to slow development of mental healthcare resources globally include the lack of straight-forward biological diagnostic paradigms for mental health disorders, the continued stigmatization of mental illness, and perceptions in the global health movement that mental healthcare is a "luxury add-on" to be provided after other more basic health service needs are met (Kohrt, Mendenhall, & Brown, 2015, p. 27).

These global trends are especially salient in Latin America, which has a disproportionately high burden of psychiatric illnesses when compared to other regions of the world (Hyman, Chisholm, Kessler, Patel, & Whiteford, 2006). Throughout Latin America, more than 20 percent of all disease-related disability is caused by psychiatric disorders (Rodríguez, Kohn, & Aguilar-Gaxiola, 2009). Historically, particular reasons for the lack of development of adequate mental health services in Latin America have included minimal public health budgetary allocations, heavy concentrations of resources in urban centers, and limited medical training programs (Rodriguez, 2010).

In terms of mental health service provision, Guatemala ranks near the bottom among Latin American countries. In Guatemala, there is only 1 psychiatrist for every 200,000 inhabitants (Rodríguez et al., 2007). The issue of inaccessibility is even more profound than this statistic indicates, however, since virtually all of these providers work in urban areas such as the capital city, leaving the 45 percent of the population that lives in rural areas without any access to psychiatric or psychological services (Alarcón, 2003; Alarcón & Aguilar-Gaxiola, 2000; Rodríguez et al., 2007). The government of Guatemala spends less than 1 percent of its total health budget on mental healthcare, which is the smallest budgetary allocation for any medical specialty and one of the lowest allocation rates in all of Latin America (Paiz, 2012; Rodríguez et al., 2007). Of this budget, virtually all is spent on maintaining the government's flagship psychiatric hospital, the National Hospital for Mental Health. This hospital's unsanitary conditions, deteriorating equipment, and safety abuses by poorly-trained personnel have given it a notorious reputation for human rights violations (Attorney for Human Rights Office [PDH], 2010). Indeed, the US-based advocacy group Disability Rights International (2012) has described it as the "most dangerous facility our investigators have witnessed anywhere in the Americas."

Detailed information on the prevalence of specific mental illnesses in Guatemala is limited by a lack of comprehensive surveys. One of the only available studies is a community-based survey conducted in departmental capitals by researchers at the University of San Carlos of Guatemala. This study found an overall prevalence for mental health disorders of 27.8 percent. The most common conditions were post-traumatic stress disorder, depression, and alcohol abuse or dependence (University of San

Carlos [USAC], 2009). At the same time, however, the survey found that only 2.3 percent of affected individuals sought any kind of professional help from a psychiatrist, other medical doctor, or spiritual guides (USAC, 2009). *Curanderos,* common folk healers who practice primarily plant-based medicine, while included as an option in the survey, were not endorsed by respondents as a mental healthcare resource (USAC, 2009). Low rates of care seeking for mental health are partly explained by the scarcity and distribution of resources, as noted above. In addition, in rural communities, if mental health services are available, they are typically in private sector clinics, which are financially inaccessible to the majority of Guatemalans. Finally, stigmatization of mental illness contributes to the marginal status of mental healthcare services (Pezzia, 2013).

PANAJACHEL

This chapter is based on an ethnographic study of mental healthcare seeking I conducted in the town of Panajachel in the Western highlands of Guatemala. Panajachel sits off the shores of Lake Atitlán and has a population of approximately 17,000 inhabitants, consisting of local, national, and foreign-born residents. Approximately 70 percent of inhabitants are indigenous, primarily Kaqchikel Maya (Instituto Nacional Estadistica [INE], 2013). Panajachel has seen a significant increase in population in the last century with an accompanying shift in social, economic, and political dynamics (Hinshaw, 1975; Tax, 1963). A tourist stronghold for over a century, the town currently ranks among the most popular tourist destinations for Guatemala, due to its striking vistas of Lake Atitlán and surrounding volcanoes. The main streets of Panajachel are full of restaurants, hotels, and transportation and tour centers, and droves of tourists and backpackers arrive and depart each day. The town also serves as a central point for tourists to boat to other towns around the lake, which boast a range of luxury resorts, spas, markets, and artisanal cooperatives. Although some of the local Guatemalan population lives in Panajachel itself, many commute to the town on a daily basis from its outlying hamlets and smaller towns close by, which do not benefit as much from the tourism infrastructure.

Panajachel has a multi-sectorial healthcare system that includes local folk healers, public health institutions, private for-profit facilities, and charitable or non-governmental organizations (NGOs). Interestingly, though the historical anthropological literature about this region has described the role of *curanderos,* Mayan spiritualists (*ajq'ija'*), and Evangelical religious healers in providing all types of healthcare, including mental health services (Hinshaw, 1975; Logan, 1979; B. Paul, 1967; Paul & Paul, 1975), my interviewees considered these healers mostly for physical health conditions and as either inappropriate or ineffective for mental healthcare. This finding is also mirrored in USAC's community-based survey (USAC, 2009). Indeed, my research indicates that Panajachelenses are increasingly engaging with biomedical resources for mental healthcare, thus necessitating a better understanding of care-seeking within a "new" context of medical pluralism discussed throughout this volume.

As described in detail in this volume's introduction, public health infrastructure in many areas of Guatemala, including Panajachel, has historically been minimal. This trend has only continued with healthcare reforms in the 1990s, which encouraged care provision through the NGO and private sectors while de-emphasizing the role of the Ministry of Health. In the context of healthcare privatization, Panajachel has seen a surge of NGOs and private for-profit clinics that offer health services, but mental healthcare continues to be poorly addressed. For example, although Panajachel possesses both one large central health center and several outlying public health posts, these facilities do not offer any mental healthcare services—except when an occasional psychology intern requires a practicum site, as described in Magda's story. Within the past two decades, private and NGO sector services have proliferated, and Panajachel also attracts many foreign-sponsored short-term medical and surgical missions each year (Berry, 2014), as well as longer-term development and health projects. Indeed, Panajachel's streets are dotted with NGO offices and teeming with Euroamerican foreign aid workers and volunteers. Medical staff at both longer- and short-term aid programs are primarily comprised of teams of transient visiting medical professionals, who generally do not speak Spanish or local indigenous languages. Mental healthcare is not prioritized among medical missionaries, who generally prefer to offer services for acute medical problems. Furthermore, due to language barriers between largely English-speaking providers and Kaqchikel- and Spanish-speaking patients, foreign volunteers often remain unaware of patients' mental health complaints.

Notably, there is only one public sector psychiatrist, Dr. Mayra Benavidez, serving the entire department to which Panajachel pertains. Dr. Benavidez is employed by the government health system and works at multiple public facilities in the region. However, she only sees patients during the local health facilities' typical morning work hours. As is common for many public health physicians in the area, she then holds office hours in her private clinic in the afternoons, where she charges 200–300 quetzales an hour (approximately 26–39 USD). Dr. Benavidez is currently the only specialist in the area who can provide both counseling and prescriptions. Previously, a group of private psychologists opened a private clinic in early 2011. Although that clinic's hourly fee for counseling was lower than Dr. Benavidez's private clinic fees, lay community members still considered the costs too high, given that a treatment program usually consisted of a minimum of six hours of counseling sessions held over several weeks. Within one year of opening, the private psychology clinic had closed due to lack of business.

Local public health leaders in the region described to me how mental health problems, namely, depression, anxiety, schizophrenia, and alcoholism, are all on the rise. One local physician told me, "In this past year alone, I have seen more people with psychiatric issues than I have in more than thirty years of practicing medicine." My epidemiological work, documented elsewhere, indicates that 35.1 percent of Panajachelenses suffer from a mental health issue (Pezzia, 2013). Suicidal ideation (15.9 percent), depression (10.2 percent), alcohol use disorders (9.5 percent), and generalized anxiety (7.7 percent) were the most common mental health disorders (Pezzia, 2013), in comparison to national data indicating post-traumatic stress disorder (6.9 percent), depression (6.4 percent), and alcohol use disorders (5.2 percent) as the most common (USAC, 2009). In the face of these high rates of mental illness, local political leaders, including the mayor and other elected representatives whom I interviewed, all expressed to me their preoccupation with the lack of available resources for mental illness and the lack of funds or plans to develop them. For example, at one closed-door community meeting that I attended, a community leader recommended opening a drug and alcohol rehabilitation facility in town. One of the political officials in attendance interrupted him stating, "While there are a lot of things that would be nice, we need to be realistic here." The official suggested that with a limited budget other issues, such as malnutrition and education, take priority, reflecting the global health discourse that often classifies mental health services as a "luxury add-on" (Kohrt et al., 2015, p. 27).

The research for this article is drawn from fifteen months of ethnographic research in Panajachel. I conducted in-depth semi-structured interviews with 126 community members, including people with mental health issues, their family members, NGO directors, health program volunteers, religious leaders, physicians, psychologists, pharmacists, municipal and indigenous mayors, members of local political offices, and local political sector representatives. My interviews focused on mental health and healthcare experiences, provider practices, and potential interventions, especially within the biomedical sector. The following sections reflect the experiences of interviewees with mental illnesses as well as those of their family members (n=30). Their pathways to care reveal common themes of slippage and serendipity, and their stories below are organized by these concepts.

INADEQUACIES, INTERCONNECTIONS, AND SLIPPAGE: FROM PUBLIC TO PRIVATE

Gustavo is a middle-aged Kaqchikel Maya man with a history of alcohol-related problems. Gustavo was very up-front with me about his drinking problem, but he also told me that he had been suffering for almost a year from various symptoms he did not attribute to his alcohol use. Over six months, he went to a public health facility nearly once a month, complaining of trouble sleeping, abdominal pain, numbness and tingling in his extremities, and pain radiating from the base of his skull to his forehead. Nurses and physicians attributed this problem to his history of alcohol abuse. "Because I am indigenous, they only see an alcoholic. They do not think I have anything really wrong with me," he told me. At each visit, he was referred to a public gastroenterologist, who subsequently diagnosed Gustavo with "gastritis nerviosa" (stress-related dyspepsia) and prescribed medications that gave him "no relief." Unsure what else to do, Gustavo then visited the local market, where he bought "herbal remedies" from a traveling salesperson. Yet these, too, gave Gustavo no relief. On recommendation from a cousin, he visited a Catholic faith healer who told Gustavo that he only cured spiritual illnesses and could not help him because Gustavo's problem was purely physical.

I arranged for Gustavo to meet with a psychology intern from Guatemala City who, after a thirty-minute counseling session, recommended that Gustavo visit with Dr. Benavidez for a prescription. Gustavo agreed that seeing a psychiatrist would be beneficial. Indeed, he stated that he had hoped to see Dr. Benavidez each time he had formerly visited the public health facility, but that he had never successfully obtained an appointment. He asked if I would accompany him to the public health facility, because he felt that my status as a foreigner would grant him easier access and minimize the likelihood of the nurses and general physicians simply referring him to the gastroenterologist again. I agreed to visit the public health clinic with him.

When we reached the reception desk, Gustavo turned to me for help when the receptionist, a non-indigenous woman in her twenties, did not appear to understand when he asked to see "*el médico de los nervios*" (the "nerves" doctor), a common moniker for psychiatrists in the area. I jumped in, indicating that Gustavo wanted to see Dr. Benavidez. The receptionist stared at me blankly for a couple of seconds before permitting us to enter the waiting room. Gustavo went in to meet with Dr. Benavidez alone. He emerged rapidly from the consultation room, after only five minutes, with a diagnosis of general anxiety disorder and a prescription for an anti-anxiety medication. Afterwards, we stopped by a private pharmacy to fill his prescription. Although the public facility was technically supposed to stock psychiatric medications (Rodriguez et al., 2007), none were available.

Gustavo's case reflects the phenomenon of "slippage," where patients are diverted to the private sector for care when the public healthcare system does not adequately meet their needs. Although Gustavo was able to see a psychiatrist in a public health facility, the brief encounter ended with a prescription and a referral to a private-sector pharmacy. Per other interviewees, this sort of encounter with Dr. Benavidez was fairly typical. The average time Dr. Benavidez spent with a patient at the public health facility ranged from five to ten minutes, and she always ended these visits by writing a prescription. In the overburdened, under-resourced government-sponsored health facilities, one can imagine how psychiatrists like Dr. Benavidez become nothing more than prescription writers. Because public facilities rarely stock psychiatric medications, patients who present for public-sector care are automatically pipelined into the private sector, since they are required to fill all their prescriptions at for-profit pharmacies. This "slippage" from government facilities to private sector pharmacies is built into the structure of public mental healthcare, and it renders the notion of "free public sector care" meaningless for many care-seekers. Given the overwhelming demands placed on Dr. Benavidez, she is unable to provide counseling to most patients she sees in the public clinic—a service which would be "free" and of long-standing benefit to the patient. Instead, she simply prescribes medications, which are not free. Gustavo was able to purchase the recommended medications at a pharmacy through the income he generated from running his own business, but the monthly costs of psychiatric medications often exceed 100 USD. This amount of money is far beyond the reach of most care-seekers, who earn minimal wages in the informal economy.

Gustavo's experience of mental healthcare contrasts sharply to that of Hilda, a European woman residing in Panajachel. Back home, Hilda had been diagnosed with depression, and in Guatemala, she was experiencing an exacerbation due to recent marital troubles. Hilda visited a local public health facility, where, in contrast to Gustavo, she easily secured a consultation with Dr. Benavidez. Indeed, from my observations, Euroamerican foreigners generally spend less time waiting in line to see public sector practitioners, and secretaries and nurses are quicker to bring their cases to the attention of more specialized practitioners than they are while serving local Guatemalan patients. When Dr. Benavidez saw Hilda, she spent approximately five minutes speaking with her and wrote her a prescription for two different medications. She encouraged Hilda to visit her in her private clinic where they would have more time to talk. Hilda agreed, and when she visited the private clinic, Dr. Benavidez provided one hour of counseling and suggested therapeutic exercises to help Hilda with her marital problems. After a year, Hilda told me she could no longer afford the monthly doctor visits or one of her medications: "It was different when I first got here, and I was working for a foreign company. Now, I'm making Guatemalan wages. There is no way I can afford regular appointments or medications, and that's even with a discount I supposedly receive from Dr. Benavidez because she likes me." Even though she could no longer meet with Dr. Benavidez, Hilda was able to continue at home the therapeutic exercises Dr. Benavidez had taught her while in their private sessions.

While Gustavo's case demonstrates slippage due to systemic shortcomings, Hilda's case illustrates the deliberate commoditization of mental healthcare when public sector providers steer their patients to their private, fee-based services. Based on other interviews and participant-observation, Hilda's experience is also common: when Dr. Benavidez perceives that a patient at a public health facility has the financial resources to access the private sector, she recruits him or her into her private practice. White foreigners like Hilda are preferentially recruited over darker-skinned people with characteristically indigenous last names like Gustavo, who are presumed to be poorer. Motivations for recruiting patients from one sector to another are complex and interconnected. In my interactions with Dr. Benavidez, she always expressed passion and enthusiasm for helping people suffering from mental illnesses. However, Dr. Benavidez also recognizes that she can provide better care in her private clinic where she can control the number of patients she sees and give each the attention and time they need. Like other civil servants, Dr. Benavidez is underpaid and often does not receive paychecks on time due to government shortages. Indeed, she told me at one point that she had not received her public sector salary for nearly twelve months. She continued to work in the public sector, she told me, mostly for the social security benefits she would receive, but could not depend on the job for a living wage. Pipelining public patients into her private clinic was a strategic maneuver to ensure her livelihood and her family's wellbeing.

At times, those seeking mental healthcare turn to non-specialist private sector providers. Private internists operating general medicine clinics sometimes prescribe medications for depressive and anxiety disorders, as in Magda's case. However, all seven private internists I interviewed in Panajachel reported that that they did not feel comfortable addressing patients' specific psychological and psychiatric complaints.[2] Most non-specialist physicians in Panajachel instead referred their patients with symptoms they deemed "severe" to other facilities and showed limited awareness as to whether specialists were available there. For example, when I asked Dr. Perez, a popular private physician who provides care on a sliding scale based on income level, about his typical line of treatment for patients with mental illness, he stated that he referred them to the psychologist at the public health clinic. When I told him that the public health clinic no longer had a psychologist on staff, he responded that the public health center could help the patient better than he could regardless. Such referrals from private generalists only contribute to the circularity of the public-private mechanism: successfully obtaining an appointment at the public facility would, as Gustavo's and Hilda's stories illustrate, only lead patients back to the private sector—either to fill a prescription at a pharmacy or into Dr. Benavidez's private clinic.

Sometimes, health seekers bypass care at public and private clinics altogether and go directly to the pharmacies. As in much of the Global South, in Guatemala, most medications can be dispensed by a pharmacist without a prescription. However, pharmacies do not represent a safe or reliable source of psychiatric care. Indeed, many pharmacies are staffed by untrained personnel (Amorim, 2012; see also Hall-Clifford, this volume). In Panajachel the majority of small pharmacies are family businesses run by non-licensed proprietors who are only familiar with the most common medications for colds, fevers, and diarrhea. Despite dispensing psychotropic medications, these pharmacists are unable to properly monitor dosages and adverse drug reactions. Additionally, stock-outs make it difficult for patients to adhere to a daily regimen when they pursue this option. For example, for many years, Tobias worked two jobs to purchase an anti-psychotic medication that stabilized the mood of his twenty-seven-year-old daughter Maria, who has schizophrenia. I went one day with Tobias to attempt to refill Maria's medication. We visited four pharmacies before finding one—the most expensive in town—that had the medication in stock. At each of the first three pharmacies, we were told the medicine would not be refilled for at least several days to a week. As Tobias related, he knew he had to be vigilant to not let Maria's medication supply run too low before going to refill her prescription, but he often could not be as proactive as he wished due to his own unstable income situation.

SERENDIPITY AND TRANSITORY SERVICES: BEING AT THE RIGHT PLACE AT THE RIGHT TIME

Fabiola is a Tz'utujil Maya woman in her mid- 20s. In her late teens, she had what she considered a serious problem with alcohol: "I would drink a bottle of XL [rum] each night, first only on the weekends. Then I started drinking on Thursdays and sometimes Wednesdays. I would go to work still drunk some times." One night, while drinking with a male friend, she was sexually assaulted by her drinking companion. For weeks, she cycled through various emotions: disbelief, rage, humiliation, numbness, and self-loathing. She did not tell her family out of fear that they would think less of her, nor did she tell her friends what had happened. Years prior, she had told her "best friend" something in private, and by the next day her secret had become common knowledge within her community. Since then, she was cautious about revealing personal information. Fabiola tried looking for a psychologist to talk about the sexual assault and her drinking, as she felt she could trust a psychologist not to discuss her problems with others. At the time, the closest one she could find worked in a public hospital a few hours away by bus, and she could not take the time off from work to make the trip. From time to time, she would lock herself in her room at night and drink by herself. "I feel like I'm going crazy. I just drink and cry myself to sleep," she told me at the time.

When I first interviewed Fabiola, she seemed to have given up on finding a mental healthcare provider to speak with. Indeed, initially, our conversations revolved around finding help for her ailing mother-in-law with early-stage dementia. It was not until our fifth encounter that Fabiola trusted me enough to tell me the particulars of her story. Around that time, undergraduate and graduate psychology students from Guatemala City were working on their practicum hours at the public health clinic, and I set up a time for Fabiola to meet with the students. After their first session, there was a notable change in Fabiola's demeanor. She seemed happier, more carefree. She met with the students one more time before they completed their practicum and left Panajachel. Fabiola would like to continue receiving psychological guidance, but she is not sure where to go.

My presence as an ethnographer and a foreigner facilitated Fabiola's entrée with the psychology students. In this regard, her pathway to care resembles that of Gustavo, who attributed obtaining an appointment with Dr. Benavidez at the public health facility to being accompanied by me, a foreigner who local public health staff was less likely to dismiss. Both Fabiola and Gustavo actively sought mental health resources through their social networks. In this way, their pathways to care depended on what Whyte (2014b) refers to as "contingent sociality" and "technical know-who" in Uganda; social relations, connections to others—including visiting anthropologists—enable health seekers to access care.

What I wish to emphasize here, however, is that serendipity is a key element of Fabiola's trajectory to health services. My interviews with Fabiola happened to occur during the window of the psychology interns' practicum in Panajachel. Unfortunately, Fabiola's access to care was fleeting, as was Magda's, as introduced at the beginning of this chapter. Both Magda and Fabiola happened to visit the public health center at the precise moment when a psychology intern was there. Both women actively sought care, but its availability was a matter of chance due to institutional shortcomings. If they had not showed up at the times they did, it is likely that neither would have ever accessed psychological services. The director of the public health facility does not plan to hire anyone to attend to mental health needs. Instead, he prefers to wait for students completing internships, as this arrangement does not cost the center anything. However, it also results in an inability to provide continuous care, as well as uncertainty among locals about whether counseling services are available at any given time. This theme was borne out by interviews I conducted with parents of children traumatized by landslides and ensuing destruction of homes and roads resulting from Hurricane Agatha, which ravaged the Western highlands in 2010. Immediately after the tropical storm, psychologists from Guatemala City provided counseling for the children on multiple occasions. However, these services stopped after several weeks, leading to confusion among community members and further reinforcing perceptions of the transient presence of mental health providers in the area.

Psychologists are sometimes available on a more regular basis via long-term NGO programming. For example, a local NGO called the Women's Rights Association employs a psychologist. Because the group's primary objective is to provide legal counseling and services to encourage women to press charges against their abusers, the psychologist is only called to work with women experiencing domestic abuse. Patients experiencing psychological or psychiatric problems unrelated to domestic abuse cannot avail themselves of the psychologist's services. These services are not widely announced and known throughout the community. To access services, legal or psychological, a woman is usually referred by another woman who has received services previously or by someone who knows NGO staff. In a similar vein, some residents of Panajachel manage to access medications and private sector consultations through friendships with foreign aid workers who offer to assist them. For example, during my fieldwork, Melinda, a long-term volunteer from the United States working for a local NGO, regularly bought psychotropic medications for Heidi, one of her Guatemalan friends in a neighboring town. While this arrangement is benefitting Heidi temporarily, it is not a long-term solution, as Melinda may soon be leaving Guatemala altogether. These examples again demonstrate how health seekers actively utilize their social networks in attempts to access care.

Notably, however, mental healthcare is not mobilized only through extant social relations in Panajachel. Sometimes, health seekers' chance first-time encounters with empathetic volunteers at NGOs provide avenues to care. For example, Helping Hands is a faith-based organization whose primary purpose is organizing construction projects. In the past, the organization's social workers have provided volunteer support for community members recently discharged from rehabilitation programs, and some foreign volunteers have collected funds to pay for community members' treatment at private rehabilitation facilities nearby. As a result, individuals suffering from alcoholism and other addictions sometimes approach Helping Hands staff in hopes of accessing these types of resources. The volunteer social work program no longer offers psychological support to those recovering from addictions, but Dennis, the sympathetic long-term director of the organization, is sometimes touched by the plights of those seeking support to enter private rehabilitation programs and funds their treatment. Individuals often relapse after leaving the rehabilitation center as they lack long-term follow-up care. Dennis recognizes that the assistance Helping Hands provides meets with limited success, but takes great pride in the support the NGO extends to a small number of individuals facing addiction: "I like to think we're continuing Jesus' work. He didn't help the rich but the prostitutes and the mentally ill. But we're a long way off from being as effective." It is worth emphasizing that health seekers who arrive at Helping Hands and manage to interact with Dennis are likelier to gain access to health resources than if they interact with other staff members. For some health seekers, this leads to the perception that access to care through NGOs is based on "luck." As also documented by Chary in this volume, it can also lead to strategic visits to an NGO in hopes of encountering a staff member with a reputation for generosity. Central to these stories is the role that serendipity and chance encounters play in accessing mental health services, as well as how they constitute important parts of health seekers' overall understanding of how accessing mental health services "works."

CONCLUSION

This chapter has explored two major aspects of the experiences of mental healthcare seekers in Panajachel within a setting of proliferating nonprofit and for-profit private-sector resources. The first of these is slippage of patients between public, private, and nongovernmental sectors. Slippage is not simply a result of NGOization and health service fragmentation. Rather, my ethnographic data foreground institutional tendencies to systematically lead health seekers from one sector to another. In Panajachel, the public sector effectively serves as a pipeline to recruit patients into private clinics and pharmacies (for other examples, see Chary; Flood & Rohloff, this volume). Slippage appears to result primarily from the budgetary and human resources shortcomings of the public mental health system. Mental health professionals like Dr. Benavidez recognize that they are able to provide higher quality services outside the public sector and so, when able, they use their public positions to recruit away patients that they perceive as being willing or able to pay. Although on the surface this is done with the goal of providing better patient care, it is impossible to separate out the conflict of interest inherent to needing to build a successful private practice to counterbalance the financial constraints of the public system. Selective public to private recruitment also may theoretically worsen the care provided by the public system by siphoning away lower-risk, higher-functioning patients with higher amounts of social capital, effectively concentrating the number of high-risk, marginalized patients within the public system.

Slippage also functions by funneling public sector patients towards private pharmacies. Overworked and pressed for time, Dr. Benavidez focuses most of her attention on writing prescriptions; other elements of her clinical practice repertoire, such as counseling and behavioral techniques, are only available in her private clinic. Such pharmaceuticalization of public sector psychiatric care, in which consultations revolve around medications, is common in both resource-rich and resource-poor contexts (Biehl, 2005). What is notable here is the linkage between pharmaceuticalization and public-private slippage: since the public facilities are almost always stocked out of psychiatric medications, a public consultation effectively becomes a mechanism for referring individuals to pharmacies for expensive medications. Those least likely to be able to afford medications are most likely to be directed to purchase them, without the benefit of receiving counseling or other non-pharmaceutical treatments that might help them experience symptom relief without incurring significant costs.

Second, in a "resource-rich" tourism- and aid-heavy community like Panajachel, accessing mental healthcare often depends on serendipitous encounters, such as stumbling upon a psychology intern, as Magda did, or a charitable aid worker, as those who approach Helping Hands hope to do. With the concept of serendipity, my intent is not to ignore how health seekers actively and strategically mobilize resources through social networks, as discussed in other contexts (Nguyen, 2010; Scherz, 2014; Whyte, 2014b). Rather, in the context of healthcare privatization in Guatemala, I wish to highlight the ways that institutional inadequacies and inconsistencies shape health seekers' trajectories. Psychologists are only transiently available at public sector facilities; care through NGOs occurs through idiosyncratic personalistic arrangements; the supply of medications in private pharmacies is unpredictable. Sometimes, serendipity may serve to mitigate the inadequacies of the public sector and the financial inaccessibility of the private for-profit sphere and pharmaceutical market. More often, access to care is ephemeral.

In this environment of shifting priorities and shifting opportunities, though health seekers are aware that their attempts to access care will often be fruitless, they rationally hope for serendipitous encounters. A description by Susan Reynolds Whyte, Michael A. Whyte, Lotte Meinert, and Jenipher Twebaze (2013) of Ugandans' navigation of abundant but ever-changing HIV/AIDS care organizations is apropos to mental health seekers in Panajachel: "[T]here's a kind of gambling element at play, a hoping for luck ('you never know') that makes much support-seeking more like a lottery than a systematic investigation of available possibilities" (p. 149). Mental healthcare in Panajachel is ad hoc, episodic, and discontinuous, but for many, slippage and serendipity provide the only avenues to care.

NOTES

1. To maintain confidentiality, I use pseudonyms throughout the chapter.

2. Globally, non-specialist primary care workers commonly have little to no training in proper indications for psychiatric treatment and monitoring (World Health Organization [WHO], 2011).

SEVEN

Hysterectomies and Healer Shopping

Cervical Cancer and Therapeutic Anarchy in Guatemala

Anita Chary

Gloria Puac,[1] *53 years old, vaginal discharge,* read the handwriting scrawled on the clinic intake form. On the exam table sat a heavy-set woman wearing a lacy turquoise blouse and a matching woven indigenous skirt. Beads of perspiration dotted her hairline. For several hours, she and her husband had been waiting in an endless line of patients to see the "American doctors" sponsoring a weeklong medical mission in the coastal Guatemalan town of Santa Clara.

"Doctor," Gloria's husband Ovidio addressed the volunteer staffing the consultation room, "we went to see a private doctor last week. He told us to get these exams." Ovidio produced a manila folder of pelvic ultrasound images, which highlighted a mass against a dark background.[2] "Suspicious for cancer," read bolded words above the interpreting physician's frilly signature.

Two years ago, Gloria related, she had developed persistent vaginal discharge. "At the health center, they don't do anything," Ovidio explained their decision to bypass Santa Clara's government-run clinic. In theory, free government-sponsored healthcare is a constitutional right for Guatemalan citizens. Santa Clara's health center, however, was chronically short-staffed and often closed. Therefore, Gloria and her husband traveled to a nearby city and paid for a consultation at *Salud Guatemala,* an NGO-sponsored reproductive health clinic. There, a physician performed a Pap smear, a screening exam for cervical cancer.

"He told me, just from looking at my uterus, that there was something very serious and I needed an emergency operation," Gloria related, her Spanish reverberating with the fricative consonants of her native language, K'iche'. The physician personally arranged for an ambulance to transfer Gloria to his private clinic. There, he charged Gloria's husband 3000 quetzales (~390 USD) for initial exams. The surgery itself would cost an additional thousand dollars. "I felt he was just taking the money, not actually helping me," Gloria said, so she left before receiving the surgery.

Distrustful, she sought out a second opinion with a private gynecologist, Dr. Guillermo Ordoñez, who performed a hysterectomy for a lower fee of 4000 quetzales (~520 USD). For one year, Gloria felt fine. Then the discharge returned. Ovidio took Gloria to another private doctor, who told them he would need imaging exams to help them, but, knowing they were poor agricultural laborers, recommended that they seek help with the "American doctors" who would be in Santa Clara the next week.

"We can't know without further exams, but I would highly suspect recurrent cervical cancer," stated one of the volunteer OB/GYNs in English, as he palpated Gloria's tumor during a pelvic exam. "She'll need to go to the oncology hospital in Guatemala City for treatment."

Curious about what exam results had led Dr. Ordoñez to perform Gloria's hysterectomy, I called him at his private clinic. He briefly commented that he had operated based on her symptoms and physical exam, but had not done a biopsy prior to the surgery. Instead, he "took a swabbed sample from the vaginal vault" after he had removed her uterus and sent it to a pathologist friend who confirmed that Gloria had cervical cancer. "I told her husband that he had to take her to Guatemala City for more treatment," Dr. Ordoñez said, "but I don't know if they followed up."

Dr. Ordoñez quickly excused himself from the call to attend another patient. I hung up feeling deeply disturbed: standard clinical practice, in suspected cancer cases, is to obtain a biopsy—not jump straight into surgery—and, if the biopsy reveals cancer, perform staging exams to determine the extent of the spread of the disease. Women with early-stage cervical cancer can be treated with surgery, but at more advanced stages, chemotherapy and radiation are the recommended treatments and surgery is contraindicated. Gloria may have been cured if Dr. Ordoñez had followed the standard protocol and sent Gloria to the oncology hospital initially. Was Dr. Ordoñez unfamiliar with oncological protocols? Had profit potential motivated him to perform a gratuitous operation? Had he assumed Gloria, a poor farmer, would never make it to Guatemala City for care, and decided on her behalf to perform a palliative operation that might alleviate her symptoms? After our initial brief conversation, Dr. Ordoñez did not answer or return my phone calls. Regardless of his original reasons for operating, however, Gloria's only current option was palliative care.

This chapter examines the complex pathways to care taken by Guatemalan women with cervical cancer. Healthcare privatization has encouraged the emergence of multiple biomedical resources in Guatemala, which, as stories like Gloria's indicate, is changing the nature of healthcare decision-making. Health seekers for complex conditions like cervical cancer now face a chaotic milieu of public, private, and NGO-sector biomedical providers, who sometimes compete or collaborate with each other and practice medicine using different clinical standards. In this environment, women like Gloria commonly visit multiple biomedical providers to search for the "best deal." Anthropological studies of medical pluralism historically referred to such behavior—seeking out multiple health practitioners for the same problem without referral from one provider to the next—as "healer shopping" (Kroeger, 1983). This consumerist metaphor is potentially problematic, as it depicts health-seeking as an economic act, implies that the "buyer" and the "seller" have defined, relatively straightforward roles and mutual expectations, and envisions the "shopper" as an informed and rational consumer—assumptions which do not neatly apply to poor sick Guatemalans like Gloria who need care immediately. By employing this metaphor in this chapter, I do not intend to reduce complex acts of health-seeking to these economic terms. Rather, the term illuminates the ways in which Guatemala's contemporary healthcare landscape resembles a marketplace. As health seekers increasingly engage with private and NGO sector health resources, they strategically attempt to optimize the cost and perceived quality of a service, aware that many providers are driven by profit motives. Additionally, as others in this volume show, Guatemalans increasingly conceptualize health and healthcare as commodities, as goods that some aspire to purchase as a sign of status or upward mobility (see Flood & Rohloff, Hall-Clifford). In these ways, the label of "shopping" does capture some important dynamics of health-seeking in Guatemala. I argue that as healthcare options expand through privatization and NGO-ization in Guatemala, healer shopping becomes the norm, and health outcomes are unpredictable.

CERVICAL CANCER AND THE HEALTH SYSTEM TRANSITION IN GUATEMALA

In Guatemala, as in many low- and middle-income countries, cervical cancer is one of the leading causes of death among women of reproductive age (Ferlay et al., 2013). The disease is easily preventable through vaccination against the human papillomavirus, the sexually transmitted infection that causes cervical cancer, or through regular cervical screening exams (World Health Organization [WHO], 2006). However, vaccines are not yet widely available in Guatemala, and screening coverage is low:

only 40 percent of women have ever been screened for cervical cancer in the country (Gakidou, Nordhagen, & Obermeyer, 2008). Additionally, although the disease has high cure-rates at early stages, cervical cancer typically does not cause symptoms until late stages. Therefore, most women with cervical cancer seek out care at advanced stages, when they have developed vaginal discharge, bleeding, and/or pain. Ideally, a woman with these symptoms would be referred by a local-level healthcare provider to the *Instituto de Cancerología* (INCAN), the only oncology hospital in Guatemala that attends to impoverished public-sector patients. However, as Gloria's case illustrates, women's paths to treatment are not always so straightforward.

Over thirteen months of ethnographic research conducted from 2012–2014, I interviewed fifty Guatemalan women with cervical cancer about their trajectories to cancer care. I recruited thirty women directly from INCAN and twenty from NGOs supporting patients through treatment at INCAN. The sample included women from the eastern and western coasts, the central and western highlands, northeastern Petén, and Guatemala City and its surrounding metropolitan area. With each woman, I elicited the types of providers she had accessed and her rationales for doing so throughout the course of her illness, and in some cases, I interviewed her healthcare providers as well. While some of the women (nineteen of fifty) obtained cancer care in a fairly linear fashion—i.e., through successive referrals from the first clinic accessed to a facility performing more specialized exams (colposcopy and biopsy) to INCAN—the majority of them (thirty-one of fifty) took more complex routes to treatment through healer shopping.

Guatemala is a multicultural country that boasts a remarkable plurality of healing systems. Ethnomedical practitioners, including midwives, bonesetters, herbalists, and shamans, historically served as the immediate healthcare resort for the country's majority indigenous Maya population (Cosminsky & Scrimshaw, 1980; Paul & Paul, 1975; Valladares, 1952). As biomedicine became increasingly available through government institutions, pharmacies, and networks of health promoters over the second half of the twentieth century (Albizu, Goyo Todosantos, & Mendez, 2005; Rivera Alvarez, 1985), social scientists and public health practitioners began to study how indigenous and rural populations navigated between ethnomedical and biomedical practitioners for particular health problems (Berry, 2010; Cosminsky, 1982a; Goldman & Heuveline, 2000; Mosquera Saravía, 2002). However, in the era of privatized healthcare, it is becoming increasingly important to understand how patients choose between different *biomedical* resources, as well (i.e., how they engage with what this volume refers to as the "new" medical pluralism of expanding biomedical options).

Theoretically, health seekers can access free biomedical care through the public sector, a system of health clinics and hospitals operated through the Guatemalan Ministry of Health (MOH). In reality, however, these under-resourced facilities offer very limited services, particularly in rural areas (Garcés de Marcilla, 2004). Furthermore, as a result of healthcare reform in the 1990s, encouraged and financed by the Inter-American Development Bank, many basic health services in Guatemala are now delivered through government-contracted NGOs (Cardelle, 2003; see Maupin, this volume). At the same time, Guatemala's private for-profit medical sector has grown tremendously (United States Agency for International Development [USAID], 2008; see also this volume's introduction). As a result of these forms of healthcare privatization, Guatemalans have a variety of biomedical providers to choose from: those at government health facilities, NGO-based health programs, and private fee-for-service clinics.[3]

Among women with cervical cancer I interviewed, there were locally perceived advantages and disadvantages of resorting to each sector. Public sector care is technically free, which served as a primary motivation for one third of women I interviewed to access to MOH facilities when they developed symptoms.[4] However, as others alleged, "you only go to waste time," or "it's not worth it." Public clinics are often short-staffed and service hours unpredictable, particularly in rural areas. Patients may wait all day, only to receive a prescription that must be purchased at a pharmacy or a request to obtain an exam not available in the facility. Common complaints that "they didn't attend to me," "they didn't even do an exam," or "they didn't let me in," reflect patients' unfulfilled therapeutic expectations, as well as frustrations with outright discrimination (Berry, 2008; Chary et al., 2013). Sentiments that "they don't do anything," as Gloria's husband put it, lead many health seekers to avoid the public sector entirely.

Attending a private fee-for-service clinic allows patients to bypass waiting lines and receive care more akin to one-stop medical shopping. Private clinics tend to have laboratory facilities and diagnostic equipment on site, which reduces the time and effort patients must expend conducting medical errands and returning for follow-up appointments. Consultations with private physicians also tend to be less rushed than those in public clinics. "The private doctor talks to you, gives you a nice explanation," reported one woman, contrasting her experiences at a private clinic with visits to the regional public hospital.

A major deterrent to private health services is their cost. Initial consultation fees tend to start at Q150 (~20 USD)—more than twice the daily minimum wage (Ministerio de Trabajo y Previsión Social [MTPS], 2014). Although one might not expect the poor to avail themselves of private sector health services, they often incur debt or liquidate their minimal material assets to afford consultations with private doctors (see Flood & Rohloff, Pezzia, this volume). Gloria and her husband, for example, spent their life savings and borrowed money from a local lender at high interest in order to afford her initial consultations and surgery. These exorbitant expenses are justified by understandings that if one pays for the service, the quality of care must be superior to that offered in public health facilities.[5] "It's better with a private doctor," many told me.

NGOs offer a third option for biomedical care. NGOs often have high penetration into rural areas, which tend to lack other biomedical resources, and typically offer free or relatively low-cost care (Rohloff, Kraemer Díaz, & Dasgupta, 2011). Additionally, though many NGOs are run by Guatemalans, "*proyectos*" (projects, NGOs) and "*jornadas*" (daylong or weeklong medical clinics) are often associated with the presence of foreign US or European volunteers. Notions abound about *gringos'* (Euroamerican or European foreigners') wealth and generosity, and indeed, lead many to approach NGOs in hopes of receiving charitable care from people who "work from the heart." Foreign doctors—particularly from Cuba, the United States, or Europe—are also often thought to be better trained than local Guatemalan physicians. "The Guatemalan physician leaves you swollen and infected [after your surgery]," stated Sandra, a K'iche' woman who had visited a U.S.-sponsored surgical mission trip. "In contrast, the *gringo* doctor operates well."

Though there are certain advantages to seeking NGO care, many rural Guatemalans do not have easy access to these organizations, due to the country's uneven landscape of aid. Areas of Guatemala that offer natural attractions and opportunities for cultural tourism, such as Antigua, Lake Atitlán, and Quetzaltenango, three of Guatemala's most popular tourist destinations, each house hundreds of NGO projects (Foro de Coordinaciones de ONG de Guatemala, 2002). In contrast, the density of NGOs is much lower in Guatemala's hotter, less visibly indigenous areas, such as the southwestern coast and the eastern desert. Additionally, the populations NGOs cover and packages of services they offer vary widely by organization. Many NGOs attend only to patients enrolled in a particular program or residing within a particular catchment area. The majority of NGOs turn away patients with complex medical conditions due to budget constraints or lack of clinical capacity. Healthy Families International, for example, referred Gloria to INCAN, but did not offer her any form of assistance or follow-up care.

Given the distinct features of public, private, and NGO-sector care, Gloria's pattern of interacting with multiple providers across these sectors on the quest for therapy was not uncommon. Indeed, the majority of the cervical cancer patients I interviewed (31 of 50) ended up visiting multiple biomedical practitioners without being referred from one to the next. The following vignette offers a complicated case of healer shopping that further explores women's motivations in obtaining second opinions.

HERMINIA: BIOMEDICAL SHOPPING

"I have faith that God will do His work," said Herminia, dying of cervical cancer. At age forty-eight, shortly after her husband died in a car accident, Herminia developed a gray vaginal discharge with bleeding. The pills the nurse at the local MOH post gave her for a presumed "infection" had no effect, so Herminia borrowed money from an adult son to visit a private doctor. "He told me it was cancer, that I had to go to the capital [to INCAN]."

Herminia was a subsistence farmer in a small Jacaltec Maya village on the border of Guatemala and Mexico. A mother of seven, she was still raising two young children and did not have the money for bus fare to make the two-day journey to Guatemala City. Herminia's eldest daughter, Delmi, wary of the private doctor's advice, suggested that they seek out a second opinion "to see if it [was] true." Delmi took her mother to Huehuetenango, the closest major city—about four hours away by bus—where a second private doctor confirmed that Herminia would need to go to the capital.

Both of the private doctors had warned Herminia that she would need to take "a lot of money" to INCAN, which is technically a private hospital. Because the Guatemalan MOH does not have the funding to operate its own oncology facility, INCAN accepts referrals of poor patients suspected to have cancer. Although INCAN receives some governmental funding to offset the costs of public sector patients' initial laboratory exams and diagnostic procedures, patients must pay out-of-pocket for their treatment. The cost of chemotherapy alone—several thousand dollars, an amount greater than several years' worth of salary for many of Guatemala's poor—deters the majority of patients from completing treatment at the hospital. Indeed, as the hospital director revealed in an interview, one-third of patients never even begin treatment after their initial cancer diagnosis at INCAN. Herminia's case was no different, as she related:

> We went to Guatemala City, but lamentably, because of the money, we didn't do anything. The chemotherapy was expensive! And each exam was worth over 1000 quetzales (130 USD)! And my daughter went to talk with the social worker. She told my daughter that there weren't discounts—that it was a fixed price. I told her, maybe it's cheaper in zone 5 [at another hospital], but as we were already paying [in INCAN], we didn't have more money, and we didn't go elsewhere. I didn't return.

Over the following months, Herminia grew weaker from blood loss. "I was changing my underwear two, three times a day," she remarked. Delmi helped her scrounge together the money to visit another private doctor, recommended by relatives, to see if any other treatment options existed.

"They told me they were going to take out my uterus," Herminia stated. After the operation, the bleeding and discharge stopped, and Herminia felt she had been "cured." Months later, however, Herminia began to experience discharge again. "I would carry corn on my head," Herminia related, "and a discharge started to come down when I would walk home [from the fields]." The thought of cancer did not cross her mind. Rather, thinking she might have an infection, Herminia asked one of her sons for money to see a private physician who operated a closeby clinic across the border in Mexico.[6] "The doctor from Mexico told me that I would have to go to Mexico for treatment, for chemotherapy, because she couldn't offer me what I needed anymore," Herminia said, confused. "I thought, why are they going to do chemotherapy to me if I'm already cured?"

Herminia, distrustful of the Mexican doctor's advice, sought out a second opinion at *ProMujer*, a reputable women's health NGO in Santo Tomas, two hours away from her village. Iris, the nurse who initiated Herminia's pelvic exam, recalled that the exam table was immediately covered in blood. *ProMujer* had forged an alliance with a physician at the National Hospital in Huehuetenango, and Iris quickly arranged for Herminia to obtain a biopsy there. Dipping into *ProMujer* funds, Iris gave Herminia money for her bus fare and instructed her to return with her results. Herminia, however, did not return. She reported that once again, after the exam, the doctor told her, "There's no medicine for you. The only thing we can do is hospitalize you here and give you food. The best thing to do would be to go to the capital." Skeptical and discouraged, Herminia went home and decided to endure the discharge.

Several months later, Herminia's daughter informed her that a team of U.S. doctors was visiting Santo Tomas to hold "a campaign of exams for women." Herminia decided to try her luck with the "*gringos*." She was surprised to find that the U.S. volunteers were working with Iris at *ProMujer*—the NGO clinic she had already visited. The U.S. medical team, representatives of an international NGO that had partnered with *ProMujer*, offered to fund Herminia's treatment at INCAN. Iris began to coordinate Herminia's care and accompanied her to appointments in the capital, where she received a course of palliative radiation that would likely extend her life by two to three years. "The doctors say there's no cure anymore, but there's nothing impossible for God," Herminia told me. "I'm putting all my trust in him."

HOW HEALER SHOPPING BECOMES THE NORM

Herminia's pathway to treatment reflects an increasingly common pattern of healer shopping: by the time she accessed cancer treatment at INCAN, she had interacted with four private doctors, two public sector practitioners, and two NGOs. In some ways, Herminia's story is exceptional. Among the thirty-one women I interviewed who sought second opinions, twenty-eight had "shopped" between two to four providers, and only two had accessed as many providers as Herminia. In other ways, however, Herminia's experiences are broadly representative: they illustrate how misdiagnoses, medical mismanagement, and heterogeneity in clinical standards breed mistrust of biomedical practitioners in general. In this context, healer shopping becomes a form of "common sense." Clifford Geertz (1983) describes "common sense" as a dynamic body of knowledge about how to cope with "everyday problems in an everyday way with some effectiveness" (p. 75). He emphasizes that common sense is far from a set of universal truths, but rather a cultural system based on local models of apprehending reality. Along these lines, in Guatemala, consulting with multiple healers for a particular health issue is a historically and culturally conditioned response to the "everyday problems" of poor-quality, unaffordable, and inaccessible biomedical services.

This theme figured prominently in the narratives of women who had been repeatedly misdiagnosed while seeking cancer care. Apart from Herminia, twelve other women reported that when they first began to experience vaginal hemorrhage, public and private doctors failed to perform physical exams and simply prescribed pills and injections that "did not have any effect." Some were told that they were going through "menopause" or had "irregular menstruation" that would "go away on its own," only to have symptoms last for many months afterwards.

Misdiagnoses are so common that many pre-emptively seek second opinions. Janet, a forty-five-year-old woman of mixed descent with vaginal hemorrhage, told me she had gone to six private and NGO clinics before she was definitively referred to INCAN for cervical cancer. When I asked her why she had seen so many doctors, she replied, "It is because they are not sure. The first one doesn't diagnose well, and it's not until you see a fourth one, a fifth one, that you see what it is that you truly have." It was only at Janet's fourth medical consultation that she was told she might have cervical cancer. Her fifth doctor suggested fibroids, and the sixth performed the biopsy that confirmed the recommendations of the fourth to go to INCAN. Indeed, a nurse reflecting on Janet's case remarked, "You always have to go to two or three doctors. It's always the custom. People say if three say the same thing, it's true. But if two say yes and another says no, then no, you have to keep searching."

Healthcare inaccessibility also feeds into seeking second opinions. Herminia resisted multiple referrals to higher levels of care at INCAN in part due to economic and geographic barriers to care. In this setting, patients look for "easier options," which healthcare providers are quick to provide—in Herminia's case, likely due to profit motives, lack of specialized oncological training, or unfamiliarity with clinical standards of care. The medical mismanagement that results fuels healer shopping. When Herminia's symptoms returned after her hysterectomy, she sought out care with multiple additional providers. However, because she thought she was "cured" by the surgery, she was suspicious of their advice to go to INCAN.

Physicians at INCAN reported that they routinely saw cervical cancer patients like Herminia and Gloria, who had prior hysterectomies without having had biopsies or staging exams. These patients rarely receive a record of what was done and why. Josefina, a sixty-three-year-old woman from eastern Guatemala, offered one such story. Four years before our interview, she visited a private physician, complaining of vaginal bleeding. The physician did a Pap smear, told Josefina it had "turned out badly," and performed a hysterectomy. Four years later, Josefina began to have trouble urinating. She went to another private doctor, who discovered masses impinging on Josefina's ureters. "He said my kidneys were blocked up," she told me. The doctor referred Josefina to INCAN.

"She was operated on by a doctor of the street (*médico de la calle*)," said Dr. Rosas, the INCAN physician managing Josefina's care, showing me radiographic images of metastases throughout Josefina's chest and pelvis. For Dr. Rosas and other Guatemalan physicians I spoke with, the term "doctor of the street" refers to a physician who tricks impoverished and uninformed patients out of their money. While Dr. Rosas stated that it was impossible to know what stage of cancer Josefina had four years ago when she had gotten the hysterectomy, she suspected that the "doctor of the street" had operated on Josefina to extract money from her, rather than referring her to INCAN as he should have.

Indeed, rather than attributing these outcomes to private physicians' lack of training in cancer management, most Guatemalan healthcare professionals I spoke with interpreted such hysterectomies as acts of economic predation. They pointed out that hysterectomies are lucrative, because they are relatively simple surgeries for general physicians to perform and require minimal investment in surgical equipment and infrastructure. One gynecologist related, "After a gynecologist graduates, he wants to buy himself a new car, a new house. He knows that if he goes to the [rural areas] and starts operating on people, he'll be able to buy his own plantation soon." This physician, and others, referred to such entrepreneurial and ethically unsound gynecologists as "*ginecopatas*," or "gyneco-paths," a play on the words for "gynecologist" and "sociopath."

Various physicians reflected about how economic motivations to perform hysterectomies allow for a loosening of clinical standards of practice. One INCAN physician, only half in jest, suggested that hysterectomies are so profitable that "the only contraindications to having a hysterectomy in Guatemala are previous hysterectomy, being born without a uterus, or being a man." A Guatemalan physician working for an NGO similarly quipped, "In our country, we have the culture of doing hysterectomies for whatever reason. If you have fibroids, goodbye, uterus! If you have pain, goodbye, uterus (*adiós a la matriz*)!"

For these reasons, several physicians opined that patients should not trust a surgical recommendation without seeking an additional opinion. For example, Dr. Menendez, a gynecological oncologist at INCAN, described that he had recently seen a woman who had received a recommendation for an "immediate hysterectomy" from a private doctor. When Dr. Menendez performed a physical exam, he found an invasive necrotic mass that was beyond the point of surgery. "I congratulated her for not getting the operation," he said. "Patients have to seek out second opinions. But not all patients do. More commonly, they are taken in by the private doctor who tells them they need to get the operation."

CELESTINA AND NGO CARE

"It's not only the private physicians who are screwing patients over. The foreigners are also screwing patients over. It's everyone," opined Sylvia Keith, a volunteer physician from the U.S. Dr. Keith had just finished a consultation with Celestina, a forty-one-year-old Kaqchikel Maya woman with advanced cervical cancer and a disturbing treatment history. Two years before meeting Dr. Keith, Celestina, who lived in a village near Lake Atitlán, had developed continuous vaginal bleeding and sought out medical assistance with one of the many NGOs in the area. Visiting the local health center, she felt, would be "useless," and as a recently widowed subsistence farmer and mother of six, she had no money to see a private doctor. Rather, Celestina first attempted to access care through Samuel, a generous *gringo* she had seen distributing school supplies to orphaned children in a nearby town.

"Thanks to God, Samuel didn't deny my request," Celestina described. Samuel had initially founded the Maya Children's Foundation to provide educational scholarships for children in Panajachel, a tourist hub. However, moved by the chronic poverty and suffering of the local population, Samuel also supported patients with complex medical needs from a wide catchment of surrounding towns and villages on an ad hoc basis. "People deserve to have whatever care you can give them, to have a chance," he said compassionately.

Samuel quickly arranged a consultation for Celestina at a private clinic in the nearby town of Sololá. There, a physician revealed that Celestina had a tumor on her uterus and would require a hysterectomy. He offered to perform the operation himself for several hundred dollars.

"We don't have funds [for clinical care], that's the problem," Samuel told me. Hoping to find a cheaper option, he reached out to contacts at the Surgeons' Cooperative, a US-based NGO coordinating an upcoming weeklong surgical mission trip to the central highlands. They offered to perform the surgery for free.

"There, with Samuel's help, I got cured," Celestina explained. After the surgery, the bleeding stopped, allowing Celestina to care of her children, cook and clean, and tend to the family's fields as she had not been able to do for over a year. Her respite from illness, however, was short-lived: "Nine months after the operation, [the blood] suddenly started to come down again." Celestina, frightened, reached out to Samuel once more. Samuel had recently heard of an NGO called Maya Clinic, which coordinated specialized treatments for patients with complex medical problems. He reached out to Dr. Keith, one of the organization's volunteer physicians from the US, who agreed to see Celestina.

Dr. Keith immediately suspected recurrent cervical cancer. She contacted the Surgeon's Cooperative to access Celestina's surgical report, which contained a brief and uninformative note that surgeons had performed a hysterectomy. However, imaging exams ordered by Dr. Keith showed that Celestina's uterus was intact. With further investigation, Dr. Keith discovered that the surgical team had resected half of the mass, discarded it, rather than sending it to a pathologist for analysis, and "sent her home to die." When I asked Celestina what the Surgeon's Cooperative doctors told her about the operation, she responded:

> They operated on me there, but they didn't tell me what they did to me. They didn't give me any papers, either, nothing. They told me, "We will talk with the people who sent you." So the papers stayed with the *gringos*.

A visit to a Surgeons' Cooperative medical mission trip illuminated the chaotic environment in which such communication failures occur. Between triaging hundreds of potential surgical candidates and performing operations, the surgeons and their support staff were busy around the clock. Very few of the foreign volunteers spoke Spanish proficiently and none were familiar with Q'eqchi', the locally spoken indigenous language. Though the organization had hired English-Spanish and Spanish-Q'eqchi' translators from the area, very few were present on the surgical wards. As a result, well-meaning, already overburdened volunteers with very rudimentary Spanish often ended up conveying important information to patients in short bursts. For example, instructions about fasting prior to receiving anesthesia took the simple form of "nothing in your mouth" ("*nada en tu boca*"), with no temporal indications or explanations otherwise. Providers also tended to assume that all patients spoke Spanish, unaware that their conversations were entirely lost on monolingual Q'eqchi' patients. Out of respect and gratitude to the healthcare providers, patients typically nodded along blankly, their eyes betraying their confusion. Like Celestina, none of the patients received written records about their operations.[7]

While the Surgeons' Cooperative team did not provide Celestina with comprehensible information about her operation, they did inform Antonio, the local Maya Children's Foundation staff member who had coordinated the referral, that Celestina had cancer and that "nothing could be done." Antonio recalled that the surgeons had "removed part of a mass on her cervix to help her live a little bit longer," but estimated that Celestina had "only six to eight months to live." Antonio shared the prognosis with Celestina's family, but no one dared tell Celestina herself. Informing Celestina that she had cancer, they agreed, might emotionally devastate her, which could accelerate her death. Such understandings form the basis of non-disclosure of cancer diagnoses and fatal prognoses in biomedical practice in Guatemala and many other countries (Gordon & Paci, 1997).

"The question is, why was she operated on in the first place?" Dr. Keith asked rhetorically. The private Guatemalan doctor who first recommended the hysterectomy—known by nurses and physicians working in the area as the "butcher of Sololá" for his willingness to perform unnecessary operations—did not release Celestina's medical records. However, Celestina's examiner at the Surgeons' Cooperative had noted in her record that the tumor extended from her cervix into her vagina and to her bladder, indicating at least Stage IIB disease. The appropriate treatment at this stage, according to international clinical guidelines, is radiation and chemotherapy, rather than surgery (Edge et al., 2010). Although I was unable to speak with the surgeons who performed Celestina's operation, other Surgeons' Cooperative providers universally stated that they always referred women with advanced cancers to INCAN. What made Celestina's surgical team operate remains unknown. Dr. Keith guessed that the volunteers, unaware of the availability of oncological services in Guatemala, had "assumed there were no other options."

HUMANITARIAN INTENTIONS, UNPREDICTABLE RESULTS

Anthropologists in many contexts have described how "compassion" and "humanitarian" sentiments inspire medical volunteers—particularly upper-middle class North Americans and Europeans working with NGOs, university programs, and church groups—to provide care for those deemed needy and vulnerable (Bornstein & Redfield, 2010; Fassin, 2011; James, 2010). While foreigners' motivations for medical volunteering are complex, and may include opportunities for tourism or resume building (Brada, 2011; Wendland, 2010), much of North American- and European-sponsored NGO care in Guatemala appears to be motivated by desires to "do good" (Berry, 2014). Overwhelmingly, the short- and long-term volunteers and NGO staff I interviewed shared expectations of helping the poor.

Good intentions may lead medical volunteers astray. I encountered several cases like Celestina's—women who had received ill-advised NGO-sector operations—during participant-observation at INCAN. NGO providers I interviewed were well aware of this problem. A European OB/GYN described her horror at meeting volunteer surgeons who operated on women with metastatic disease; they thought it was better to "at least [do] something" for rural women they assumed would never otherwise access any form of care. Others accused such surgeons of behaving like "cowboys" and "waltzing in, doing whatever they want, and then leaving."

At the same time, humanitarian sentiments can be mobilized in productive ways. Celestina did eventually access stage-appropriate biomedical treatment. Maya Clinic arranged for her to receive palliative radiation in Guatemala City, which will likely "extend her life by a few years," as Dr. Keith put it. At the time of this writing, Dr. Keith continues to conduct home visits with Celestina to assist with pain management. Medical assistance programs may also broaden the domain of care to include the creation of social safety nets for the sick and their families: Celestina's young children are receiving scholarships and monthly food rations through the Maya Children's Foundation, and Samuel has pledged to continue supporting the family after Celestina dies.

Celestina's case illuminates the heterogeneity of clinical practice and capacity in the NGO-sphere. Organizations like the Maya Children's Foundation, which dabble in healthcare provision, "[don't always] know the best places to go" or "the right follow-up to have," as Samuel admitted in an interview. Groups such as the Surgeons' Cooperative can offer specialized services, but rely on a rotating base of short-term service providers who may have little awareness of locally available resources. But just as NGO care can spell disaster, it can offer possibilities for positive health outcomes. NGOs like Maya Clinic, which operate long-term programs integrated into extant in-country services, may offer care that is better tailored to the needs of the rural and indigenous poor.

CONCLUSION

Global health policy in 1980s and 1990s encouraged privatization and NGO-ization of health services in many poor countries under neoliberal assumptions that a market-based approach to care would encourage efficiency and improved quality of medical services by fostering competition among healthcare providers. Reform policies were also based on visions of health seekers as rational economic actors with the capacity to choose between healthcare services as consumers (Castro & Singer, 2004; Keshavjee, 2014; Kim, Millen, Irwin, & Gershman, 2000; Pfeiffer & Chapman, 2010; see also this volume's introduction). Gloria's, Herminia's, and Celestina's complex pathways to cancer care contrast with and complicate these assumptions.

With respect to cervical cancer care in Guatemala, a privatized market-based approach to healthcare promotes "therapeutic anarchy," rather than efficiency or quality. Stefan Ecks and Ian Harper (2013) coined the term to describe the plethora of divergent tuberculosis treatment protocols that have emerged among unregulated private practitioners in India. The cases presented here similarly demonstrate that clinical practice in Guatemala is incredibly heterogeneous and goes largely unregulated. Treatment protocols deviate from standard radiation and chemotherapeutic regimens to idiosyncratic hysterectomies. Clinical decisions are not always based on professional therapeutic standards, but rather revolve around profit motives, among some private physicians, or anticipation of losing patients to biomedical follow-up, among some NGO volunteers. These private physicians' economic predation and medical volunteers' humanitarian acts gone wrong can spell premature death for their patients. Yet at the same time, some practitioners do follow norms of referring women to specialty care, with some international NGOs even supporting women through cancer treatments.

Further contributing to therapeutic anarchy, biomedical practitioners' identities, capacities, and relationships vary greatly. Some work across sectors and recruit public and NGO patients into their private clinics, as Gloria's first physician did and as the "butcher of Sololá" attempted to do with Celestina. Such slippage between the public, NGO, and private sectors is common, with the former two increasingly serving as pipelines for the latter (see also Flood & Rohloff; Pezzia, this volume). In light of these connections and diversions, the results of care-seeking can be disparate. Some interactions, like Gloria's visit to Healthy Families International, end with a referral letter; others, like Celestina and Herminia, end up receiving accompaniment through referral networks of NGOs, public, and private clinics to access follow-up care. Outcomes depend, at least in part, on accessing the right provider at the right time (see also Pezzia, this volume).

In a setting of therapeutic anarchy, in some ways, health seekers cannot act as rational informed consumers envisioned by neoliberal policymakers. Poor Guatemalans lack information about their illnesses and appropriate therapies that might help them "shop" for care; they struggle to navigate an ever-increasing number of private- and NGO-sector biomedical resources. In other ways, however, the sick respond to their environment very rationally. As already minimal public sector infrastructure is withdrawn, impoverished patients attempt to search for the most affordable or convenient option among private practitioners. Patients, used to low-quality biomedical care and wary of extractive practitioners, become suspicious of misdiagnoses and mistreatment and seek out second opinions, a finding Clara Han (2013) has also reported in Chile. And as Guatemala's landscape becomes "projectified," to borrow a term from Susan R. Whyte, Michael A. Whyte, Lotte Meinert, and Jenipher Twebaze's (2013) description of a Ugandan landscape overrun with HIV programs, appeals to sympathetic *gringos* become one of the easiest ways to access care (see also Nguyen, 2010; Pezzia, this volume). As health-seekers continually negotiate the vagaries of market- and humanitarian-driven care, they rely on their experiential knowledge and local wisdom to tactically shop between providers for the best deal or the most supportive practitioner. Healer shopping becomes a "custom," a common-sense strategy (Geertz, 1983) to deal with low-quality health services, unchecked profit motives, and medical malfeasance and malpractice. In these ways, in Guatemala, therapeutic anarchy promotes a particular model of health seeking, in which patients increasingly act as pro-active, even entrepreneurial "consumers" of healthcare, and employ creativity and exert agency in seeking care (see also Flood & Rohloff; Pezzia, this volume).

In these ways, healthcare decision-making against the backdrop of the "new medical pluralism"—an expanding quasi-marketplace of biomedical resources—looks very different from historical accounts of medical pluralism, which emphasized tensions between ethnomedicine and biomedicine as at the heart of therapeutic choice among Maya people. Today, health seekers do not simply access care, but "achieve" it (Whyte, 2014b), and impoverished women with cervical cancer strategically resort to healer shopping in order to do so. Notably, to date, most discussions of biomedical shopping concern relatively high socioeconomic status populations in the Global North. "Doctor shopping behavior," in these contexts, is commonly discussed in terms of health-seekers confirming difficult diagnoses with specialists (Chang, Yang, & Chung, 2013; Chiou, Wang, Liu, & Yuang, 2012) or seeking prescriptions drugs (Sansone & Sansone, 2012). However, a handful of studies about "doctor shopping" in the Global South reach the same conclusions that this chapter draws. Health system fragmentation, medication inaccessibility, inadequacy of public sector care, and poor regulation of private practitioners have been found to drive healer shopping in South Africa (Moshabela, Pronyk, Williams, Schneider, & Lurie, 2011), Pakistan (Shafiq, Shaikh, & Kumar, 2011), and India (Sen, Iyer, & George, 2007; Sheehan, 2009). Various ethnographers have also shown that the proliferation of private and NGO-sector HIV/AIDS care resources in sub-Saharan Africa can have similar effects on health seeking strategies (Benton, 2015; Prince, 2014; Whyte, 2014b). Taken together, these studies suggest that the relationship between healer shopping and healthcare privatization is ripe for further scholarly investigation.

While ethnographic data herein highlight the perils of privatization-associated healer shopping, for rural, poor, and indigenous Guatemalans with complex medical conditions like cervical cancer, the practice may offer a sliver of hope: a lucky few, like Celestina and Herminia, may eventually stumble into NGO safety nets (see also Flood & Rohloff; King, Chary, & Rohloff; Pezzia, this volume). Here, privatization—specifically, projectification—may present apertures to improve access to care for vulnerable populations. However, where therapeutic anarchy reigns, health outcomes will remain unpredictable.

NOTES

1. All names herein of people, villages, and organizations are pseudonyms.
2. While some public, private, and NGO clinics document clinical consultations and exams in formal records, impoverished health-seekers in Guatemala must typically maintain their own records of laboratory and imaging exams and carry them to subsequent clinical interactions. It is often difficult for providers to obtain access to a patient's medical records from a previous clinical encounter without having a personal relationship with the prior provider.
3. Pharmacies and ambulatory vendors of pharmaceuticals represent another important biomedical option for health seekers. Though a few women I interviewed did report resorting to these resources, I do not consider them in this chapter. Hall-Clifford and Pezzia consider this topic in depth in this volume.
4. Of the fifty women I interviewed, six had their cancers detected through routine screening exams and reported no symptoms. Of the forty-four women who sought care after developing symptoms of vaginal discharge or hemorrhage, fourteen first turned to a government-sponsored clinic; eight to a private clinic; fifteen to an NGO; two to health care providers within their social networks; two to herbalists; and three attempted self-cure with home remedies.
5. This perception is also reported in Puerto Rico (Mulligan, 2014).
6. For patients living in rural villages at national borders, seeking care outside of Guatemala can involve less travel and fewer expenditures.
7. Most NGOs and medical missions keep written records about their patients, but do not provide patients with these records for a variety of reasons. Patients are often illiterate and do not speak Spanish or English, the languages used in medical records. Providers sometimes neglect the fact that patients may require and seek follow-up care. In Celestina's case, the chaotic nature of the mission also likely contributed to the failure to provide her with records.

EIGHT

Leveraging Resources in Contemporary Maya Midwifery

Nora King, Anita Chary, and Peter Rohloff

Rosa,[1] a forty-five-year-old Kaqchikel Maya woman from a rural community, recalls that her interest in health and healing began soon after her husband died of stomach cancer. In order to send her three young sons to school, Rosa held jobs outside the home and dedicated her nights to commissioned weaving. Slowly, and perhaps because of her life experiences and resilience, women began to approach Rosa for advice about various issues, including health concerns. Rosa was flattered, but often found herself unable to answer her confidants' health questions. She sought out any medical training she could find, attending health education sessions sponsored by non-governmental organizations (NGOs) in a nearby town. Eventually, she stumbled on a midwifery course offered at a government health center. As a result of her excellent performance in the course, she connected with lay midwives participating in a cooperative, and she began to attend their monthly self-directed education sessions.

Rosa was not called to midwifery through dreams or a spiritual experience—the common vocational paths documented by many scholars (Lang & Elkin, 2006; Paul & Paul, 1975). Nor was her adoption of midwifery a simple matter of professional choice, which contemporary accounts suggest is increasingly common among young secular Maya midwives (Berry, 2006; Hinojosa, 2004; Maupin, 2008). Rather, Rosa's practice grew organically out of her social position in her community. Her experience in childrearing, homemaking, and weaving—as well as the relative breadth of her medical experience—place her in confidence with all kinds of women in her village. At the same time, through attending NGO- and government-sponsored health courses, she has become well versed in biomedical perspectives on the physiology of pregnancy and birth and has developed the skills to work with a variety of women's health issues outside of childbirth. For example, she treats simple urinary tract infections, offers women advice about birth control methods, and refers patients to a local NGO or to the health center when there is a problem beyond her scope of practice. In these ways, Rosa simultaneously maintains strong ties with traditional Kaqchikel life and actively engages biomedical resources, on her own terms, to craft her own style of practice.

This chapter analyzes how healthcare privatization has induced changes in Guatemala's healthcare landscape, which increasingly positions indigenous Maya midwives like Rosa to leverage multiple resources, engage with biomedicine on their own terms, and define the scope of their own practice. In Guatemalan indigenous communities, lay midwives[2] have overseen childbirth for millennia. Lay midwives continue to play a crucial role in delivering care in Guatemala today. While Guatemalan women are, in theory, guaranteed access to free prenatal, delivery, and post-partum care through a government system of health posts, clinics, and hospitals, these facilities are underfunded and often geographically inaccessible (see this volume's introduction). Prenatal vitamins, laboratory exams, and sterile materials for surgeries are often unavailable through the public system, with the result that impoverished women must pay for these items at private clinics. Furthermore, public health facilities are understaffed, as government-employed physicians and nurses avoid rural assignments, receive salaries only for part-time work, and earn their living primarily through private fee-for-service clinical work (see also Pezzia, this volume). These factors compound women's cultural and religious preferences to deliver at home with a midwife (Berry, 2010). Indeed, lay midwives attend half of all births nationwide, and up to 70 percent of all births in rural indigenous communities (Ministerio de Salud Pública y Asistencia Social [MSPAS], 2010; United Nations Statistics Division [UNSD], 2014).

Guatemala has one of the highest rates of maternal mortality in Latin America, at 140 per 100,000 live births in 2010 (World Bank, 2014b), and this figure often doubles or triples within rural and indigenous communities (Schieber & Stanton, 2000). In attempts to reduce maternal mortality nationwide, the government of Guatemala has regulated lay midwives' practices for many decades. As described below, this trend has only continued with healthcare privatization reforms of the 1990s. Notably, healthcare privatization in Guatemala has entailed a rapid expansion of NGOs—both those associated with a government health service contracting system and those working independently—as well as other private providers. This has promoted a greater availability of biomedical resources as well as international funding and partnerships related to lay midwives' work. In response to these opportunities, lay midwives are redefining their work and transforming their roles within both their communities and the national healthcare system. As they do so, they resist and subvert two disparate but paradoxically aligned discourses, which have historically circumscribed midwives' roles. The first of these discourses is the historical perspective of anthropological literature on Guatemalan lay midwives, which situates them as "ethnomedical" practitioners by focusing on the idiosyncratic and ritualistic elements of their vocation and ignoring their contemporary multisectorial engagements. In contrast, this chapter demonstrates how indigenous midwives increasingly integrate biomedicine into their practices in creative and productive ways while still fulfilling traditional social and community-based roles. The second of these discourses is that of national public health policy and the development agenda, which have attempted to limit lay midwives' scope of practice by insisting on their "backwardness" and inability to effectively assimilate biomedical techniques into their practice. However, Maya midwives do not let these policies define the boundaries of their practice. Rather, they readily access private and nongovernmental biomedical resources, expanding and reinforcing their central and traditional role as liaisons and arbiters between their communities and the biomedical healthcare system. Rather than passive subjects controlled by tradition, the development apparatus, and biomedicine, we argue that Maya midwives exert agency in expertly crafting their roles in contemporary society.

Ethnographic data presented here derive primarily from one year of Nora King's (NK) participant-observation and collaboration with the Cooperativa K'exeloma', a lay midwife cooperative in the Western highlands of Guatemala, from 2013-2014. Cooperativa K'exeloma' is a voluntary group of about 100 members who gather monthly for educational sessions. Members also have access to discounted medications, receive practical support from the cooperative's leadership, and can make referrals to a physician associated with the organization. Cooperativa K'exeloma' also serves a social role, providing a safe space for lay midwives to share best practices and voice frustrations. Many participants are monolingual speakers of Mayan languages, but others are younger women who have recently begun studying midwifery.[3] The insights presented in this chapter principally derive from NK's work with Cooperativa K'exeloma', including attending meetings, developing training sessions, providing clinical support, shadowing Maya midwives, and participating in social functions. Other data presented are based on site visits to NGOs involved in midwife training programs as well as a review of websites and strategic documents of such groups conducted by all authors.

This chapter begins with a historical outline of how the twin discourses of anthropology and biomedicine have circumscribed lay midwives' biomedical engagements. Subsequently, it provides an overview of recent trends towards privatization and diversification of the biomedical landscape in Guatemala, which are enabling lay midwives to resist these earlier characterizations as either idiosyncratic or "backward" by leveraging biomedical resources on their own terms. Finally, it explores specific examples of how lay midwives leverage these resources through three cases, offering insight into how they are redefining their social roles through these productive and creative engagements.

LAY MIDWIVES AS ETHNOMEDICAL PRACTITIONERS: THE ANTHROPOLOGICAL DISCOURSE

Guatemalan medical anthropology has a long history, and studies of indigenous midwives feature prominently in this literature. Some of the earliest medical anthropological texts from the field were extended studies of lay indigenous midwifery practices (Adams, 1952; Valladares, 1952). These accounts were heavily influenced by Latin American indigenist ideology (*indigenismo*), which viewed understanding cultural difference as critical to national assimiliationist projects, and which was promoted by Mexico's National Indigenous Institute among anthropologists working in Mesoamerica. As well, in the mid-twentieth century, public health and research institutions regularly hired medical anthropologists to document local indigenous explanatory models and healing practices, largely for the purposes of bridging communicative gaps between biomedical practitioners and local populations and facilitating community health interventions (Barrett, 1997). In the 1970s, in particular, given the prevailing philosophy in international health of primary care for all, anthropologists sought to document ethnomedical practices in hopes of contributing towards broader efforts to integrate local healers into incipient primary care systems (S. Cosminsky, personal communication, January 1, 2015). In this political environment of knowledge production, scholars focused on the ritualistic and spiritual elements of Maya midwifery in attempts to document and legitimize their unique knowledge. Tropes established by these early studies included accounts of Maya midwives' receiving their vocational calling—and sometimes even their training—through spiritual means of dreams and revelations, or by falling victim to an illness with metaphorical significance, such as chronic aching in the hands, which improves following assumption of the duties of midwife (L. Paul, 1975; Paul & Paul, 1975).[4]

Although subsequent generations of anthropologists discarded many of the assimilationist assumptions and the applied focus of these earliest studies in favor of more progressive and theoretical approaches, the scholarly focus on cultural particularity has remained relatively constant in the study of Guatemalan midwifery. For example, throughout the

1980s and 1990s, studies documented lay midwives' use of hot-cold disease classification systems, treatment of ethnomedical illnesses such as evil eye, or practices of abdominal binding and the sweatbath (Cosminsky, 1982b; Greenberg, 1982; Lang & Elkin, 1997; Messer, 1987; Villatoro, 1986). In part, these analyses were responses to feminist critiques of the medicalization of childbirth, which led many scholars to advocate for the study of cultural birthing practices as valid and coherent systems (e.g., Jordan, 1978; MacCormack, 1994; McClain, 1989; Sargent & Davis-Floyd, 1997).

Even the most recent studies of lay midwives, however, which tend to have an explicit focus on revitalizing and reasserting the public health significance and cultural authority of lay midwives, have largely recapitulated themes of indigenous cosmovision—a philosophy attributing health to cosmological, physical, spiritual, mental, and emotional balance—and vocational particularity (Eder & Garcia Pú, 2003; Rogoff, 2011; Villatoro, 2001; Walsh, 2006). Underexplored in this literature are lay midwives' engagements with biomedical knowledge and healthcare systems (Cosminsky, n.d.). Even as pharmacies, hospitals, birthing centers, and training programs proliferate around the country, these accounts continue to portray lay midwives as culturally conservative and operating in a sphere largely untouched by these other contemporary developments. Accounts that do detail lay midwives' interactions with biomedical knowledge, professionals, and systems highlight power imbalances between physicians and nurses and lay midwives, biomedical providers' and institutions' assaults on lay midwives' cultural identities, and lay midwives' limited comprehension of biomedical reasoning (Acevedo & Hurtado, 1997; Berry, 2006; Cosminsky, 2001; Hurtado & Sáenz de Tejada, 2001; Rogoff, 2011). Such phenomena do indeed occur regularly in Guatemala, but together, these studies suggest that biomedicine is supplanting midwifery practice. Few analyses take an alternative perspective that highlights indigenous Guatemalan midwives' agency in complementarily using and adding biomedical practices to their repertoires (Chary, Kraemer Díaz, Henderson, & Rohloff, 2013). In general, anthropological literature about indigenous Guatemalan midwives has not followed trends in anthropological studies of midwives in other parts of the world, which explore their complex mediation of their roles, identities, and relationships with biomedical systems (Bourgeault, Benoit, & Davis-Floyd, 2004; Davis-Floyd, 2001; Hildebrand, 2012; MacDonald, 2007).

MIDWIVES AS BARRIERS TO PROGRESS: THE BIOMEDICAL DISCOURSE

In addition to the view from the anthropological lens, indigenous midwives increasingly came under the scrutiny of the emerging biomedical and public health sectors in Guatemala in the late nineteenth and early twentieth century. As early as 1897, the Ministry of Public Education sponsored obstetrics classes for lay midwives (Carey Jr., 2014). From the 1930s onwards, the Guatemalan government increasingly formalized attempts to regulate midwifery practice through training programs and licensing requirements. Through government-sponsored training sessions, lay midwives were discouraged from using traditional therapies, such as abdominal massage and sweatbath, and were forbidden from attending certain types of high-risk deliveries (Goldman & Glei, 2000; Greenberg, 1982).

This regulation and transformation of "traditional" midwifery roles accelerated with nationwide programs following the implementation of the global Safe Motherhood Initiative (SMI) in 1987. The SMI aimed to reduce maternal mortality by strengthening community-level care, in part through more rigorous training and supervision of lay midwives (Mahler, 1987). A major documented cultural effect of these new training programs included a wave of "secular" younger lay midwives who adopted midwifery for professional reasons, but eschewed many of the more traditional vocational trappings (Hinojosa, 2004; Maupin, 2008). Nevertheless, in Guatemala and elsewhere, the SMI had minimal impact on maternal health outcomes. Hence, support for supervising and funding lay midwifery training through traditional international health sources declined, under the assumptions that lay midwives were unable to recognize danger signs and make timely referrals for obstetric emergency (Maclean, 2010).[5]

Worldwide and in Guatemala, investment in lay midwives, by governments and intergovernmental agencies associated with the SMI, was replaced with a push for "facility-based" deliveries attended by skilled birth attendants (SBAs), a term which refers to birth attendants with biomedical training, such as nurse-midwives (Cosminsky, 2012; Kestler, Walker, Bonvecchio, Sáenz de Tejeda, & Donner, 2013; Sibley & Sipe, 2006). In Guatemala, between 1995 and 2009, the percentage of deliveries that occurred with SBAs increased from 34.8 percent to 51.5 percent (UNSD, 2014). These numbers, however, belie a difficult and controversial transition. First, despite increasing pressures for women to deliver in the hospital, many continue to deliver at home with a lay midwife, given familial and cultural expectations as well as practicalities such as transportation and finances or overt experiences of racism or discrimination at government facilities (Berry, 2010; Hurtado & Sáenz de Tejada, 2001). Second, existing "skilled" attendants are often recent medical school graduates with little experience, operating unsupported in remote health centers with very few resources. The pregnant women NK worked with emphasized safety as part of preferences to deliver at home; indeed, those who deliver in health centers are more likely to have Cesarean sections or suffer from postpartum infections (Althabe & Belizán, 2006;

Kestler & Ramirez, 2000).[6] While it is difficult to assess whether physicians perform Cesarean sections out of medical necessity or for their own convenience, our interlocutors roundly wished to avoid being "operated on."

LAY MIDWIVES AND PRIVATIZATION: A THIRD WAY

Contemporary lay midwives are situated in a complex space. On the one hand, they are reified by social scientists and many activists as the final conservateurs of endangered cultural and ethnomedical knowledge. On the other hand, they are increasingly written off as irrelevant and even dangerous by the biomedical establishment. However, as the following cases studies show, Maya midwives resist both of these characterizations. In part, they are able to do this because of the unique constellation of healthcare resources that has emerged in many rural communities following the signing of the Peace Accords and the end of the civil war in 1996. As documented in this volume's introduction, the Peace Accords provided several specific measures designed to promote the health of indigenous communities, which have been historically underserved by the public healthcare system. At the same time, as in many other parts of the world, international lending institutions mandated health system reforms to privatize the provision of healthcare. Thus, measures to improve indigenous health were implemented under a government initiative known as the Program for the Extension of Coverage (PEC), which subcontracted basic healthcare provision in rural areas to NGOs (see Maupin, this volume). The PEC guidelines include a specific mandate to improve rural access to prenatal care, in part by providing oversight, supervision, training, and help with pregnancy referrals to lay midwives. Therefore, paradoxically, at just the moment when institutional and national health policy was otherwise shifting its interest away from lay midwives in favor of SBAs, the PEC was increasing funding and opportunities for lay midwives. Especially in the last decade, this has sparked a proliferation of new, bilateral training and funding initiatives (Berry, 2006; Chary et al., 2013; Foster et al., 2012). United Nations agencies, the US National Institutes for Health (NIH), the Pan-American Health Organization, and many international NGOs have allocated resources towards research, training, and policy development with lay midwives in Guatemala (A. Garcés, personal communication, July 20, 2012).

As explored below, indigenous midwife training has also become an increasingly popular initiative for NGOs and short-term medical missions not participating in the PEC. These institutions have proliferated in recent decades, and currently thousands of NGOs operate healthcare programs in Guatemala (see the introduction, this volume). Such NGO-ization represents another important aspect of healthcare privatization that has significant effects for lay midwives. In some regions of Guatemala, NGOs—both PEC-associated and independent—have filled in the gaps where SMI funding has receded. At the same time, the private for-profit healthcare market has matured considerably in recent years (United States Agency for International Development [USAID], 2008). In the towns where we work, dozens of private fee-for-service clinics and laboratories have emerged within the last decade, many of which provide exams and services unavailable in the under-resourced government health facilities. These developments create new opportunities for lay midwives who, despite being officially discounted by national and international policymakers, increasingly reach out to and network with NGOs and private biomedical practitioners for advice, referral care and supplies. In this way, they maintain their central authoritative role as a source of traditional care for their communities while incorporating new biomedical knowledge and adapting to the changing healthcare landscape. The following vignettes examine this phenomenon in detail.

JOSEFA AND THE RENEWED INTERNATIONAL INTEREST IN LAY MIDWIVES

Josefa, a middle-aged lay midwife, stood close to her client Ofelia at her home in K'echelaj, a rural Kaqchikel village in central Guatemala. She had invited Laura, a British engineer, and myself (NK), to her client's home to try out a newly designed prenatal monitoring device. I held the apparatus, a smartphone attached by a cable to a bubble-gum pink fetal heartrate monitor. The heartrate monitor, or Doppler ultrasound, is so ubiquitous in biomedical prenatal care in wealthy countries that Laura bought hers from an online retailer selling directly to expectant mothers for use at home with their own phones. Laura wanted to see whether indigenous midwives could find and record the fetal heartbeat, recordings of which could then be analyzed to help with early detection of fetal distress.[7]

Josefa and I finished explaining the function of the device to Ofelia in Kaqchikel, and she agreed to participate. She loosened her brightly colored skirt, as she had done many times before for Josefa's prenatal checkups, and lay down on her bed in the dim room. Laura showed Josefa how to connect the cable and use the touchscreen. I joked about Josefa's facility with the technology, to which she replied that she had used her son's smartphone already.

Before using the device, Josefa set it down on the bed and used her hands to feel Ofelia's abdomen. It was large; she was just one week shy of her due date. "*Ütz rub'anon,*" she murmured, implying that the baby was in a good position for delivery. She turned on the device and placed it on Ofelia's abdomen. We all fell silent, listening through the static for traces of a heartbeat. Within moments, it appeared. Ofelia beamed, and Josefa looked satisfied. "There's the heart," she said. As we cleaned up, Josefa held the device, inspecting it again. "I would love to have one," she said. "I think I could do a lot of good for the women I see." Her words rang true to us; in her isolated village, early detection and referral of obstetric problems could spell the difference between life and death for mother and child.

Lay midwives like Josefa are increasingly seeking out and incorporating biomedical and technical resources, such as Doppler ultrasounds and smartphones, into their practice. Such resources are becoming more widely available as privatization facilitates and encourages flows of humanitarians involved in research and service initiatives. Laura, for example, works with a prestigious university in England that is becoming increasingly invested in global health projects. Through a colleague with former research experience and connections in Guatemala, she contacted Cooperativa K'exeloma in hopes of finding lay midwives willing to pilot test the device for what would later be expanded into a formal small-scale clinical trial. The cooperative's leadership enthusiastically established a partnership with Laura and her colleagues, hoping that the connection might bring in resources and equipment in the future, and arranged for Laura to conduct home visits with various lay midwives in their network over several weeks.

These sorts of relationships between Guatemalan lay midwives and health professionals and volunteers, both local and foreign, are becoming increasingly common. A number of NGOs, religious missions, and foreign universities have established midwife training programs and midwifery schools throughout Guatemala (e.g., Midwife International, 2014; Midwives for Midwives, 2015; Saving Mothers, 2012). During visits we have conducted with such groups, administrators have spoken about their motivations to promote "women's empowerment" and "indigenous culture" through their programs. They have showcased specially-designed birth registration notebooks, colorful educational materials illustrating common obstetric signs of danger, and basic supplies like scissors, antiseptics, and gloves that they provide to lay midwives associated with their programs. The websites of such groups feature photos of local staff, foreign volunteers, and indigenous midwives practicing skills such as auscultation and breech deliveries with mannequins (e.g., The Hope Alliance, 2014; Kitch, 2014). A number of Guatemalan physicians in Guatemala City have also organized and delivered midwife training sessions, both through local charitable foundations and institutions receiving international grants, and some have proudly shown us awards they have received as a result of this work. Health professionals in these settings have described to us the ease of working with lay midwives as a group of readily identifiable community health workers, and thus an easy point of access for health interventions, as opposed to other types of local healers such as shamans or herbalists.

Resources have also become increasingly available to lay midwives through nursing and midwifery schools in the Global North (Foster et al., 2012). Some of these institutions promote intercultural programs, through which trainees have opportunities to visit Guatemala and shadow lay indigenous midwives. From our interactions with such exchange students, part of their tuition money goes towards financing toolkits for local lay midwives as well as healthcare costs for their clients. In some cases, foreign students pay for homestays with lay midwives, thus making direct economic contributions towards their livelihoods. These sorts of transactional arrangements are becoming more common with the explosion of academic interest in public and global health in the last two decades and the concomitant emphasis on health professional students' participation in service learning programs abroad (Merson & Chapman Page, 2009).[8]

The Doppler ultrasound Josefa pilot tested with Ofelia and Laura is part of these broader flows of biomedical resources from North America and Europe to Guatemala. By accommodating the Doppler ultrasound into her home visits with clients, Josefa demonstrates that incorporation of biomedicine into midwifery practice does not necessarily equate with the disassembly of traditional values, nor does it require absolute conformity to a facility-centered model. Josefa interacts with her client in Kaqchikel in her home, where she establishes her trust through repeated visits and receiving payment in kind. At the same time, Josefa is acutely aware of the medical consequences of obstetric emergencies. Her willingness to participate in extra-local global health initiatives in order to further opportunities for her clients demonstrates lay midwives' capacity to expand the scope of their practice within a pluralistic and privatized medical landscape.

FLOR AND BEATRIZ: ACCESSING RESOURCES

On a Sunday morning, I (NK) received a call from Flor, a middle-aged lay midwife in the rural village of Pa Ch'ab'aq. One of her clients, Adelina, had given birth to Karina, a baby girl—her second child—two days prior at the national hospital. Adelina was healthy, but when her labor began, she bled even before the baby was born. Flor recognized this as potentially dangerous and referred her to the hospital. When Adelina arrived at the hospital with her husband, doctors closely monitored her labor. Although the labor and birth went well and the bleeding could be controlled, Flor related, Karina was born with a cleft lip and palate. Doctors in the hospital discharged Adelina and Karina home quickly with instructions to follow up at the local health post.

Upon learning about the newborn's cleft lip and palate, Flor made her way to Adelina's house immediately. Flor is among one of the most proactive members of Cooperativa K'exeloma'. Despite speaking very little Spanish, she is involved with the organization's executive board and is very influential amongst her peers—a quiet sort of leader. I spent time living with Flor's family as I learned Kaqchikel, and during subsequent visits to her community, I was able to observe the services she provided in the community. Flor often attends home deliveries and remains with the family until everyone feels settled and safe. Whenever a baby is born in the community, whether delivered at the hospital or the home, Flor visits the family to weigh the baby with a handheld balance, gives the mother lactation advice, and prepares the sweatbath, among other services. From her previous experiences and participation in Cooperativa K'exeloma', Flor recognized the urgency of Karina's situation. Infants with cleft lip and palate can have trouble latching onto the nipple to breastfeed. Even those able to obtain adequate breastmilk burn more calories nursing than other infants, and therefore they are at great risk of malnutrition and dehydration if they do not receive supplemental milk formula (Reilly, Reid, Cahir, Mei, & Bunik, 2013).

Flor knew that I was a medical student involved in women's health projects and that I was connected to another NGO, Medicina Iximulew, which had supported several people in her community with complex illnesses. She called me in hopes that I could connect Adelina and her baby to urgently needed resources—both milk formula and health education. The morning following the phone call, I met up with Flor to visit Adelina and Karina. Karina was strong and healthy and did not show signs of dehydration. I arranged for them to consult with Dr. Brown, a pediatrician working for Medicina Iximulew, the following day. This organization scheduled regular weight checks, provided the family with supplemental milk formula, and arranged for Karina to have surgery with a reputable surgical mission at nine months of age. Flor continued to visit Adelina to provide her usual postpartum care. Flor also enlisted the help of her own daughter, a community health worker, to negotiate with Adelina when she considered going to a poorer-quality surgical mission when Karina was three months old. Flor reminded Adelina that a well-done surgery would have lasting effects. Ultimately, Adelina waited to perform the surgery, which turned out successfully.

Several months later, I was talking with another lay midwife, Beatriz, at the Cooperativa K'exeloma' office. Like Flor, seventy-year-old Beatriz primarily spoke Kaqchikel and could not read or write. Beatriz was one of three lay midwives serving a very large geographical area, which included two neighboring villages: Pachimos, an indigenous Kaqchikel village where Beatriz lived, and San Pedro, a primarily Spanish-speaking village where the majority of residents are of mixed indigenous and European descent. Both villages are quite poor, and women prefer midwife-attended deliveries for cultural and economic reasons. Although Pachimos is physically close to the departmental capital, Beatriz had related stories to me about trucks getting stuck in the mud on the notoriously decrepit road. Beatriz's clients in both villages faced economic and transportation barriers to accessing nearby health centers, and hospital births were seen as expensive, cold, impersonal, disrespectful, and even dangerous.

Recently, Beatriz related, Sara, one of her clients from San Pedro, the nonindigenous village, had given birth to a baby boy with a cleft lip and palate. Beatriz delivered the infant in the family's house, an adobe and bamboo shelter accessible only over muddy footpaths, without incident. As she usually does, Beatriz stayed with the family until the infant was nursing well, but she was still worried. She knew the baby needed further care, which would only be available at the government health center. However, Sara was anemic and malnourished and had a domineering husband and eight other children. Because Sara was unable to leave the house, Beatriz decided to take the infant to the health center herself.

As a resident of Pachimos, Beatriz was registered as a lay midwife at the government health center of Ixcal, the majority indigenous municipality charged with providing health services for her village. She was familiar with the staff there, even though they were not on the best of terms. San Pedro, however, pertains to a different municipality, Santa Ana, and village inhabitants must attend the Santa Ana health center. Beatriz is not registered as a lay midwife at the Santa Ana health center and reported that she had only been there a handful of times. She felt that the discrimination she normally faced as an indigenous midwife in Ixcal's health center was immensely magnified in Santa Ana. In Ixcal, Beatriz was at least known for her long tenure and hard work as a lay midwife. In Santa Ana, her indigenous clothes and heavily accented Spanish made her seem "backwards," a term that many lay midwives used to describe how they felt in the presence of biomedical providers.

Beatriz's attempts to help her client Sara seek care for the newborn with cleft palate proved this point once again. "I went four times," said Beatriz, "carrying the baby twice. They refused me each time." When I pressed her to explain why, she admitted that her *carnet*, a document granting permission to lay midwives to work, had expired because she had forgotten to submit her renewal paperwork. It is not uncommon for health posts to heavily emphasize bureaucratic procedures, such as documenting visits, over delivering care (see Dasgupta-Tsikinas & Wise, this volume), and staff simply refused to perform a clinical evaluation of the child. Frustrated, Beatriz told me, "We took him to Dr. Ivan." Dr. Ivan is a locally well-known physician who runs a part-time private clinic in San Jorge. Beatriz often refers patients with general medical complaints to him, and she successfully arranged a private consultation with him for Sara and the baby. Unfortunately, by this point the child was very dehydrated and malnourished, and died shortly thereafter. The baby's death was a reminder that simply because lay midwives have access to diverse resources does not mean that they and their clients will be well served.

COOPERATIVA K'EXELOMA': DEFINING ROLES

An elderly Maya midwife kneeled over scatterings of pine needles and colorful floral arrangements and offered a soft blessing in Kaqchikel. Cameras flashed from a large audience of about one hundred people attending the inauguration of Cooperativa K'exeloma's new clinic. "We began on the ground," said Cristina, the executive director of the cooperative. "No one has ever ensured that midwives have had a dignified place to work. This is a dream, and it is only the beginning." Representatives from local health centers and supporting organizations in Guatemala City, the United States, and Europe listened on at an honorees' table as the founding members of Cooperativa K'exeloma' related the group's story, which had officially begun nearly ten years before the celebration taking place that day.

In 2004, a group of Maya midwives in San Jorge grew frustrated with how they were treated at the local health center. During meetings and conversations at the Cooperativa K'exeloma' office, midwives enumerated a number of complaints about their antagonistic relationship with biomedical providers there. First, they realized that local government providers were blaming them for maternal and infant mortality. Any adverse events, even those that occurred at a health center, were recorded as midwife-related if the woman began labor under a lay midwife's care, making lay midwives look irresponsible. Second, the lay midwives saw little personal benefit to their participation in the required training and felt the information they received at the health center was repetitive, simplistic, and often given in incomprehensible Spanish, rather than their native language of Kaqchikel.[9] Third, they felt that the health center granted licensure to practice arbitrarily. Maintaining one's *carnet* was supposed to be contingent on attending training sessions and submitting paperwork in accordance with deadlines. However, retaining licensure meant that midwives were also required to perform humiliating tasks, such as mopping the center's buildings. They were also required to participate in health promotion activities, assist with vaccination campaigns, and record vital statistics in areas covered by the health center. Though the lay midwives recognized the value of some of these activities, they felt that the health center staff did not recognize that they were already burdened with other responsibilities, and indeed, that the health center used them as a free workforce to carry out activities in the most remote villages without compensating them for their time or transportation expenses. In a way, the lay midwives felt they had become the drones of under-resourced health centers. These problems discouraged them from seeking help at the health centers when problems arose among their clients who were in labor.

"We had to come together to defend our rights," says Cristina, who is now the group's executive director, "since there was no guarantee that the health center would treat us fairly." Cristina, a middle-aged woman who had worked as a health promoter in her youth and had been a lay midwife for decades, was a natural leader and spearheaded organizational activities. She began talking with like-minded colleagues, and a small group formed. The fledgling group began to meet monthly, usually in their own homes, to talk about the treatment they received at the health center. If they were able to get a critical mass of participants, they thought, perhaps they could influence local policy towards lay midwives. At the very least, they enjoyed sharing advice and experiences. In addition, participants wanted to learn about the topics that health centers should be teaching them: complications of labor, gynecologic complaints, and basic medication use, for example. Cristina and her colleagues had no trouble finding participants. As it turned out, even the lay midwives that health center staff saw as the most "backwards"—those who were older, monolingual in Kaqchikel, and supposedly reluctant to give up traditional practices—were excited about the opportunity to learn more biomedicine.

Cristina quickly saw that the group was expanding beyond what she had anticipated. When participants' homes could no longer accommodate their large meetings, she began reaching out to external resources. She led petitions to incorporate the group into San Jorge's civil society, began to arrange meetings with NGOs in the area that might serve as allies, and performed internet searches for grants to support the group's work. Initially, the group received sponsorship from local NGOs and government offices to rent space. With funds from an international NGO, they hired Dr. Ivan, a non-indigenous Guatemalan physician, to provide primary care to their clients and assist with hospital referrals. Working with Dr. Ivan and a second international NGO, the lay midwives began to organize their own training sessions; they also, in some cases, received scholarships from supporting NGOs to attend workshops in other towns of Guatemala and share their knowledge with other lay midwives. Soon afterwards, they began collaborating with a group of German physicians who ran a primary care clinic in Ixcal and with an international reproductive rights organization, which had a regional office in Guatemala City. Through pledges of support from these groups, Cristina and her colleagues secured funding to build a new birth center adjoining the clinic. This center was inaugurated in a public celebration, attended by health center staff, regional Ministry of Health officials, and a number of NGOs and other supporters as described above. At the celebration, an administrator of a local health center gave a public speech about how "there no longer needs to be competition between us, but collaboration," and a leader from the regional hospital asserted that the founding of the clinic represented "a new era of collaboration between the Ministry of Health and the midwives." International organizations continue to be instrumental in the cooperative's day-to-day activities, such as procuring medications, providing practical training and helping with data management.

Cooperativa K'exeloma' demonstrates not only that successful collaboration between lay midwives and biomedical establishments is possible, but that lay midwives are eager to engage biomedical resources and forge such collaborations on their own terms. Cristina's enterprising attitude, and her colleagues' desire to integrate biomedicine into their practice, enabled the cooperative's formation and success. Privatization facilitated the presence of diverse medical actors in San Jorge, including private physicians, small NGOs, foreign governments, and large international organizations.

CONCLUSION

Lay midwives remain one of the most significant healthcare resources available to rural indigenous communities in Guatemala. They have long been subject to significant external scrutiny and analysis, both that emanating from anthropological scholarship about Guatemala as well as from public health policy at the international and national level. These analyses have tended to emphasize cultural particularities of lay midwifery while failing to appreciate its agile engagements with multiple sectors within Guatemalan society and the international community. Although originating from two disparate sites of political and theoretical engagement, anthropological portrayals of the Guatemalan midwife as "ethnomedical" practitioner and guarantor of cultural knowledge and the biomedical portrayal of the midwife as an unskilled, "backward" healthcare provider have tended to reinforce each other.

These predominant understandings of lay indigenous midwives do not capture the complexity of their contemporary practice, particularly in light of Guatemala's privatized healthcare landscape. The rapid growth of the private healthcare sector in the years following the signing of the Peace Accords and the surge of interest among the international donors in lay midwifery have given Maya midwives new opportunities for leveraging resources. The case studies presented in this chapter demonstrate the ways in which, through access to these resources, Maya midwives gain social and financial capital that allow them to engage productively the biomedical and public health sectors on their own terms. In doing so, they also demonstrate their capacity to negotiate their public identities, which are neither exclusively ethnomedical nor exclusively biomedical. Rather, they are able to incorporate and transform key elements of the contemporary practice of biomedicine in ways that both remain "effective" on biomedicine's own terms while also reinforcing and reinvigorating their central authoritative roles as a source of traditional and local caring. As they do so, their visibility increases within biomedical establishments, the public health system, internationally-funded health projects, and among indigenous clients, many of whom prefer providers who can straddle and incorporate valuable elements from various styles of healing.

In these ways, the lay midwives of Cooperativa K'exeloma' exemplify Davis-Floyd and Davis's (1997) concept of the "postmodern midwife," whose practices do not fall neatly into distinct categories of traditional, professional, or biomedical. Rather, they move between systems of knowledge; they integrate into their repertoires practices they see as beneficial to their clients and their own professional longevity (Davis-Floyd, Pigg, & Cosminsky, 2001; Hildebrand, 2012). Postmodern midwives are "educated, articulate, organized, political, and highly conscious of both their cultural uniqueness and their global importance" (Davis-Floyd & Davis, 1997, pp. 319–320). They actively create spaces for their own work in response to multiple processes and policies, including, for example, their marginalization from or inclusion in biomedical environments, increased availability of technological interventions in childbirth, or broader political and economic shifts (Davis-Floyd, Pigg, & Cosminsky, 2001).

In Guatemala, we suggest that what has significantly influenced the emergence of postmodern midwives is privatization, and associated flows of material and human resources from the Global North to the Global South. Lay midwives are well-poised to take advantage of these resources, given contextual factors such as limited access to high-quality birthing care, the large rural indigenous population's ongoing dependence on lay midwives, and the global political foci of the SMI. The role of NGOs and foreign aid in driving midwives' professionalization has similarly been documented in other parts of the world. For example, Davis-Floyd (2001) highlights how North American certified midwives make available educational and material resources that help lay midwives in Mexico organize and cast themselves as "professional midwives." As well, Price (2014) describes how NGOs' promotion of biomedical discourse about and among SBAs in India shapes understandings of midwives' professional identities. In contrast to these cases, which describe professionalization of middle-class midwives or skilled birth attendants, in Guatemala, this process is occurring among indigenous women of low socioeconomic status at a grassroots level.

Our findings provide a provocative counter-example to prevailing empirical analyses of the interactions between lay midwives and biomedicine. In various countries, scholars have highlighted the ways in which biomedicine, as an institution, erodes lay midwives' autonomy (Cosminsky, 2012; Geurts, 2001; Jenkins, 2001; Kruske & Barclay, 2004; Towghi,

2004). Often, when lay midwives interact with biomedicine on terms not their own—whether through government-imposed training courses (Torri, 2012), co-optation into reproductive health services beyond pregnancy and childbirth (Schneider, 2006), or increased surveillance (Cosminsky, 2001; Triolo, 1994)—the results are inevitably disempowering. However, as our cases demonstrate, the flourishing of private and civil sector resources in recent years in Guatemala can change the rules of the game. Privatization has facilitated the emergence of a more autonomous and entrepreneurial lay midwife, at once ethnomedical and biomedical, who increasingly solidifies her own caregiving position both within her community and in the national healthcare landscape.

NOTES

1. All subjects' names, the names of their villages, and other details, have been changed to protect identity.
2. We use the term "lay midwife" to describe women who are elsewhere called "traditional birth attendants" (TBAs) or "traditional midwives." Commonly, in Guatemala, they are known as *comadronas*. In Kaqchikel, the language spoken by the women we describe, midwives are called *k'exeloma'* or *iyoma'*, although *comadrona* is most commonly used. In this chapter, "indigenous midwife" and "Maya midwife" also refer to lay midwives. Nurse-midwives do not have a formal designation in Guatemalan biomedicine.
3. Midwives voluntarily attend the cooperative. In order to maintain the license to practice, they must attend training sessions at the local health posts and avoid government-prohibited activities (see Berry, 2006; Hinojosa, 2004).
4. A notable exception to this trend is Brigitte Jordan's (1978) famous study of Yucatec Maya midwives in Mexico. Jordan highlights these lay midwives' savvy in blending local and biomedical birthing practices and in creating social networks.
5. Recently, oppositional voices have emerged, arguing that midwives were not given appropriate training and tools before being judged by the SMI. For example, recent studies have shown improvements in knowledge and safe behaviors (Sibley, 2006) and impacts on perinatal and maternal mortality (Jokhio, Winter, & Cheng, 2005).
6. In contrast to the World Health Organization's recommended Cesarean section rate of 5–10 percent of all pregnancies, in Guatemala City, the Cesarean section rate is 23.8 percent in public hospitals and 63.9 percent in private practices (Althabe & Belizán, 2006).
7. This is similar to fetal monitoring practices in the Global North, which aim to detect poor placental oxygenation and fetal acidosis, particularly during late pregnancy and delivery—harbingers of hypoxic injury and perinatal death.
8. Notably, the presence of these programs tends to be short-term, due to inadequate long-term funding mechanisms. The leadership of Cooperativa K'exeloma was quite familiar with these issues, but generally sought to take advantage of such relationships while possible.
9. Medical care and most midwife training sessions are conducted in Spanish rather than indigenous languages (Berry, 2006; Chary et al., 2013; Maupin, 2008).

NINE

Conclusion

A Bad Conscience of Justice!

Peter Benson

> "The forces of grief that curse the human and cosmic villainy are the source of all the religion and ethics there have been and are in the world."
> —(A. Lingis, 2000, p. 74)

Guatemala is a country of striking social disparity, especially when it comes to health access and outcomes. Deep patterns of marginalization and stigmatization, confounding connections to the capitalist world system, and ideologies of harmony and nationalism make for a country in which poor and indigenous people face trying conditions and comparatively worse life chances, even as things are said to be—and in many ways apparently are—improving. Much of the disparity comes out of Guatemala's long colonial history, the civil war of the past half century, and international free trade policies. The War on Drugs that continues to be waged by the United States and its political allies has also entailed substantive impacts throughout Latin America. The prevalence and danger of organized crime and drug and human trafficking is related to this punitive and martial approach to what can otherwise be reckoned a public health issue. Much of what is happening in Guatemala looks a lot like what is happening in many other countries. Stark health and socioeconomic disparities persist, institutional and clinical capacity is woefully lacking or chaotically organized, the state has never really played an effective role in delivering progressive outcomes, and conflictual divisions worsen even as a broad rhetoric of improvement and opportunity, of equality and enfranchisement, seeks to boost hopes and assure affected populations that things are getting better.

This situation might be described by the social theorist Lauren Berlant (2011) as "cruel optimism." Cruel optimism is a "structure of feeling" (Williams, 1977). It is an aspect of the cultural logic of late capitalism. Affects, sentiments, feelings, and attitudes accompany the worldwide structuring of a neoliberal economy. This logic encourages people to feel optimistic even as life chances diminish, economies of violence flourish, traditions are swallowed up in the incessant marketing of the new, and communities become increasingly hierarchical, fragile, or displaced. That life entails such basic features as illness and death, and that these facts are inescapable for all of us, is obscured in smooth surfaces of the marketable, the consumable, the curable, and the moveable. Upward mobility, financial success, and freedom from illness, aging, and death are marketed as things that we ought to expect, while the vast majority of people live everyday life in a state of critical coping and struggle to make ends meet.

We live amid wars and struggles and incursions of various kinds. Yet the messages of consumer culture and the strategic posturing of the nation-state encourage a view of life as anything but conflictual. Consider the endless stream of colorful ads for the cell phone companies Tigo and Claro along Guatemala's highways. Brightly painted, they are visible everywhere: on the outer walls of small stores, on billboards, and on jackets worn by poor vendors who sell cell phone minutes in passing traffic. *Tigo* implies an embrace, an outward reach. The company markets itself as *tigo* (as in *contigo* [with you]). *Claro* [clear] implies clarity. Things seem rational and reasonable, life organized by a market that makes sense. But these are cruelly optimistic brands that mask the real. Cell phone technology connotes civil society, interconnectedness. But in the real world, for people who cannot afford gated communities or are daily exposed to violence, crime, and extortion, life is anything but *claro* or *tigo*.

Cruel optimism eschews a commitment to objective reality and obfuscates an elegiac sensibility. Neoliberal rhetoric and policy instruct us that market-based solutions and interventions that flow from the Global North to the Global South represent our best, perhaps our only way out of our mounting anthropogenic crisis. But in historical perspective, this very dynamic of sourcing solutions and interventions from wealthy countries is part and parcel of how present conditions have been made. The cultural logic of capitalism has long been based on the notion that the West is the best. The American economist Walt Rostow was special assistant for national security affairs for president Lyndon Johnson. A staunch anti-communist, Rostow powerfully shaped U.S. foreign policy and the Cold War and is best known for his book *The Stages of Economic Growth: A Non-Communist Manifesto* (1960). Rostow argues that all societies progress through stages of "development," from "traditional society" to the era of "high mass consumption," and this era of advanced consumption represents the pinnacle of human achievement. This model of "development" became a leading model for thinking about and directing international economic policy in the last half century.

Here is someone who had all the power in the world. And he argued that consumption—*consumption*—is the best of what humans can do. Maya peoples, with deep traditions of community and morality, should apparently give up these moorings and embrace the stuff of Walmart. To parlay tragedy and objective reality for marketable optimism is to forget that problems like malnutrition and obesity and poverty are not inherent to Maya communities, but rather stem from how these communities have been historically integrated into Western systems of rule and the lifestyle, and morality—the high mass consumption—that they promote.

Multinational capitalism promises to deliver the goods to even the most marginal of places. Tecpán, Guatemala, a town in which I have lived and conducted ethnographic research over many years, is a bustling market town along a major highway and an excellent example of these dynamics. The economy in Tecpán is changing. Nontraditional forms of agriculture have sprouted up alongside traditional peasant ways of life. The town is increasingly becoming connected to distant places. Products like snow peas and apparel flow out (Fischer & Benson, 2006; Thomas, 2013). Sugary sodas and cell phones and other apparel flow in. Corn, long the subsistence crop of the Mayas, remains a core feature of the diet, although now largely in the form of corn syrup sold in sodas and processed foods at Walmart. Community life is changing. Entrepreneurs on farms and in apparel workshops desire *algo más* (something more or something better) and face heightened risk in their pursuit of money or reputation (Fischer & Benson, 2005). New hierarchies of value and worth are emerging. Some families can afford to build two-story houses, and traditions of work and vibrancy are evolving into new forms of industry and labor. Livelihoods are complex and confounded. People are trying to make do and attain some purchase in a world in which high mass consumption is touted as the apex. Rostow was willing, indeed eager to wage war to promote such a lifestyle, and in many ways he achieved the world that he wanted.

The ontology of a place like Tecpán—what it means to be there—cannot be understood apart from an understanding of the institutions and regimes that shape livelihoods and shift the texture of what community means. "Ordinary ethics" (Lambek, 2010) and "ordinary affects" (Stewart, 2007) are changing on the ground as some families prosper more than others in a new economy of enterprise and consumerism. Importantly, healthcare is now more widely available as nongovernmental organizations bring novel clinical services to populations. Ethnographers are ideally positioned to document how interpersonal and institutional relationships affect the cloth of care that makes up everyday life in towns like Tecpán, and how this is linked to emerging hierarchies of affluence and prominence and a burgeoning "republic of NGOs" (Schuller, 2012). And this is the proper analytical context for thinking about living and dying in a shifting world. To probe the particularities of illness and medicine in Tecpán requires a constant and critical probing of the town's changing economy and relationship to the state and the capitalist world system and the emergence of new social forms and relationships centered on privatized interventions in the healthcare domain. It is precisely this kind of manifold perspective that the chapters in this volume embrace.

Guatemala is a place of contradictions. Because the long civil war is formally over, the country is said to now be in a "postwar" stage. But the War on Drugs endures, mining operations are transforming ecologies in spite of vibrant local opposition, supermarket chains are massifying a Western diet on the cheap and, as of this writing, a former military commander responsible for some of the worst atrocities of the war is the country's leader. Life in Guatemala is still life during wartime. Insufficient structural orientations that make a meager patchwork of medical institutions and public health responses better than nothing, governments that embody corruption and control as steadfast commitments, corporations that place profits over the basic needs of living, breathing, heaving people—these are the diacritics and critical realities of an unkind world. Careful historical and ethnographic study provides important conceptual tools for coming to grips with inequalities and interventions in countries that are said to exist beyond or apart from war. What Chary and Rohloff and their colleagues have done is to write chapters that speak truth to cruel optimism and place illness, health, ethics, and politics at the center of efforts to make sense of the contradictions that define "postwar" Guatemala.

Part of the picture of optimism and contradiction in Guatemala is the emergence of a complex regime of private healthcare. This volume's pioneering introduction provides us with the best overview to date of the evolving terrain of healthcare and medicine in Guatemala, reflecting critically on the new possibilities for care that exist as well as the certain dangers and disparities inherent in this phase. The detailed chapters of the book help us to think about how indigenous Mayas navigate an often confusing meshwork, how disparate coverage and outcomes are impressed upon bodies and communities, and how the whole gamut of where Mayas get their healthcare is changing. The theme of medical pluralism is not surprisingly on the minds of the authors. What makes this volume especially relevant is the incisive approach demanded by Chary and Rohloff. Moving beyond dated models predicated on a strict divide between biomedical and indigenous forms of medicine, this book stresses a more mobile and richly ethnographic method. Families and individuals make decisions in contexts that reflect a great number of institutional factors and available options. Decisions are increasingly complex, multiple kinds of biomedicine are considered, various nongovernmental organizations are engaged, and practitioners working within and across private and public sectors contend with a double burden of disease. Plainly put, there is a lot going on. There is no single "system" of healthcare. The story is about networks and patchworks. It is about ordinary people and practitioners putting pieces together.

The first section of the book is about changing relationships between the civil, public, and private sectors. The general pattern is familiar to students and scholars of neoliberalism. Responsibility and accountability are devolved onto private actors. Nongovernmental agencies serve state functions, structuring how people access services and identify as citizens and members. Funding might be scarce and priorities established at a distance. As Maupin describes, the very parameters of civic participation are changing as health conditions and solutions evolve. Dasgupta-Tsikinas and Wise discuss how Maya women are particularly impacted by logics of responsibility that place risk and resolve related to care on their shoulders while restructuring their relationship to the government and the economy through cash transfer programs. Colom's analysis of child-focused services critiques how a diminished state makes for a situation in which the complex life conditions of mothers and children are inadequately addressed in public-private partnerships. Across this section, we see patients and sufferers become "biological citizens" (Petryna, 2003), their medical conditions the basis for making claims and entering into new relationships with agencies and institutions.

The second section examines the marketplace of healthcare seeking. Hall-Clifford's chapter takes us into the depths of the neoliberal medical economy in its ranging analysis of the cruel optimism entailed in pyramid schemes. Flood and Rohloff's chapter on diabetes further helps us to think about how health is being seen as a commodity, only affordable by the upwardly mobile and rich and something that people must aspire to—*algo más*. These chapters also help us to query the epidemiological transition, where infectious diseases coexist with emerging chronic conditions that increasingly define health seekers' interactions with a patchwork of healthcare options.

The third section examines the complexities of how indigenous Maya patients and healers navigate multiple healthcare resources in an era of privatization. Individualism and self-reliance are promoted. Sickness becomes a context of entrepreneurship. Struggles to cope bring affected individuals and families into a dizzying array of institutions and interventions. Pezzia's focus on mental health helps us to grasp how optimism is fleeting. The system plays mind games. Public sector care is so inadequate that it merely functions as a recruiting ground for private practitioners, and accessing care is increasingly interpreted in terms of chance encounters. Cancer too is part of this epidemiological picture, as Chary's chapter demonstrates. Systemic problems of inadequate screening and treatment put women in harm's way and make cervical cancer a most pernicious pathway to premature mortality. Pezzia's and Chary's accounts demonstrate how families and communities are pressured into fending for themselves in the face unpredictable health resources. Maya midwives are also fending for themselves and their communities through diverse engagements, as King, Chary, and Rohloff's chapter shows. We witness the enduring social and political roles midwives continue to play in the lives of Maya communities. Maya midwives extend durable cultural traditions while tactically mobilizing resources to meet timely challenges and predicaments.

It might seem cliché to talk about structural violence and the "double burden" of disease. But this language is important and appropriate. Guatemala is straight-up strapped. To talk about Guatemala or any other country as a "failed state" neglects the fact that "success" or "development" for such countries and constituencies have been forestalled by external forces. The double burden happens not in a vacuum, but because Guatemala was thrown into colonial and postcolonial predicaments where poverty and a lack of health resources, malnutrition and overconsumption have been normalized. Politicians and whole societies have become enamored of Rostow's idea that the free flow of products like soda, sweatshop-produced garments, and plastic toys is indicative of progress. Powerful, wealthy countries like the United States, which have long sucked the wind out of places like Guatemala, overconsume resources, disproportionately pollute the world, and express "care" towards postcolonies through corporate philanthropy, "foreign aid," and "development" assistance, rather than through radical commitments to reparations and responsibility.

A key take-away message from this volume involves a renewed concept of medical pluralism capable of taking into account changing cultural and institutional circumstances. What Chary and Rohloff propose as a "new medical pluralism" is characterized by a diminishing authority of traditional ethnomedical resources and the proliferation of multiple competing biomedicines. It sometimes exposes individuals to previously unknown social hazards. The massive, unregulated proliferation of the nongovernmental sector has created a disorienting network of services and many practical difficulties when it comes to navigating them. Some new interventions are oriented towards profits and are inherently predatory. Maya families and communities face debt loads as a result of illness and an inability to pay for fees and services. But the optimism of a global culture bent on rendering responsibility a matter of entrepreneurship or corporate philanthropy, commodifying hope and relief, pinning aspiration on the afflicted, divorcing accountability from wholesome senses of what it means to exist as part of a collective universe, and pushing people into predatory schemes finds a critical counterpoint in the stories of people like Julia, with which this volume begins.

Julia's story tells us that in the face of obstacles we find powerful efforts to make do. Julia has walked the Earth with little access to education or healthcare. She has endured living in a remote area distant from comprehensive clinical and preventive services. She has faced difficult subjective experiences related to physiological changes and the fear of disease and death. She was forced to access healthcare in a colonial language and in the face of a healthcare system geared towards benefitting those who are wealthier and whiter. She scrounged up enough money to purchase minimal services and faced the brutal decision of having to sell long-held assets in order to survive. Her decision to parlay tradition for consumption did not reflect the abstract theoretical modeling about "development" of a Walt Rostow. It was a basic existential choice having to do with a "will to live" (Biehl, 2009). Julia understandably turned to faith and pursued whatever treatment options were available because the tumor grew. She sought out missionary organizations that turned her away. She consulted with physicians who sell optimism, charge a lot for treatment, and do their important work within a dangerous moral economy of aspiration and desperation. Julia hooked up with an NGO. She realized some success, and her story shows how people traverse a complicated patchwork where pathways and possibilities are an improvement over an older public health infrastructure that was long absent from rural regions and provided no services whatsoever.

Emergent relations of care and compassion exist amid anecdotes about people facing obstacles. In a country in which no substantial welfare state ever really existed, the notion that neoliberal reforms have led to a diminishment of the state does not neatly fit. What we find instead is a hodgepodge that devolves responsibility onto vulnerable people, empowers private actors and organizations, and brings them into relation with entanglements and futures that seem comparatively better. Julia's "pathway to healthcare in post-reform Guatemala involved a non-transparent array of healthcare institutions, charitable organizations, and complex financial and personal risks," Rohloff and Chary point out. However, they assert that healthcare privatization has not necessarily adversely affected her trajectory to care, because "the situation in Guatemala prior to neoliberal reform and privatization was not one of affordable, publicly-financed care, with a transition to private, expensive care. Rather, it was one of *no care*."

Some care is of course better than no care. There is bountiful compassion in a republic of NGOs. Philanthropy is infilling. Giving is a gift in itself and expressive of something innately human. The institutions that helped Julia reflect the brave efforts of people who want to make a difference and deliver quality healthcare to people who deserve it and have long been denied. Practitioners and experts and social workers from all over the world are struggling alongside patients and their families to make do in the absence of sufficient resources. They are "improvising medicine" (Livingston, 2012). Indeed, this theme of emergent possibility and patchwork services reflects a developing focus throughout medical anthropology. Joao Biehl's book *Will to Live: AIDS Therapies and the Politics of Survival* (2009) chronicles the struggles of people living with HIV/AIDS in Brazil to access treatment and sustain viable life chances amid an expanding field of private and public health options and pathways. Vinh-Kim Nguyen's book *The Republic of Therapy: Triage and Sovereignty in West Africa's Time of AIDS* (2010) documents the complicated work of nongovernmental organizations and the difficult decisions and daily struggles of people living with illness. Because many postcolonial states have not been capable of providing publicly available healthcare to their populations or developing a robust welfare system, vacuums must be filled and life chances must be conjured around the work of nongovernmental organizations, charitable groups, expatriates and development workers, and patients and sufferers like Julia who live outside of gated communities.

The chapters in this volume paint this picture. They are about new and emergent possibilities and long-standing challenges. They are about struggle and reality, options and opportunities, and the maelstrom of what is happening as ordinary people, practitioners, and professionals seek to attend to the basic contours of living and dying in an unkind world partially inspired by the likes of Rostow. But high mass consumption is out of control. The kind of "development" envisioned by Rostow—a predictable transition from tradition to modernity accompanied by the clear benefits of economic growth—is simply not the order of the day. Disparity and difficulty still define life for most. As much as privatization might not have "negatively impacted" Julia, the current patchwork environment of healthcare did push her into and out of zones of abandonment and demanded tremendous diligence on her part.

Who is responsible for Julia? Where does responsibility lie when it comes to defining and attending to her tumor and the structural and infrastructural conditions that helped it to grow? Is she responsible as an individual? Does accountability reside within the family and the immediate community? Does responsibility belong to private agencies and organizations that interact with and provide care for people like Julia? Can we talk about responsibility as something that is more thoroughly social and historical and more interestingly transverse? Can we implicate the United States, which ousted a democratically-elected Guatemalan president in 1954 because the economic interests of U.S. corporations were at stake? Should we consider the fact that this coup helped to launch the long Guatemalan civil war? Does Spain owe something in the way of education, healthcare, or prosperity to Julia because of its long heritage of stripping Guatemala of resources? We can go on. These are questions about responsibility that take history and geopolitics seriously and see structural violence not so much as an analytical framework but a long-lived reality.

The late French philosopher Emmanuel Levinas emphasized themes of ethics and morality. In his major work, *Totality and Infinity* (1969), Levinas argued that ethics is the "first philosophy," taking precedence over ontology and epistemology. While it is important to know about the world, how things work and what it means to exist, for Levinas the pursuit of knowledge, truth, and being can dangerously entail a withdrawal from the immediacy of lived experience and a failure to acknowledge that responsibility to and for other people defines human life in constitutive ways. Levinas was arguing against Heidegger's ruminations on Being, which emphasized enclosure, selfhood, and isolation. For Levinas, ethics as first philosophy is grounded in phenomenology—life lived in an ordinary way, in the rise and repetition of the face-to-face encounter with other people. Others call us into relations of responsibility because they face us and we are bound up in their lives and struggles. "The very sense of having a separate existence," writes the American philosopher Alphonso Lingis (2000), "can be malevolent and pernicious" (p. 95). An esoteric model of rational actors pursuing self-interests to maximize Utility is a particular way of seeing that favors competition and makes individuation and circumscription seem natural. The prefabricated arc of "development" and "progress" that the likes of Rostow proposed took us down the low road in failing to prioritize the social, a core value that indigenous and ancient peoples have within their traditions of healing, ritual life, land tenure, and communal organization.

For Levinas, we might say, society is most basically about *tigo*. It is about living with others and taking up shared stakes. And the ancient societies—the ones that Rostow cast as backward—valued these values. Medicine is an ancient practice. Ancient societies saw healing not as a sold or scarce resource but, rather, it defined a central orientation of how people organized and sought to sustain themselves. Impulses to heal and nurture run deep in the course of human evolution. Evolutionary models emphasizing individualism, "selfish genes," and competition fail to acknowledge that altruism, sociality, and cooperation are in fact the primordial stuff of human existence and have played central roles in directing the biological and social evolution of the species (Sussman & Cloninger, 2011). And impulses of kind coexistence perdure in the dynamics of care and compassion that institutions and charities carry out today in countries like Guatemala.

But is this "system" sufficient? How are ancient impulses to care converted into forms of relating and reacting that stress individuation and even distance and render health a commodity or a carrot, as motives of profit, measures of cost-effectiveness, geographies of privatization and privation, and epistemologies of progress models come to predominate? Healing should not be a patchwork phenomenon. Healing should define the essence of society at the most foundational level. What paths of moral imagination and lines of flight can push us to think about how a patchwork approach to healthcare—doubtless relevant and sustaining given the limited resources available for people like Julia—is at the same time simply not enough? More robustly universal and systemic moves in social medicine and global health—such as the "Health For All" vision articulated in the Declaration of Alma-Ata in 1978—are what someone like Julia deserves (see Farmer, Kleinman, Kim, & Basilico, 2013). In the concluding pages, my goal is not to map out simple pragmatic solutions, but rather to draw on Levinas and other intellectual resources as a means of emphasizing that any viable solutions for addressing problems of poverty and illness in a place like Guatemala necessarily require historical thinking, a reprioritization of values, a reconsideration of lifestyles, and an eagerness to reorganize society in substantive, far-reaching ways.

Chary and Rohloff argue that the appropriate theoretical perspective for thinking about a story like Julia's is not simply "to decry the phenomenon of privatization and the proliferation of biomedicines." They instead call for "detailed and reflective ethnography" that "spell[s] out the ground-level effects of the health system phase transition" and points the way towards "new collective futures." I agree that ethnography and concept-work are important for figuring things out and pointing towards more positive directions. This commitment to empiricism links this volume to the best kind of ethnographic research and writing. I also agree that the tidal shift to an era of private healthcare is realistically too forceful to repel in an abstract way and entails concrete benefits that must be acknowledged. Many nongovernmental organizations are doing redeeming work in Guatemala and there is no reason why a range of institutions cannot play an important role in the kind of kind society that Levinas envisions. Ethics as first philosophy is precisely about developing new collective futures. It is not about having a strong state do everything for everyone. It is not about simply privileging the public over the private. It is about the "primacy of the ethical" (Scheper-Hughes, 1995). What kinds of critical policies and appraisals need to happen in order to attend to people like Julia in more encompassing and ready ways? What would Guatemala look like were "development" to be modeled on the Alma-Ata declaration, which emphasized universal access to healthcare and was linked to a spirit of social justice, rather than on Rostow's vision?

Morality for Levinas is about infinity. He drew on Jewish philosophy and theology in talking about responsibility. For Levinas, the creation of the human being is different from the way a commodity is made. Humans are not interchangeable or replaceable. Their destruction or loss is not the same as the destruction or loss of an object. "[To] create a man was to create in one creature two," writes Levinas (1990, p. 165). Each human has two sides—one of radical singularity and non-substitutability (each person is unique) and one of eternity and entirety (each person is stamped with the impression of the whole universe). "[Certainly] one must not think it strange that God," Levinas writes, "in creating me, has placed in me this idea as the mark of the craftsman stamped on his work; and it is not as necessary that this mark be something different from this very work" (2001, p. 48). Levinas was thinking about the ways that we have a sense of infinity within ourselves. This interior space, subjectivity itself, is what Derrida (1996), critically engaging with Levinas, would later define as "God." Julia, like everyone, has the divine inside of her because she is incomparably singular, a creature of infinite depth whose death would mean not simply the end of an object, but the annihilation of a subject, the closure of consciousness, an infinite web of relations, the whole universe, all of Creation.

Ideas from the Mishnah and the Talmud, parts of Jewish tradition, are found everywhere throughout Levinas's thinking about ethics. Here is a passage from the Mishnah:

> Therefore man was created uniquely, to teach you that whoever destroys a single soul of Israel, Scripture accounts it as if he had destroyed a full world; and whoever saves one soul of Israel, Scripture accounts it as if he had saved a full world. . . . Again to declare the greatness of the Holy One, blessed be He, for man stamps out many coins with one die, and they are all alike, but the King, the King of kings, the Holy One, blessed be He, stamped each man with the seal of Adam, and not one of them is like his fellow. (Cited in Fagenblat, 2010, p. 30)

Different economies are here juxtaposed. We are responsible for the other person not because of abstract principles, but because in relating to other people we do not relate to coins. We can think through Levinas about a tendency to treat people (and their health and su stenance) as commodities. Making a kind society requires different forms of valuation than Rostow's political economy. Making a kind society is about ensuring that Julia's story be read as the story of a "full world," the story of everything. This is about predicating forms of coexistence on responsibility and dignity and the infinite depth of the other person. Levinas (1990) writes:

> This humanity is defined, not by liberty . . . but by responsibility prior to all initiative. Man answers for more than his freely chosen acts. He is the hostage of the universe. Extraordinary dignity. Unlimited responsibility. Man does not belong to a society which bestows limited responsibility upon its members. He is the member of a society of unlimited responsibility. (p. 171)

Making a kind society is about putting people over profits, a society in which "people come first" (Biehl & Petryna, 2013). It is about insisting that patchwork healing is not enough, however promising or improved. It is about thickening a context of care so that health, sustenance, and flourishing are readily available to Julia, and to everyone, while at the same time acknowledging that this reordering of the social order must also entail a serious reevaluation of whose knowledge and experience and expertise inform institutional work, where solutions are sourced, who gets to make decisions about collective futures, and what counts as progress. It is about taking into account history and time and geopolitics and the ways that a primordial present makes all of us responsible for the fullness and infinity of the other person, indeed the whole world. It is about critically redistributing resources. It is about deep democracy and a penchant for reparations. Levinas (1998) writes:

> That is perhaps the very excellence of democracy, whose fundamental liberalism corresponds to the ceaseless deep remorse of justice: legislation always unfinished, always resumed, a legislation open to the better. It attests to an ethical excellence and its origin in kindness from which, however it is distanced—always a bit less perhaps—by the necessary calculations imposed by a multiple sociality, calculations constantly starting over again. Thus, in the empirical life of the good under the freedom of revisions, there would be a progress of reason. A bad conscience of justice! It knows it is not as just as the kindness that instigates it is good. (pp. 229–230)

All of this might seem idealistic. On the contrary, it is not at all abstract or removed. Junk food is not "magically delicious," as the ad for Lucky Charms breakfast cereal states. *That* is the abstract, fanciful, charming, cruelly optimistic idea—commodity fetishism. The objective, *claro* perspective is that junk food is manmade and harmful and unfortunately compulsory consumption for many people. But why cannot society be organized otherwise, around an aversion to the mass production of anthropogenic diseases, or a profound predilection for social justice, or a planetary potlatch? Indeed, Rohloff and Chary underscore a similar point when they write that the "possibilities are especially rich in Guatemala, which has a long tradition of indigenous Maya activism and still a small, committed civil society sector with a social justice agenda."

Looking at the above quotation, what "reason" or clarity mean for Levinas involves a "bad conscience" and a "deep remorse of justice." What "progress" means has nothing to do with scoring a pinnacle of achievement, as it did for Rostow, who, in mass consumption, assumed that humans had reached the "end of history" (Fukuyama, 1992). For Levinas, making a kind society is about "legislation always unfinished, always resumed," and the critical standpoint that actual empirical life simply does not live up, that society "is not as just as the kindness that instigates it is good." This is an altogether different model of progress that flips the script.

Bread and butter in anthropology is the idea that the societies of Melanesia and the Amazon and other parts of the world are more attuned to the needs of people and ecologies than modern societies defined by high mass consumption. Maring rituals prevent the degradation of the environment. Kwakiutl potlatch helps to balance the distribution of food across social segments. Ndembu curing, initiation, and hunting rituals allay social conflict and impart sustaining norms and relations (see Ortner, 1984). Maya culture is an ancient culture that has long been about reverence for sacred sites, connections to the land and ancestors, careful considerations of envy and distribution, investments in the meaning and sustenance of communal groupings and collective labor, respect for elders and myth and custom, insistence upon the social and cultural importance of ritual and critical events, and various forms of traditional healing. Lately Mayas are sold optimism amid continued and concentrated calamity and are saddled with the desperation and desire of life during wartime.

I romanticize and satirize to make polemical if also quintessentially anthropological points. Anthropology has historically involved a conscientious perspective on indigenous and ancient ways of life. It has often been a mode of "cultural critique" (Marcus & Fischer, 1986), considering how geopolitically marginalized communities might have an instructive handle on how to organize society and cope with human conditions, finding in their experiences and struggles rich fodder for critical reflection on the postcolonial global field. The chapters collected here reflect this important heritage because they emphasize the ongoing value of traditional medicine among Mayas and a critical understanding of the diminished role of these traditions as a complex field of medical pluralism takes shape. These chapters encourage us to see in the new medical pluralism not so much a simple challenge to tradition that ought to be reversed as much as a manifestation of human impulses to heal and care, innovate and invent that are emerging in the present to make something better than nothing and work within enduring and evolving traditions.

Making a kind society is about undoing the possessive investment in "progress" models that define human achievement in terms of overconsumption and materialistic and militaristic amassment and articulate a certain audacity in believing that history is over. Making a kind society is about finding within our we-have-never-been-modern (Latour, 1993) selves the humility to learn from indigenous peoples and constantly refresh primordial impulses to respect and revere the universe because it is at stake. The French sociologist Bruno Latour (2008) writes:

> [The] gigantic sins that were to be committed would be hiding a much greater sin that it has been upon our generation to finally atone for: not technology itself, but the absence of love for the technology we have created, as if we had decided that we were unable to follow through with the education of our own children. The question is not to stop innovating, inventing, creating, intervening, etc. The real question is to have the same type of patience and energy as God the Creator Himself. And the comparison is not blasphemous if it is true that we have been

> taking the whole of Creation on our shoulders and have now become literally (and not metaphorically in our actions) coextensive to the Earth. This is another gloss, this time techno-theological, of the Biblical assertion that we have been created in His image. . . . We want to develop, not withdraw. (para. 30)

Returning to Levinas, making a kind society is about maintaining and advocating a shared "bad conscience," a basic phenomenological "reason" motivated by remorse and the pursuit of ever more careful and considerate modes of coexistence with each other and environments. The chapters in this volume tell us that the story of Guatemala is the story of the universe—not a failed state, but rather a state that never really had a chance and remains reeling. It is a full world of historical and global connections, struggles that are shared or not shared, and a politics of legislation and reason that for Julia's sake, for God's sake, for goodness sake must be left open for the better. Patchwork care is *algo más*, something more or something better. This volume helps us to understand the complexities of how things are improving for people like Julia even as there remain limitations and disparities. The chapters insist that improvement be reckoned in terms of what is realistic and relevant and provide us with a moral compass for critically assessing patchwork and limited healing orientations as a framework that, with links to the important work of social medicine and social justice activism, is still not as just as the kindness that instigates it is good.

References

Abadia, C. E., & Oviedo, D. G. (2009). Bureaucratic itineraries in Colombia: A theoretical and methodological tool to assess managed-care health care systems. *Social Science & Medicine, 68*(6), 1153–1160.

Acevedo, D., & Hurtado, E. (1997). Midwives and formal providers in prenatal, delivery, and post-partum care in four communities in rural Guatemala: Complementarity or conflict. In A. R. Pebley & L. Rosero-Bixby (Eds.), *Demographic diversity and change in the Central American isthmus* (pp. 271–326). Santa Monica, CA: RAND.

Adams, R. (1952). Un análisis de las creencias y prácticas médicas en un pueblo indígena de Guatemala (con sugerencias relacionadas con la práctica de medicina en el área Maya). Guatemala: Instituto Nacional Indígena.

Adams, R., & Rubel, A. J. (1967). Sickness and social relations. In M. Nash (Ed.), *Handbook of Middle American Indians:* Vol. 6. *Social relations* (pp. 333–356). Austin: University of Texas Press.

Adams, V. (2013). *Markets of sorrow, labors of faith: New Orleans in the wake of Katrina.* Durham, NC: Duke University Press.

Aguilar, V. (2005). *El modelo de la motivación y el desarrollo personal empleado en el sistema multinivel* (Masters thesis). Instituto Politécnico Nacional de México.

Akinladejo, O. H., Clarke, M., & Akinladejo, F. O. (2013). Pyramid schemes and multilevel marketing (MLM): Two sides of the same coin. *Journal of Modern Accounting and Auditing, 9*(5), 690–696.

Alarcón, R. D. (2003). Mental health and mental health care in Latin America. *World Psychiatry, 2*(1), 54–56.

Alarcón, R. D., & Aguilar-Gaxiola, S. A. (2000). Mental health policy developments in Latin America. *Bulletin of the World Health Organization, 78*(4), 483–490.

Albizu, J. L., Goyo Todosantos, M., & Mendez, E. (2005). *El efecto Guatemala: Un viaje con las promotoras y los promotoras de salud a través de la vida del 0 a 2012.* Guatemala City, Guatemala: Magna Tierra Editores.

Althabe, F., & Belizán, J. M. (2006). Caesarean section: The paradox. *The Lancet, 368*(9546), 1472–1473.

Alvarado Browning, F., Carrera Guerra, M., & Girón, A. (1998). *Perfil de las organizaciones no gubernamentales en Guatemala.* Guatemala City, Guatemala: Foro de Coordinaciones de ONG de Guatemala.

Amorim, C. (2012). *"Health is a business for everyone and is not a right to anyone": Neoliberal health care provision in rural Guatemala* (Masters thesis). University of Kansas, Lawrence, KS.

Anson, A., Ramay, B., Ruiz de Esparza, A., & Bero, L. (2012). Availability, prices and affordability of the World Health Organization's essential medicines for children in Guatemala. *Globalization and Health, 8*(22).

Arellano-López, S., & Petras, J. F. (1994). Non-governmental organizations and poverty alleviation in Bolivia. *Development and Change, 25*(3), 555–568.

Arévalo, L. (2015, February 4). Salud reducirá las ONG en programa de cobertura. *La Nación.* Retrieved from http://www.lanacion.com.gt/salud-reducira-las-ong-en-programa-de-cobertura.

Armada, F., & Muntaner, C. (2004). The visible fist of the market: Health reforms in Latin America. In A. Castro & M. Singer (Eds.), *Unhealthy health policy: A critical anthropological examination* (pp. 29–42). Walnut Creek, CA: AltaMira Press.

Arvelo, W., Degollado, J., Reyes, L., & Álvarez, A. (2013). Perceptions regarding oral rehydration solutions for the management of diarrhea in Guatemalan children: Implications for diarrheal management in the Americas. *Revista Panamericana de Salud Publica, 43*(2), 121–126.

Attorney for Human Rights Office (PDH). (2010). [*Special report on the right of every person to receive the highest standard of care for physical and mental health: The right to health*]. Guatemala City, Guatemala: Procurador de los Derechos Humanos.

Awah, P. K., Unwin, N., & Phillimore, P. (2008). Cure or control: Complying with biomedical regime of diabetes in Cameroon. *BMC Health Services Research, 8*, 43.

Baer, H. A. (2012). Rejoinder: A long and convoluted journey. *Medical Anthropology Quarterly, 26*(2), 299–303.

Baer, H., & Singer, M. (1995). *Critical medical anthropology*. Amityville, NY: Baywood Publishing.

Barcelo, A., Aedo, C., Rajpathak, S., & Robles, S. (2003). The cost of diabetes in Latin America and the Caribbean. *Bulletin of the World Health Organization, 81*(1), 19–27.

Barcelo, A., Gregg, E. W., Gerzoff, R. B., Wong, R., Perez Flores, E., Ramirez-Zea, M., Cafiero, E., . . . Villagra, L. (2012). Prevalence of diabetes and intermediate hyperglycemia among adults from the first multinational study of noncommunicable diseases in six Central American countries: The Central America Diabetes Initiative (CAMDI). *Diabetes Care, 35*(4), 738–740.

Barrett, B. (1997). Identity, ideology, and inequality: Methodologies in medical anthropology, Guatemala 1950-1995. *Social Science & Medicine, 44*(5), 579–587.

Bebbington, A. (1993). *NGOs and the state in Latin America*. London: Routledge.

Beck, E. (2014). Countering convergence: Agency and diversity among Guatemalan NGOs. *Latin American Politics and Society, 56*(2), 141–162.

Behrhorst, C. (1975). The Chimaltenango development project in Guatemala. In K. W. Newell (Ed.), *Health by the People* (pp. 30–52). Geneva, Switzerland: World Health Organization.

Behrhorst, C. (1983). Introduction. In U. Stelzter (Ed.), *Health in the highlands: The Chimaltenango Development Program of Guatemala* (pp. xi–xxxv). Seattle: University of Washington Press.

Behrhorst, C. (n.d.). *Health and development: The Chimaltenango Development Program: Its evolution 1961-1982*. Unpublished manuscript.

Belmartino, S., & Baris, E. (2000). *Reshaping health care in Latin America: A comparative analysis of health care reform in Argentina, Brazil, and Mexico*. Ottawa, Canada: International Development Research Center.

Beltran, A. (1992). El proceso de aculturación (4th ed.). México: Fondo de Cultura Económica.

Benavides, J. (2013). Conditional cash transfers program in Guatemala policy simulation and cost effectiveness analysis. Retrieved from: http://www.gdn.int/admin/uploads/editor/files/GDN_PEMRP_FUNDESA_PS_Education_Health.pdf.

Benton, A. (2015). *HIV exceptionalism: Development through disease in Sierra Leone*. Minneapolis: University of Minnesota Press.

Berger, P. (2010). Max Weber is alive and well, and living in Guatemala: The Protestant ethic today. *The Review of Faith & International Affairs, 8*(4), 3–9.

Berger, S. A. (2006). *Guatemaltecas: The women's movement 1986-2003*. Austin: University of Texas Press.

Berlant, L. (2011). *Cruel optimism*. Durham, NC: Duke University Press.

Berry, N.S. (2006). Kaqchikel midwives, home births, and emergency obstetric referrals in Guatemala: Contextualizing the choice to stay at home. *Social Science & Medicine, 62*(8), 1958–1969.

Berry, N.S. (2008). Who's judging the quality of care? Indigenous Maya and the problem of "not being attended." *Medical Anthropology, 27*(2), 164–189.

Berry, N.S. (2010). *Unsafe motherhood: Mayan maternal mortality and subjectivity in post-war Guatemala*. New York, NY: Berghahn Books.

Berry, N.S. (2014). Did we do good? NGOs, conflicts of interest and the evaluation of short-term medical missions in Sololá, Guatemala. *Social Science & Medicine, 120*(2014), 344–351.
Biehl, J. (2005). *Vita: Life in a zone of social abandonment.* Berkeley: University of California Press.
Biehl, J. (2009). *Will to live: AIDS therapies and the politics of survival.* Princeton, NJ: Princeton University Press.
Biehl, J., & Petryna, A. (Eds.). (2013). *When people come first: Critical studies in global health.* Princeton, NJ: Princeton University Press.
Bird, S. M., Wiles, J. L., Okalik, L., Kilabuk, J., & Egeland, G. M. (2008). Living with diabetes on Baffin Island: Inuit storytellers share their experiences. *Canadian Journal of Public Health, 99*(1), 17–21.
Birn, A.E. (2014). Philanthrocapitalism, past and present: The Rockefeller Foundation, the Gates Foundation, and the setting(s) of the international/global health agenda. *Hypothesis, 12*(1): e8.
Bornstein, E., & Redfield, R. (Eds.). (2010). *Forces of compassion: Humanitarianism between ethics and politics.* Santa Fe, NM: School for Advanced Research Press.
Bourgeault, I. L., Benoit, C., & Davis-Floyd, R. (Eds.). (2004). *Reconceiving midwifery.* Montreal: McGill-Queen's University Press.
Bowser, D. M., & Mahal, A. (2011). Guatemala: The economic burden of illness and health system implications. *Health Policy, 100*(2-3), 159–166.
Brada, B. (2011). *Botswana as a living experiment.* (Doctoral Dissertation). Retrieved from ProQuest Dissertation and Theses. (Accession No. 3460154).
Branas, C. C., Dinardo, A. R., Puac Polanco, V. D., Harvey, M. J., Vassy, J. L., & Bream, K. (2013). An exploration of violence, mental health and substance abuse in post-conflict Guatemala. *Health, 5*(5), 825–833.
Burleigh, E. (n.d.). *Guatemala. Pro Redes salud: Rapid scale-up of primary health care through NGOs.* Unpublished manuscript.
Burleigh, E., Dardano, C., & Cruz, J. R. (1990). Colors, humor, and evil eye: Indigenous classification and treatment of childhood diarrhea in highland Guatemala. *Medical Anthropology, 12*(4), 419–441.
Burrell, J. (2014). *Maya after war: Conflict, power, and politics in Guatemala.* Austin: University of Texas Press.
Bustamante, A. V., & Méndez, C. A. (2014). Health care privatization in Latin America: Comparing divergent privatization approaches in Chile, Colombia, and Mexico. *Journal of Health Politics, Policy and Law, 39*(4), 842–886.
Cahn, P. S. (2006). Building down and dreaming up: Finding faith in a Mexican multilevel marketer. *American Ethnologist, 33*(1), 126–142.
Camey Huz, J. (2000). *Disponibilidad de las Organizaciones no Gubernamentales (ONGs) para incorporarse al Sistema Integral de Atención en Salud (SIAS).* Guatemala City, Guatemala: Universidad de San Carlos de Guatemala.
Cardelle, A. J. (2003). *Health care reform in Central America: NGO-government collaboration in Guatemala and El Salvador.* Coral Gables, FL: North-South Center Press at the University of Miami.
Carey Jr., D. (2001). *Our elders teach us.* Tuscaloosa: University of Alabama Press.
Carey Jr., D. (2006). *Engendering Mayan history: Kaqchikel women as agents and conduits of the past, 1875-1970.* New York, NY: Routledge.
Carey Jr., D. (2014, February). *Transnational knowledge and violence: Guatemala's lethal embrace of science.* Paper presented at Freie Universität Workshop: Encountering Transnational (In)Security and Violence in Guatemala, Berlin, Germany.
Carlsen, R. S. (1997). *The war for the heart and soul of a highland Maya town.* Austin: University of Texas Press.
Carmack, R. M. (Ed.). (1992). *Harvest of violence: The Maya Indians and the Guatemalan crisis.* Norman: University of Oklahoma Press.
Carrera Guerra, M. (2002). *Características del sector ONG en Guatemala.* Guatemala City, Guatemala: Cromográfica.

Castro, A., & Singer, M. (Eds.). (2004). *Unhealthy health policy: A critical anthropological examination.* Walnut Creek, CA: AltaMira Press.
Cecchini, S., Leiva, A., Madariaga, A., & Trucco, D. (2009). *Desafíos de los programas de transferencias con corresponsabilidad: Los casos de Guatemala, Honduras y Nicaragua.* Santiago, Chile: United Nations.
Chang, H., Yang, M., & Chung, K. (2013). Can cancer patients seeking a second opinion get better care? *American Journal of Managed Care, 19*(5), 380–387.
Chary, A., Dasgupta, S. N., Messmer, S. E., & Rohloff, P. (2011). "But one gets tired": Breastfeeding, subjugation, and empowerment in rural Guatemala. In N. McPherson & M. Walks (Eds.), *An anthropology of mothering* (p. 172–182). Bradford, Ontario: Demeter Press.
Chary, A., Greiner, M., Bowers, C., & Rohloff, P. (2012). Determining adult type 2 diabetes-related health care needs in an indigenous population from rural Guatemala: A mixed-methods preliminary study. *BMC Health Services Research, 12*(1), 476.
Chary, A., Kraemer Díaz, A., Henderson, B., & Rohloff, P. (2013). The changing role of indigenous lay midwives in Guatemala: New frameworks for analysis. *Midwifery, 29*(8), 852–858.
Chary, A., Messmer, S., Sorenson, E., Henretty, N., Dasgupta, S., & Rohloff, P. (2013). The normalization of childhood disease: An ethnographic study of child malnutrition in rural Guatemala. *Human Organization, 72*(2), 87–97.
Chase-Dunn, C. (2000). Guatemala in the global system. *Journal of Interamerican Studies and World Affairs, 42*(4), 109–126.
Chiou, S. J., Wang, S. I., Liu, C. H., & Yaung, C. L. (2012). Outpatient-shopping behavior and survival rates in newly diagnosed cancer patients. *American Journal of Managed Care, 18*(9), 488–496.
Chu, M., & Segre, J. (2010). A note on direct selling in developing economies. Harvard Business School note 9-310-068. Retrieved from www.hbsp.harvard.edu/educators
Cleland, J., Conde-Agudelo, A., Peterson, H., Ross, J., & Tsui, A. (2012). Contraception and health. *The Lancet, 380*(9837), 149–156.
Colectiva por el Derecho a Decidir. (n.d.). *Embarazo en niñas: Un embarazo impuesto como resultado indiscutible de la violencia.* San Jose, Costa Rica: Colectiva por el Derecho a Decidir.
Comisión Económica para América Latina y el Caribe (CEPAL). (2011). *Salud de la población joven indígena en América Latina.* Santiago, Chile: United Nations.
Commission on Social Determinants of Health (CSDH). (2008). *Closing the gap in a generation: Health equity through action on the social determinants of health* (Final Report of the CSDH). Geneva, Switzerland: World Health Organization.
Cook, G., & Offit, T. (2008). Pluralism and transculturation in indigenous Maya religion. *Ethnology 47*(1), 45–59.
Coperacha Nacional. (2012). ¿Qué es tengo algo que dar? Retrieved from http://www.coperachanacional.org/index.php/qsomos.
Corral, J. E., Arnold, L. D., Argueta, E. E., Ganju, A., & Barnoya, J. (2012). Clinical preventive services in Guatemala: a cross-sectional survey of internal medicine physicians. *PLoS One, 7*(10), e48640.
Cosminsky, S. (1982a). Childbirth and change: A Guatemalan study. In C. P. MacCormack (Ed.), *Ethnography of fertility and birth* (pp. 205–230). New York, NY: Academic Press.
Cosminsky, S. (1982b). Knowledge and body concepts of Guatemalan midwives. In M. Kay (Ed.), *Anthropology of human birth* (pp. 233–252). Philadelphia, PA: F.A. Davis.
Cosminsky, S. (2001). Midwifery across the generations: A modernizing midwife in Guatemala. *Medical Anthropology, 20*(4), 345–378.
Cosminsky, S. (2012). Birth and blame: Guatemalan midwives and reproductive risk. In L. Fordyce & A. Maraesa (Eds.), *Risk, reproduction, and narratives of experience* (pp. 81-102). Nashville, TN: Vanderbilt University Press.
Cosminsky, S. (n.d.). *Maria's world: Midwives and medicalization.* Austin: University of Texas Press.

Cosminsky, S., & Harrison, I. E. (1984). *Traditional medicine* (Vol. 2). New York, NY: Garland.

Cosminksy, S., & Scrimshaw, M. (1980). Medical pluralism on a Guatemalan plantation. *Social Science & Medicine; Medical Anthropology, 14B*(4), 267–278.

Coston, J. M. (1998). A model and typology of government-NGO relationships. *Nonprofit and Voluntary Sector Quarterly, 27*(3), 358–382.

Danaei, G., Finucane, M. M., Lu, Y., Singh, G. M., Cowan, M. J., Pacjorek, C. J., . . . Ezzati, M. (2011). National, regional, and global trends in fasting plasma glucose and diabetes prevalence since 1980: Systematic analysis of health examination surveys and epidemiological studies with 370 country-years and 2.7 million participants. *The Lancet, 378*(9785), 31-40.

Danel, I., & La Forgia, G. M. (2005). Contracting for basic healthcare in rural Guatemala: Comparison of the performance of three delivery models. In G. M. La Forgia (Ed.), *Health system innovations in Central America: Lesson and impact of new approaches* (pp. 49-88). Washington, DC: The World Bank.

Davies, J. (n.d.). *The pharmaceutical and healthcare industry in Latin America.* Retrieved from http://www.citibank.com/transactionservices/home/about_us/online_academy/docs/JDavis.pdf.

Davis, S. H., & Hodson, J. (1982). *Witnesses to political violence in Guatemala: The suppression of a rural development movement.* Boston, MA: Oxfam America.

Davis-Floyd, R. (2001). La partera professional: Articulating identity and cultural space for a new kind of midwife in Mexico. *Medical Anthropology, 20*(2/3), 185–243.

Davis-Floyd, R., & Davis, E. (1997). Intuition as authoritative knowledge in midwifery and home birth. In R. Davis-Floyd & C. F. Sargent (Eds.), *Childbirth and authoritative knowledge: Cross-cultural perspectives* (pp. 315–349). Berkeley: University of California Press.

Davis-Floyd, R., Pigg, S. L., & Cosminsky, S. (2001). Daughters of time: The shifting identities of contemporary midwives. *Medical Anthropology, 20*(2/3), 105–139.

de Certeau, M. (2011). *The practice of everyday life.* (S. Rendall, Trans.). Berkeley: University of California Press.

DeBoer, M. D., Lima, A. A., Oria, R. B., Scarf, R. J., Moore, S. R., Luna, M. A. & Guerrant, R. L. (2012). Early childhood growth failure and the developmental origins of adult disease: Do enteric infections and malnutrition increase risk for the metabolic syndrome? *Nutrition Reviews, 70*(11), 642–653.

de-Graft Aikins, A. (2005). Healer shopping in Africa: New evidence from rural-urban qualitative study of Ghanaian diabetes experiences. *The BMJ, 331*(7519), 737.

de-Graft Aikins, A., Awuah, R. B., Pera, T. A., Mendez, M., & Ogedegbe, G. (2014). Explanatory models of diabetes in urban poor communities in Accra, Ghana. *Ethnicity and Health, 20*(20141212), 1–18.

del Valle Escalante, E. (2009). *Maya nationalisms and postcolonial challenges in Guatemala.* Santa Fe, NM: The School for Advanced Research.

Derrida, J. (1996). *The gift of death.* (D. Wills, Trans.). Chicago, IL: University of Chicago Press.

Disability Rights International (DRI). (2012). *Guatemala: Precautionary measures petition to the Inter-American Commission on Human Rights.* Retrieved from http://www.driadvocacy.org/media-gallery/our-reports-publications.

Dougherty, M. L. (2011). The global gold mining industry, junior firms, and civil society resistance in Guatemala. *Bulletin of Latin American Research, 30*(4), 403–418.

Dubois, P., & Rubio-Codina, M. (2012). Child care provision: Semiparametric evidence from a randomized experiment in Mexico. *Annals of Economics and Statistics, 105/106*, 155–184.

Ebdon, R. (1995). NGO expansion and the fight to reach the poor: Gender implications of NGO scaling-up in Bangladesh. *IDS Bulletin, 26*(3), 49–55.

Ecks, S., & Harper, I. (2013). Public-private mixes: The market for antituberculosis drugs in India. In J. Biehl & A. Petryna (Eds.), *When people come first: Critical studies in global health* (pp. 252–275). Princeton, NJ: Princeton University Press.

Eder, K., & García Pú, M. M. (2003). *Model of indigenous Maya medicine in Guatemala: Joint investigation in Sipacapa, San Marcos, San Martín Jilotepeque, Chimaltenango and San Juan Ixcoy, Huehuetenango.* Chimaltenango: Asociación de Servicios Comunitarios de Salud (ASECSA).

Edge, S., Byrd, D. R., Compton, C. C., Fritz, A. G., Greene, F. L., & Trotti, A. (Eds.). (2010). *AJCC [American Joint Cancer Committee] Cancer Staging Manual* (7th ed.). New York, NY: Springer. Retrieved from http://www.springer.com/medicine/surgery/book/978-0-387-88440-0.

Espina, C. (2015, February 12). PDH califica crisis de salud como situación sin precedentes en el país. *El Periódico.* Retrieved from http://www.elperiodico.com.gt/es/20150212/pais/8448/PDH-califica-crisis-de-salud-como-situaci%C3%B3n-sin-precedentes-en-el-pa%C3%ADs.htm.

Fagenblat, M. (2010). *A covenant of creatures: Levinas's philosophy of Judaism.* Stanford, CA: Stanford University Press.

Farmer, P., Kleinman, A., Kim, J. Y., & Basilico, M. (Eds.). (2013). *Reimagining global health: An introduction.* Berkeley: University of California Press.

Fassin, D. (2009). Another politics of life is possible. *Theory, Culture & Society, 26*(5), 44–60.

Fassin, D. (2011). *Humanitarian reason: A moral history of the present.* Berkeley: University of California Press.

Fassin, D. (2013). Children as victims: The moral economy of childhood in the times of AIDS. In J. Biehl & A. Petryna (Eds.), *When people come first: Critical studies in global health* (pp. 109–129). Princeton: Princeton University Press.

Fee, M. (2006). Racializing narratives: Obesity, diabetes and the "aboriginal" thrifty genotype. *Social Science & Medicine, 62*(12), 2988–2997.

Ferguson, J. (1990). *The anti-politics machine: "Development," depoliticization, and bureaucratic power in Lesotho.* Cambridge, England: Cambridge University Press.

Ferguson, J. (2010). The uses of neoliberalism. *Antipode, 41*(Suppl. 1), 166–184.

Ferguson, J. (2013). Declarations of dependence: Labor, personhood, and welfare in southern Africa. *Journal of the Royal Anthropological Institute, 19*(2), 223–242.

Ferguson, J., & Gupta, A. (2005). Spatializing states: Towards an ethnography of neoliberal governmentality. In J. X. Inda (Ed.), *Anthropologies of Modernity: Foucault, Governmentality, and Life Politics* (pp. 105–132). Malden, MA: Blackwell Publishing.

Ferlay, J., Soerjomataram, I., Ervik, M., Dikshit, R., Eser, S., Mathers, C., Rebelo, M., Parkin, D.M., Forman, D., & Bray, F. (2013). GLOBOCAN 2012: Cancer incidence and mortality worldwide. IARC CancerBase No. 11 [Internet]. Lyon, France: International Agency for Research on Cancer. Retrieved from: http://globocan.iarc.fr

Ferzacca S. (2001). *Healing the modern in a Central Javanese city.* Durham, NC: Carolina Academic Press.

Fiedler, J. L. (1996). The privatization of health care in three Latin American social security systems. *Health Policy and Planning, 11*(4), 406–417.

Fischer, E. F., & Benson, P. (2005). Something better: Hegemony, resistance, and desire in Guatemalan export agriculture. *Social Analysis, 49*(1), 3–20.

Fischer, E. F., & Benson, P. (2006). *Broccoli and desire: Global connections and Maya struggles in postwar Guatemala.* Stanford, CA: Stanford University Press.

Fisher, W. F. (1997). Doing good? The politics and antipolitics of NGO practices. *Annual Reviews in Anthropology, 26,* 439-464.

Fiszbein, A., & Schady, N. (2009). *Conditional cash transfers: Reducing present and future poverty* (a World Bank policy research report). Washington, DC: World Bank.

Foro de Coordinaciones de ONG de Guatemala. (2002). *Directorio ONG en Guatemala 2002: Una herramienta para la difusión del quehacer de las ONG en Guatemala.* Mixco, Guatemala: Coordinación de ONG y Cooperativas.

Forster, C. (1999). Violent and violated women: Justice and gender in rural Guatemala, 1936-1956. *Journal of Women's History, 11*(3), 55–77.

Fort, M., Mercer, M. A., Gish, O., & Gloyd, S. (Eds.). (2004). *Sickness and wealth: The corporate assault on global health.* Cambridge, MA: South End Press.

Foster, J., Houston, J., Davenport, A., Anderson, A., Lamprecht, V., & Frenkel, G. (2012). Weaving traditional and professional midwifery: The story of midwives, a birth center, and the empowerment of midwives in Guatemala. In R. White (Ed.), *Global case studies in maternal and child health* (pp. 25-50). Burlington, MA: Jones and Bartlett Learning.

Foxen, P. (2008). *In search of Providence: Transnational Mayan identities*. Nashville, TN: Vanderbilt University Press.

Frantz, T. R. (1987). The role of NGOs in the strengthening of civil society. *World Development, 15*, 121–127.

Frenk, J., Gómez-Dantés, O., & Langer, A. (2012). A comprehensive approach to women's health: Lessons from the Mexican health reform. *BMC Women's Health, 12*(42), 2–7.

Fukuyama, F. (1992). *The end of history and the last man*. New York, NY: Free Press.

Funcafé. (2014, October). Funcafé Express. Retrieved from http://www.anacafe.org/glifos/index.php?title=14FUN:Noticias-Funcafe#Jornada_de_Planificación_Familiar.

Fundación Juan Bautista Gutierrez. (2013). Fundación Juan Bautista Gutierrez. Retrieved from www.fundacionjuanbautistagutierrez.org.

Fundación para el Desarrollo de Guatemala (FUNDESA). (2015a). Consejo de fiduciarios. Retrieved from http://www.fundesa.org.gt/cms/es/consejo-de-fiduciarios.html.

Fundación para el Desarrollo de Guatemala (FUNDESA). (2015b). Quiénes somos. Retrieved from http://www.fundesa.org.gt/cms/es/conozcanos/quienes-somos.html.

Fundación Sobrevivientes. (2011). *Violación y embarazo, sistematización de casos atendidos en Fundación Sobrevivientes*. Guatemala City, Guatemala: Fundación Sobrevivientes.

Gaia, E. (2010). Mi Familia Progresa: Change and continuity in Guatemala's social policy. In I. Greener, C. Holden, & M. Kilkey (Eds.), *Social policy review 22: Analysis and debate in social policy, 2010* (pp. 199–225). Bristol, UK: Policy Press.

Gakidou, E., Nordhagen, S., & Obermeyer, Z. (2008). Coverage of cervical cancer screening in 57 countries: Low average levels and large inequalities. *PLoS Medicine, 5*(6), e132.

Garcés de Marcilla del Valle, A. L., & Garcés de Marcilla del Valle, C. I. (2008). ¿A quién acudimos cuando buscamos salud? El Sistema de Salud en Guatemala: ¿Hacia dónde vamos? : Programa de las Naciones Unidas para el Desarrollo. Retrieved from http://desarrollohumano.org.gt/sites/default/files/Serie_Salud_5.pdf.

Garcés de Marcilla, M.A. (2004). *Capacidad de respuesta y equidad de los servicios públicos de salud, ante la crisis económica del país*. Guatemala City, Guatemala: Dirección General de Investigación (DIGI), Universidad de San Carlos.

Garrard-Burnett, V. (2010). *Terror in the land of the Holy Spirit: Guatemala under General Efraín Ríos Montt 1982-1983*. New York, NY: Oxford University Press.

Gauster, S., & Sigüenza, P. (2008). *El impacto de los altos precios de los commodities: Guatemala*. Guatemala City, Guatemala: Cholsamaj.

Geertz, C. (1983). *Local knowledge: Further essays in interpretive anthropology*. New York, NY: Basic Books.

Geissler, P. W. (Ed). (2015). *Para-states and medical science: Making African global health*. Durham, NC: Duke University Press.

Gershman, J., & Irwin, A. (2000). Getting a grip on the global economy. In J. Kim, J. Millen, A. Irwin, & J. Gershman (Eds.), *Dying for growth: Global inequality and the health of the poor* (pp. 11–43). Monroe, ME: Common Courage Press.

Geurts, K. (2001). Childbirth and pragmatic midwifery in rural Ghana. *Medical Anthropology, 20*(4), 379–408.

Gideon, J. (1998). The politics of social service provision through NGOs: A study of Latin America. *Bulletin of Latin American Research, 17*(3), 303–321.

Gillespie, S., Haddad, L., Mannar, V., Menon, P., Nisbett, N., & the Maternal and Child Nutrition Study Group. (2013). The politics of reducing malnutrition: Building commitment and accelerating progress. *The Lancet*, 382(9891), 552–569.

Giroux, H. A. (2008). Beyond the biopolitics of disposability: Rethinking neoliberalism in the New Gilded Age. *Social Identities: Journal for the Study of Race, Nation, and Culture, 14*(5), 587–620.

Glei, D., Goldman, N., & Rodríguez, G. (2003). Utilization of care during pregnancy in rural Guatemala: Does obstetrical need matter? *Social Science & Medicine, 57*(12), 2447–2463.

Godoy, A. S. (2013). *Of medicines and markets: Intellectual property and human rights in the free trade era*. Stanford, CA: Stanford University Press.

Godoy, A. S., & Cerón, A. (2011). Changing drug markets under new intellectual property regimes: The view from Central America. *Americal Journal of Public Health, 101*(7), 1186–1191.

Godoy-Paíz, P. (2005). Obstacles to achieving mental health in post-war Guatemala: The intersection of political and structural violence. *Nexus, 18*(1), 34–64.

Goldin, L. R. (2011). *Global Maya: Work and ideology in rural Guatemala*. Tucson: University of Arizona Press.

Goldman, N., & Glei, D. A. (2000). *Evaluation of midwifery care: A case study from rural Guatemala*. Chapel Hill: MEASURE Evaluation Center, University of North Carolina at Chapel Hill.

Goldman, N., & Heuveline, P. (2000). Health seeking behavior for child illness in Guatemala. *Tropical Medicine and International Health, 5*(2): 145–155.

González, A. L. (2011, June 26). ¿Y dónde está el médico? *Prensa Libre*, pp. 2–3.

Gordon, D. R., & Paci, E. (1997). Disclosure practices and cultural narratives: Understanding concealment and silence around cancer in Tuscany, Italy. *Social Science & Medicine, 44*(10), 1433–1452.

Government of Guatemala (GOG). (2012, February). *El plan del Pacto Hambre Cero.* Guatemala City, Guatemala: Government of Guatemala.

Grandin, G. (2000). *The blood of Guatemala: A history of race and nation*. Durham, NC: Duke University Press.

Grave, C. (2013, January 15). Mides entrega bono por discapacidad. *Prensa Libre*. Retrieved from http://www.prensalibre.com

Green, L. B. (1989). Consensus and coercion: Primary health care and the Guatemalan state. *Medical Anthropology Quarterly, 3*(3), 246–257.

Greenberg, L. (1982). Midwife training programs in highland Guatemala. *Social Science & Medicine, 16*(18), 1599–1609.

Gregory, C. O., Dai, J., Ramirez-Zea, M., & Stein, A. D. (2007). Occupation is more important than rural or urban residence in explaining the prevalence of metabolic and cardiovascular disease risk in Guatemalan adults. *The Journal of Nutrition, 137*(5), 1314–1319.

Guatemaltecos Mejoremos Guatemala. (2012, April). *Guatemaltecos vamos por una Guatemala más próspera, más solidaria y más segura.* Guatemala City, Guatemala: Mejoremos Guate.

Guidinelli, A. (1981). La investigación etnomédica y sectorialización. *Guatemala Indígena 16*(1–2), 1–46.

Gutiérrez, J. (2011a). *Evaluación de impacto de Mi Familia Progresa (evaluación externa de impacto del programa de transferencias monetarias condicionadas): Efectos en indicadores de salud.* Cuernavaca, Mexico: Instituto Nacional de Salud Pública. Retrieved from http://www.insp.mx.

Gutiérrez, J. (2011b). *Evaluación de impacto de Mi Familia Progresa (evaluación externa de impacto del programa de transferencias monetarias condicionadas): Síntesis ejecutiva.* Cuernavaca, Mexico: Instituto Nacional de Salud Pública. Retrieved from http://www.insp.mx

Gutiérrez, J. (2011c). *Evaluación de impacto de Mi Familia Progresa (evaluación externa de impacto del programa de transferencias monetarias condicionadas): Efectos en indicadores de nutrición.* Cuernavaca, Mexico: Instituto Nacional de Salud Pública. Retrieved from http://www.insp.mx.

Gutiérrez, J. (2011d). *Evaluación de impacto de Mi Familia Progresa (evaluación externa de impacto del programa de transferencias monetarias condicionadas): Efectos en indicadores de educación.* Cuernavaca, Mexico: Instituto Nacional de Salud Pública. Retrieved from http://www.insp.mx.

Hale, C. R. (2006). *Más que un indio: Racial ambivalence and neoliberal multiculturalism in Guatemala.* Santa Fe, NM: School of American Research.

Hall-Clifford, R. (2009). *Oral rehydration therapy in highland Guatemala: Long-term impacts of public health intervention on the self* (Doctoral dissertation). Retrieved from ProQuest Dissertations and Theses. (Accession No. 3334541).

Han, C. (2012). *Life in debt: Times of care and violence in neoliberal Chile.* Berkeley: University of California Press.

Han, C. (2013). Labor instability and community mental health: The work of pharmaceuticals in Santiago, Chile. In J. Biehl & A. Petryna (Eds.), *When people come first: Critical studies in global health* (pp. 276–301). Princeton, NJ: Princeton University Press.

Harrison, I. E., & Cosminsky, S. (1976). *Traditional medicine: An annotated bibliography of Africa, Latin America, and the Caribbean.* New York, NY: Garland.

Harvey, D. (2005). *A brief history of neoliberalism.* New York, NY: Oxford University Press.

Harvey, T. S. (2008). Where there is no patient: An anthropological treatment of a biomedical category. *Culture, Medicine, and Psychiatry, 32*(4), 577–606.

Harvey, T. S. (2011). Maya mobile medicine in Guatemala: The "other" public health. *Medical Anthropology Quarterly, 25*(1), 47–69.

Harvey, T. S. (2013). *Wellness beyond words: Maya compositions of speech and silence in medical care.* Albuquerque, NM: University of New Mexico Press.

Hawkins, J. P., & Adams, W.R. (Eds.). (2007). *Health care in Maya Guatemala: Confronting medical pluralism in a developing country.* Norman: University of Oklahoma Press.

Heggenhougen, H. K. (1976). *Health care for the "edge of the world": Indian campesinos as health workers in Chimaltenango, Guatemala: A discussion of the Behrhorst Program* (Doctoral dissertation). Retrieved from ProQuest Dissertation and Theses. (Accession No. 7726528).

Held, V. (2006). *The ethics of care: Personal, political and global.* New York, NY: Oxford University Press.

Helman, C. G. (2014). *Culture, health and illness: An introduction for health professionals* (2nd ed.). Burlington, MA: Elsevier Science.

Herbalife. (n.d.). *Nutrición para una vida mejor.* Retrieved from http://empresa.herbalife.com.gt/Content/Global/assets/SAM/Brochure_corporativo_2013.pdf.

Hernández, M. (2013, December 11). IGSS incrementa compras sin licitar. *Prensa Libre.* Retrieved from http://www.prensalibre.com/noticias/IGSS-incrementa-compras-licitar_0_1045695443.html.

Hernández, M. (2014, April 4). IGSS es señalado de gasto irregular. *Prensa Libre.* Retrieved from http://www.prensalibre.com/noticias/IGSS-senalado-gasto-irregular_0_1114088603.html

Herrera, W., de Jesus Mari, J., & Ferraz, M. P. (2005). Mental disorders and the internal armed conflict in Guatemala. *Actas Españolas de Psiquiatría, 33*(4), 238–243.

Herrera, W., de Jesus Mari, J., Andreoli, S. B., Quitana, M. I., & Ferraz, M. P. (2008). Prevalence of mental disorder and associated factors in civilian Guatemalans with disabilities caused by the internal armed conflict. *International Journal of Social Psychiatry, 54*(5), 414–424.

Heuveline, P., & Goldman, N. (2000). A description of child illness and treatment behavior in Guatemala. *Social Science & Medicine, 50*(3), 345–364.

Hildebrand, V.M. (2012). Scissors as symbols: Disputed ownership of the tools of biomedical obstetrics in rural Indonesia. *Culture Medicine & Psychiatry, 36*(3), 557–570.

Hinojosa, S. Z. (2004). Authorizing tradition: Vectors of contention in highland Maya midwifery. *Social Science & Medicine, 59*, 634–651.

Hinshaw, R. (1975). *Panajachel: A Guatemalan town in thirty-year perspective.* Pittsburgh, PA: University of Pittsburgh Press.

Hjelm, K., & Mufunda, E. (2010). Zimbabwean diabetics' beliefs about health and illness: An interview study. *BMC International Health and Human Rights, 10,* 7.

Hommes, R. (1995). Conflicts and dilemmas of decentralization. Washington, DC: World Bank.

Howell, J., & Pearce, J. (2001). Civil society and development: A critical exploration. Boulder, CO: Lynne Rienner Publishers.

Hu, F. B. (2011). Globalization of diabetes: The role of diet, lifestyle, and genes. *Diabetes Care, 34*(6), 1249–1257.

Hujo, K., & Gaia, E. (2011). Social policy and poverty: An introduction. *International Journal of Social Welfare, 20*(3), 230–239.

Hulme, D., & Edwards, M. (1992). *Making a difference: NGOs and development in a changing world.* London: Earthscan Publications.

Hurtado, E., & Sáenz de Tejada, E. (2001). Relations between government health workers and traditional midwives in Guatemala. In B. R. Huber & A. R. Sandstrom (Eds.), *Mesoamerican healers* (pp. 211–242). Austin: University of Texas Press.

Hyman, S., Chisholm, D., Kessler, R., Patel, V., & Whiteford, H. (2006). Mental disorders. In Jamison, D. T., Breman, J. G., Measham, A. R., Alleyne, G., Claeson, M., Evans D. B., . . . Musgrove, P. (Eds.), *Disease control priorities in developing countries* (2nd ed.), pp. 605–625. Washington, DC: World Bank.

Institute for Economics and Peace (IEP). (2011). *Global peace index 2011: Methodology, results, and findings.* Sydney, Australia: Institute for Economics and Peace.

Instituto Nacional de Estadística (INE). (2011a, October). *Encuesta Nacional de Salud Materno Infantil* (ENSMI). Guatemala City, Guatemala: Instituto Nacional de Estadística.

Instituto Nacional de Estadística (INE). (2011b, December). *Primera Encuesta Nacional de Juventud en Guatemala* (ENJU). Guatemala City, Guatemala: Instituto Nacional de Estadística.

Instituto Nacional de Estadística (INE). (2013). *Caracterización Departamental Sololá 2012.* Instituto Nacional Estadística de Guatemala. Retrieved from http://www.ine.gob.gt/sistema/uploads/2013/12/09/LrQm6TxhEtYd25S0Ma1QG9aSu94hxdlQ.pdf.

Instituto Nacional de Estadística (INE). (2014, September). República de Guatemala: Estadísticas Vitales 2013. Retrieved from http://osarguatemala.org/sites/all/informa%20y%20datos/Resumen%20ejecutivo.pdf.

International Diabetes Federation. (2013). IDF diabetes atlas (6th ed.). Retrieved from http://www.idf.org/sites/default/files/EN_6E_Atlas_Full_0.pdf

Ishida, K., Stupp, P., Turcios-Ruiz, R., William, D. B., & Espinoza, E. (2012). Ethnic inequality in Guatemalan women's use of modern reproductive health care. *International Perspectives on Sexual and Reproductive Health, 38*(2), 99–108.

James E. C. (2010). *Democratic insecurities: Violence, trauma, and intervention in Haiti.* Berkeley: University of California Press.

Janes, C. R., Chuluundorj, O., Hilliard, C. E., Rak, K., & Janchiv, K. (2006). Poor medicine for poor people? Assessing the impact of neoliberal reform on health care equity in a post-socialist context. *Global Public Health, 1*(1), 5–30.

Jansen, H. G. P., Morley, S., Torero, M. (2007). *Impacto del Tratado de Libre Comercio de Centroamérica en la agricultura y el sector rural en cinco países centroamericanos: Resumen Ejecutivo.* San José, Costa Rica: Proyecto RUTA/IFPRI.

Jenkins, G. L. (2001). Changing roles and identities of midwives in rural Costa Rica. *Medical Anthropology, 20*(4), 409–444.

Johnson, J. (2009). Guatemala: The land of eternal spring. *Medical Tourism Magazine 13,* 90–95.

Jokhio, A. H., Winter, H. R., & Cheng, K. K. (2005). An intervention involving traditional birth attendants and perinatal and maternal mortality in Pakistan. *New England Journal of Medicine, 352*(20), 2091–2099.

Jonas, S. (2000). *Of centaurs and doves: Guatemala's peace process*. Boulder, CO: Westview Press.

Jordan, B. (1978). *Birth in four cultures: A crosscultural investigation of childbirth in Yucatan, Holland, Sweden, and the United States* (1st ed.). Prospect Heights, IL: Waveland Press.

Kendall, C., Foote, D., & Martorell, R. (1998). Ethnomedicine and oral rehydration therapy: A case study of ethnomedical investigation and program planning. In P. J. Brown (Ed.), *Understanding and applying medical anthropology* (pp. 415–422). London: Mayfield Publishing.

Keshavjee, S. (2014). *Blind spot: How neoliberalism infiltrated global health*. Berkeley: University of California Press.

Kestler, E., & Ramírez, L. (2000). Pregnancy-related mortality in Guatemala, 1993-1996. *Revista Panamericana Salud Pública, 7*(1), 41–46.

Kestler, E., Walker, D., Bonvecchio, A., Sáenz de Tejeda, S., & Donner, A. (2013). A matched pair cluster randomized implementation trial to measure the effectiveness of an intervention package aiming to decrease perinatal mortality and increase institution-based obstetric care among indigenous women in Guatemala: Study protocol. *BMC Pregnancy and Childbirth, 13*, 73.

Kim, J., Millen, J. V., Irwin, A., & Gershman, J. (Eds.). (2000). *Dying for growth: Global inequality and the health of the poor*. Monroe, ME: Common Courage Press.

Kitch, R. (2014). *Saving lives: Felicity Thompson and midwifery training*. Retrieved from http://faithinpractice.org/news-and-events/11-news-and-events/109-saving-lives-felicity-thompson-and-midwife-training.

Kleinman, A. (1995). *Writing at the margins: Discourse between anthropology and medicine*. Berkeley: University of California Press.

Kohrt, B. A., Mendenhall, E., & Brown, P. J. (2015). Historical background: Medical anthropology and global mental health. In B. A. Kohrt & E. Mendenhall (Eds.), *Global mental health: Anthropological perspectives* (pp. 19–36). Walnut Creek, CA: Left Coast Press.

Kolling, M., Winkley, K., & von Deden, M. (2010). "For someone who's rich, it's not a problem": Insights from Tanzania on diabetes health-seeking and medical pluralism among Dar es Salaam's urban poor. *Globalization and Health, 6*(8), 1–9.

Kroeger, A. (1983). Anthropological and socio-medical health care research in developing countries. *Social Science & Medicine, 17*(8), 147–161.

Kroeger, A., Ochoa, H., Arana, B., Diaz, A., Rizzo, N., & Flores, W. (2001). Inadequate drug advice in the pharmacies of Guatemala and Mexico: The scale of the problem and explanatory factors. *Annals of Tropical Medicine and Parasitology, 95*(6), 605–616.

Kruske, S., & Barclay, L. (2004). Effect of shifting policies on traditional birth attendant training. *The Journal of Midwifery & Women's Health, 49*(4), 306–311.

La Forgia G.M. (Ed.). (2005). *Health system innovations in Central America: Lesson and impact of new approaches*. Washington, DC: The World Bank.

La Forgia, G. M., Mintz, P, & Cerezo, C. (2005). Is the perfect the enemy of the good? A case study on large-scale contracting for basic health services in rural Guatemala. In G. M. La Forgia (Ed.), *Health system innovations in Central America: Lesson and impact of new approaches* (pp. 9–48). Washington, DC: The World Bank.

Lamas, M. (1997). The feminist movement and the development of political discourse on *voluntary motherhood* in Mexico. *Reproductive Health Matters, 5*(10), 58-67.

Lambek, M. (Ed.). (2010). *Ordinary ethics: Anthropology, language, and action*. New York, NY: Fordham University Press.

Lang, J. B., & Elkin, E. D. (1997). A study of the beliefs and birthing practices of traditional midwives in rural Guatemala. *Journal of Nurse-Midwifery, 42*(1), 25–31.

Lao Pena, C. (2013). *Improving access to health care services through the Expansion of Coverage Program: The case of Guatemala*. Washington, DC: World Bank. Retrieved from https://openknowledge.worldbank.org/handle/10986/13283.

Latour, B. (1993). *We have never been modern*. (C. Porter, Trans.). Cambridge, MA: Harvard University Press.

Latour, B. (2008, May 29). "It's development, stupid!" or how to modernize modernization. *EspacesTemps.net*. Retrieved from http://www.espacestemps.net/articles/itrsquos-development-stupid-or-how-to-modernize-modernization.
Leslie, C. (1980). Medical pluralism in world perspective. *Social Science & Medicine. Part B: Medical Anthropology, 14*(4), 191–195.
Levinas, E. (1969). *Totality and infinity: An essay on exteriority*. (A. Lingis, Trans.). Pittsburgh, PA: Duquesne University Press.
Levinas, E. (1990). *Nine talmudic readings*. (A. Aronowicz, Trans.). Bloomington: Indiana University Press.
Levinas, E.. (1998). Entre-nous: Thinking-of-the-other. (M. B. Smith & B. Harshav, Trans.). New York, NY: Columbia University Press.
Levinas, E.. (2001). *Alterity and transcendence*. (M. B. Smith, Trans.). New York, NY: Columbia University Press.
Li, T. M. (2007). *The will to improve: Governmentality, development, and the practice of politics*. Durham, NC: Duke University Press.
Lingis, A. (2000). *Dangerous emotions*. Berkeley: University of California Press.
Little, W. E., & Smith, T. J. (Eds.). (2009). *Mayas in postwar Guatemala: Harvest of violence revisited*. Tuscaloosa: University of Alabama Press.
Liu, X., Hotchkiss, D. R., & Bose, S. (2008). The effectiveness of contracting-out primary health care services in developing countries: A review of the evidence. *Health Policy and Planning, 23*(1), 1–13.
Livingston, J. (2012). *Improvising medicine: An African oncology ward in an emerging cancer epidemic*. Durham, NC: Duke University Press.
Loevinsohn, B., & Harding, A. (2005). Buying results? Contracting for health service delivery in developing countries. *The Lancet, 366*(9486), 676–681.
Logan, M. H. (1979). Variations regarding susto causality among the Cakchiquel of Guatemala. *Culture, Medicine, and Psychiatry, 3*(2), 153–166.
Lupton, D. (1995). *The imperative of health: Public health and the regulated body*. London: Sage Publications.
MacCormack, C.P. (Ed.). (1994). *Ethnography of fertility and birth*. (2nd ed.). Prospect Heights, IL:Waveland Press.
MacDonald, M. (2007). *At work in the field of birth*. Nashville, TN: Vanderbilt University Press.
Maclean, G. D. (2010). An historical overview of the first two decades of striving towards Safe Motherhood. *Sexual & Reproductive Healthcare, 1*(1), 7–14.
Mahler, H. (1987). The Safe Motherhood Initiative: A call to action. *The Lancet, 1*(8534), 668–670.
Malena, C. (1995). *Working with NGOs: A practical guide to operational collaboration between the World Bank and non-governmental organizations*. Washington, DC: Operations Policy Department, World Bank.
Marcus, G. E., & Fischer, M. M. J. (1986). *Anthropology as cultural critique: An experimental moment in the human sciences*. Chicago, IL: University of Chicago Press.
Marzal, M. (1981). *Historia de la antropología indigenista: México y Perú*. Lima: Fondo Editorial Pontificia Universidad Católica del Perú.
Maupin, J. N. (2008). Remaking the Guatemalan midwife: Health care reform and midwifery training programs in highland Guatemala. *Medical Anthropology, 27*(4), 353–382.
Maupin, J. N. (2009). "Fruit of the accords": Healthcare reform and civil participation in Highland Guatemala. *Social Science & Medicine, 68*(8), 1456–1463.
Maupin, J. N. (2011). Divergent models of community health workers in highland Guatemala. *Human Organization, 70*(1), 44–53.
Max Agüero, E. F., del Valle Quinteros, D., & Angela Gálvez, E. C. (2004). ¿Maternindad forzada? El embarazo precoz en el contexto neoliberal. Aproximación desde el trabajo social a la temática del embarazo precoz en Tucumán. *Cuadernos de la Facultad de Humanidades Ciencias Sociales. Universidad Nacional de Jujuy, 22*, 295–303.

McClain, C. (Ed.). (1989). *Women as healers: Cross-cultural perspectives.* New Brunswick, NJ: Rutgers University Press.

McAllister, C., & Nelson, D. M. (Eds.). (2013). *War by other means: Aftermath in post-genocide Guatemala.* Durham, NC: Duke University Press.

McCreery, D. (2003). Coffee and indigenous labor in Guatemala, 1871–1980. In W. G. Clarence-Smith & S. Topik (Eds.), *The global coffee economy in Africa, Asia and Latin America, 1500–1989* (pp. 191–208). Cambridge, UK: Cambridge University Press.

Mejoremos Guate. (n.d.). Alianza por la nutrición. Retrieved from http://www.mejoremosguate.org/cms/en/what-are-we-doing/alianza-por-la-nutricion.

Men, C., Meessen, B., van Pelt, M., Van Damme, W., & Lucas, H. (2012). "I wish I had AIDS": A qualitative study on access to health care services for HIV/AIDS and diabetic patients in Cambodia. *Health, Culture and Society, 2*(1), 23–39.

Menchú, R., & Burgos-Debray, E. (1983). *I, Rigoberta Menchú: An Indian woman in Guatemala.* (A. Wright, Trans.). London: Verso.

Mendis, S., Fukino, K., Cameron, A., Laing, R., Filipe, A., Jr., Khatib, O., . . . Ewen, M.(2007). The availability and affordability of selected essential medicines for chronic diseases in six low- and middle-income countries. *Bulletin of the World Health Organization, 85*(4), 279–288.

Menjívar, C. (2011). *Enduring violence: Ladina women's lives in Guatemala.* Berkeley: University of California Press.

Merson, M. H., & Chapman Page, K. (2009). *The dramatic expansion of university engagement in global health: Implications for U. S. Policy: A report by the CSIS Global Health Policy Center.* Washington, DC: Center for Strategic & International Studies (CSIS). Retrieved from http://dspace.cigilibrary.org/jspui/handle/123456789/26577.

Mesa-Lago, C. (2007). Social security in Latin America: Pension and health care reforms in the last quarter century. *Latin American Research Review. 42*(2), 181–201.

Mesa-Lago, C. (2012). The performance of social security contributory and tax-financed pensions in Central America, and the effects of the global crisis. *International Social Security Review, 65*(1), 1–27.

Messer, E. (1987). The hot and cold in Mesoamerican indigenous and Hispanicized thought. *Social Science & Medicine, 25*(4), 339–346.

Metz, B. E., & Webb, M. F. (2013). Historical sediments of competing gender models in Indigenous Guatemala. In J. Gelfer (Ed.), *Masculinities in a global era* (pp. 193–213). New York, NY: Springer.

Midwife International. (2014, April 15). *Building on the foundation in Guatemala.* Retrieved from http://www.midwifeinternational.org/news/focus-partnership-guatemala.

Midwives for Midwives. (2015). Guatemala. Retrieved from http://www.midwivesformidwives.org/guatemala

Migdal, J. S. (1988). *Strong societies and weak states: State-society relations and state capabilities in the Third World.* Princeton, NJ: Princeton University Press.

Ministerio de Desarrollo Social (MIDES). (2013). Carrera contra la desnutrición supera meta en Sololá. Retrieved from http://www.mides.gob.gt/noticias/item/1049-carrera-contra-la-desnutricion-supera-meta-en-solola.

Ministerio de Desarrollo Social (MIDES). (2014). Programas Sociales: Mi Bono Seguro. Retrieved from http://www.mides.gob.gt/programas-sociales/mi-bono-seguro.

Ministerio de Economía de Guatemala (MINECO). (n.d.). *Productos farmacéuticos.* Retrieved from http://uim.mineco.gob.gt/documents/10438/17026/F19.pdf.

Ministerio de Salud Publica y Asistencia Social (MSPAS). (2006). Normativa para la formación de encargados de ventas sociales de medicamentos, encargados de botiquines rurales y acreditación de instituciones para la formación de este personal. Retrieved from http://medicamentos.com.gt/index.php/legislacion-vigente/acuerdos.

Ministerio de Salud Pública y Asistencia Social (MSPAS). (2010). *Encuesta Nacional de Salud Materno Infantil 2008 (ENSMI-2008/09).* Guatemala: Ministerio de Salud

Pública y Asistencia Social (MSPAS), Instituto Nacional de Estadística (INE), Centers for Disease Control and Prevention (CDC).

Ministerio de Salud Publica y Asistencia Social (MSPAS). (2011). Guías para la prevención, detección, evaluación y tratamiento de las enfermedades crónicas no transmisibles. Retrieved from http://portal.mspas.gob.gt/files/Descargas/ProtecciondelaSalud/Enfermedades cronicas no transmisibles/guias_atencion_enferme dades_cronicas_2011.pdf

Ministerio de Salud Publica y Asistencia Social (MSPAS). (n.d.-a). Plan de acción 2008–2012 para la prevención y el control integral de las enfermedades crónicas y sus factores de riesgo. Retrieved from http://portal.mspas.gob.gt/files/Descargas/ProtecciondelaSalud/Bancos de Sangre/Plan_de_Accion.pdf.

Ministerio de Salud Publica y Asistencia Social (MSPAS). (n.d.-b). Plan estratégico 2014-2019. Retrieved from http://www.mspas.gob.gt/files/Descargas/LeyPresupuesto2014/17bis/Plan estrategico MSPAS 2014-2019 version 040414.pdf

Ministerio de Trabajo y Previsión Social (MTPS). (2014). Salario mínimo 2014: Acuerdo gubernativo 537-2013. Retrieved from: http://www.mintrabajo.gob.gt/index.php/salariominimo.html.

Moland, K. M., & Blystad, A. (2009). Counting on mother's love: The global politics of prevention of mother-to-child transmission of HIV in Eastern Africa. In R. A. Hahn & M. C. Inhorn (Eds.), *Anthropology and public health: Bridging differences in culture and society* (2nd ed.), pp. 447–449. New York, NY: Oxford University Press.

Molina, R. L., & Palazuelos, D. (2014). Navigating and circumventing a fragmented health system: The patient's pathway in the Sierra Madre Region of Chiapas, Mexico. *Medical Anthropology Quarterly, 28*(1), 23–43.

Molyneux, M. (2006). Mothers at the service of the New Poverty Agenda: Progresa/Oportunidades, Mexico's conditional transfer programme. *Social Policy and Administration, 40*(4), 425–449.

Molyneux, M. (2007). *Change and continuity in social protection in Latin America: Mothers at the service of the state?* (Gender and Development Programme Paper Number 1). Geneva, Switzerland: United Nations Research Institute for Social Development.

Montejo, V. (1987). *Testimony: Death of a Guatemalan village* (V. Perera, Trans.). Willimantic, CT: Curbstone Press.

Morgan, L. M., & Roberts, E. F. S. (2012). Reproductive governance in Latin America. *Anthropology & Medicine, 19*(2), 241–254.

Moshabela, M., Pronyk, P., Williams, N., Schneider, H., & Lurie, M. (2011). Patterns and implications of medical pluralism among HIV/AIDS patients in rural South Africa. *AIDS Behavior, 15*, 842–852.

Mosquera Saravía, M. T. (2002). Madres de familia, mortalidad infantil y recursos sanitarios en Rabinal, Baja Verapaz. *Revista Estudios Interétnicos, 14*(10), 103–115.

Mosquera Saravía, M. T, Gaspar Salvador, M. A, & Sucuquí Mejía, I. (2001). *Conociendo la sabiduría Achi: Salud y enfermedad en Rabinal*. Guatemala City, Guatemala: Editorial Serviprensa C.A.

Mosquera Saravía, M. T., & Kolstrup, N. (2006). *La comunicación entre paciente y trabajadores de salud en una sociedad multiétnica*. Guatemala City, Guatemala: Serviprensa, S.A.

Mosse, D. (2013). The anthropology of international development. *Annual Review of Anthropology 42*, 227–246.

Mujeres Transformando el Mundo. (2014). *Por una justicia sensible al género: Mujeres transformando el mundo*. Retrieved from http://www.mujerestransform andoelmundo.org.

Muller, F. (1991). *Pobreza, participación y salud: Casos latinoamericanos*. Medellin, Colombia: Universidad de Antioquia.

Mulligan, J. M. (2014). *Unmanageable care: An ethnography of health care privatization in Puerto Rico*. New York: NYU Press.

Muntaner, C., Guerra Salazar, R. M., Benach, J., & Armada, F. (2006). Venezuela's barrio adentro: An alternative to neoliberalism in health care. *International Journal of Health Services 36*(4), 803–811.

Murray, C. J. L., Vos, T., Lozano, R., Naghavi, M., Flaxman, A. D., Michaud, C., . . . Memish, Z. A. (2012). Disability-adjusted life years (DALYs) for 291 diseases and injuries in 21 regions, 1990–2010: A systematic analysis for the Global Burden of Disease Study 2010. *The Lancet, 380*(9859), 2197–2223.

Naqshbandi, M., Harris, S. B., Esler, J. G., & Antwi-Nsiah, F. (2008). Global complication rates of type 2 diabetes in Indigenous peoples: A comprehensive review. *Diabetes Research and Clinical Practice, 82*(1), 1–17.

Naranjo, P. (1978). Medicina indígena y popular de América Latina y medicina contemporánea. *Guatemala Indígena, 13*(1-2), 186–219.

Nash, M. (1967). *Machine age Maya: Industrialization of a Guatemalan community*. Chicago, IL: University of Chicago Press.

Nelson, D. (1999). *Finger in the wound: Body politics in quincentennial Guatemala*. Berkeley: University of California Press.

Nelson, D. M. (2013). 100 percent Omnilife: Health, economy, and the end/s of war. In C. McAllister & D. M. Nelson (Eds.), *War by other means: Aftermath in post-genocide Guatemala* (pp. 285–306). Durham, NC: Duke University Press.

Newell, K. W. (1975). *Health by the people*. Geneva, Switzerland: World Health Organization.

Nguyen, V.-K. (2010). *The republic of therapy: Triage and sovereignty in West Africa's time of AIDS*. Durham, NC: Duke University Press.

Noticias Juridicas. (2013). Código penal: Base de datos de legislación. Retrieved from http://noticias.juridicas.com/base_datos/Penal/lo10-1995.l2t7.

O'Neill, K. L., & Thomas, K. (Eds.). (2011). *Securing the city: Neoliberalism, space, and insecurity in postwar Guatemala*. Durham, NC: Duke University Press.

Observatorio de Salud Sexual y Reproductiva (OSAR). (2014a, September). Monitoreo de Partos en Niñas y Adolescentes en Guatemala, enero-agosto del año 2014. Retrieved from http://osarguatemala.org/sites/all/informa%20y%20datos/Monitoreo%20de%20Partos%20en%20Ninas%20y%20Adolescentes%20en%20Guatemala.pdf.

Observatorio de Salud Sexual y Reproductiva (OSAR). (2014b). Partos según edad de la madre de enero a diciembre 2013. Retrieved from http://osarguatemala.org/sites/all/informa%20y%20datos/Partos%20por%20edad%20de%20la%20madre%202013.pdf

Observatorio de Salud Sexual y Reproductiva (OSAR). (2014c). Notas de prensa. Retrieved from http://www.osarguatemala.org/content/notas-de-prensa

O'Donnell, G. (1994). The state, democratization, and some conceptual problems (a Latin American view with glances at some post-communist countries). In W. C. Smith, C. H. Acuña, & E. Gamarra (Eds.), *Latin American political economy in the age of neoliberal reforms: Theoretical and comparative perspectives for the 1990s* (pp. 157–180). New Brunswick, NJ: Transaction Books.

Office for the Defense of Indigenous Women. (2014, September). PLANEA 2013–2017 Progress Report. Presented at the meeting of the Office for the Defense of Indigenous Women, Guatemala City.

Oficina de Derechos Humans del Arzobispado de Guatemala (ODHAG). (1998). *Guatemala: Nunca más: Informe del proyecto interdiocesano de recuperación de la memoria histórica*. Guatemala City, Guatemala: Oficina de Derechos Humanos del Arzobispado de Guatemala.

Omnilife. (2006). Las 5 Vueltas al Mundo de Jorge. *Revista OM* 16.

Omnilife. (2015). Países. Retrieved from https://www.omnilife.com/paises.

Ong, A. (2006). *Neoliberalism as exception: Mutations in citizenship and sovereignty*. Durham, NC: Duke University Press.

Orozco, A., & Rojas, A. (2013, May 28). Laboratorios habrían acordado aumento en precios de medicinas. *Prensa Libre*. Retrieved from http://www.prensalibre.com/noticias/politica/aumento-en-precios-de-medicamentos-j-i-cohen-informe-pdh-acuerdo-entre-farmaceuticas-0-1145885594.

Ortner, S. B. (1984). Theory in anthropology since the sixties. *Comparative Studies in Society and History, 26*(1), 126–166.

Paiz, A. (2012, August 1). Mental health care in Guatemala. *Revue, 21*(6). Retrieved from http://www.revuemag.com/2012/08/mental-health-care-in-guatemala.

Pan American Health Organization (PAHO). (1998). Guatemala: Country Chapter Summary from Health in the Americas, 1998. Retrieved from http://www.ops-oms.org/english/sha/prflgut.htm.

Pan American Health Organization (PAHO). (2007). Central America Diabetes Initiative (CAMDI): Survey of diabetes, hypertension, and chronic disease risk factors. Villa Nueva, Guatemala. Retrieved from http://www.paho.org/hq/index.php?option=com_docman&task=doc_view&gid=16117&Itemid=.

Pan American Health Organization (PAHO). (2012). Health in the Americas: Country volume, Guatemala. Retrieved from http://www.paho.org/Saludenlasamericas/index

Pantelić, A. (2011). A comparative analysis of microfinance and conditional cash transfers in Latin America. *Development in Practice, 21*(6), 790–805.

Paradies, Y. C., Montoya, M. J., & Fullerton, S. M. (2007). Racialized genetics and the study of complex diseases: The thrifty genotype revisited. *Perspectives in Biology and Medicine, 50*(2), 203–227.

Paul, B. (1955). *Health, culture, and community: Case studies of public reactions to health programs.* New York, NY: Russell Sage Foundation.

Paul, B. (1967). Mental disorder and self-regulating processes in culture: A Guatemalan illustration. In R. Hunt (Ed.), *Personalities and Cultures* (pp. 150-165). Austin: University of Texas Press.

Paul, L. (1975). Recruitment to a ritual role: The midwife in a Maya community. *Ethos 3*(3), 449–467.

Paul, L., & Paul, B. (1975). The Mayan midwife as sacred specialist: A Guatemalan case. *American Ethnologist, 2*(4), 707–725.

Pearce, J. (1997). Between co-option and irrelevance? Latin American NGOs in the 1990s. In D. Hulme & M. Edwards (Eds.), *NGOs, states and donors: Too close for comfort?* (pp. 257–274). New York, NY: St. Martin's Press.

Pebley, A., Hurtado, E., & Goldman, N. (1999). Beliefs about children's illness. *Journal of Biosocial Science, 31*(2), 195–219.

Peck, J. (2010). Zombie neoliberalism and the ambidextrous state. *Theoretical Criminology 14*, 104–110.

Perera, V. (1995). *Unfinished conquest: The Guatemalan tragedy.* Berkeley: University of California Press.

Perez de Lara, O. (1987, December). El desarrollo de la antropología en Guatemala: Necesidades y perspectivas. *Boletín de Antropología Americana, 16*, 113–134.

Perez-Martini, L. F., Guerra, J., Menegazzo, A., Archila, L., Barrera, R., & McClanahan, S. (2012). Emerging opportunity in Guatemala. *Applied Clinical Trials, 21*(1), 28–32.

Perrot, J. (2006). Is contracting a form of privatization? *Bulletin of the World Health Organization, 84*(11), 910–911.

Petrakis, I. L., Gonzalez, G., Rosenheck, R., & Krystal, J. H. (2002). Comorbidity of alcoholism and psychiatric disorders: An overview. *Alcohol Research and Health, 26*(2), 81–89.

Petryna, A. (2003). *Life exposed: Biological citizens after Chernobyl.* Princeton, NJ: Princeton University Press.

Pezzia, C. (2013). *The sober self: Discourse and identity of recovering alcoholics in the Western Highlands of Guatemala (Doctoral dissertation). Retrieved from UMI Dissertation Publishing.* (Accession No. 3594605)

Pfeiffer, J., & Chapman, R. (2010). Anthropological perspectives on structural adjustment and public health. *Annual Review of Anthropology, 39*(1), 149–165.

Pierson, C. (1996). *The Modern State.* New York, NY: Routledge.

Plan International. (2013). *La inversión del Gobierno Central en niñez y adolescencia en Centroamérica 2007-2011, Informe final.* Guatemala City, Guatemala: Plan International.

Population Council. (2010). *Guatemala rising, one girl at a time: Findings from the 2009–2010 Abriendo Oportunidades Evaluation.* Guatemala City, Guatemala: Population Council.

Population Council. (2011). *Programs to address child marriage: Framing the problem—Promoting healthy, safe, and productive transitions to adulthood series, Brief #14.* New York, NY: Population Council.

Population Council. (2012). *"Safescaping" Guatemala's indigenous communities: Primary prevention of gender violence by forming and mentoring young Mayan social change agents. Progress report to the United Nations Trust Fund to End Violence against Women.* Guatemala City, Guatemala: Population Council.

Population Council. (2013). *Uniones tempranas en Centroamérica y México. Resultados de un estudio exploratorio. Hoja informativa para Guatemala.* Federal District, Mexico: Population Council.

Presidencia de la República. (2008). Acuerdo gubernativo número 273-2008. Diario de Centro América, 45, 7. Retrieved from http://old.congreso.gob.gt/archivos/decretos/2008/gtdcx58-2008.pdf.

Presidencia de la República. (2009). Acuerdo gubernativo número 52-2009. *Diario de Centro América, 37,* 2-3. Retrieved from http://old.congreso.gob.gt/archivos/acuerdos/2009/gtagx52-2009.pdf.

Price, S. (2014). Professionalizing midwifery: Exploring medically imagined labor rooms in rural Rajasthan. *Medical Anthropology Quarterly, 28*(4), 519–536.

Prince, R. J. (2014). Navigating "global health" in an East African city. In R. J. Prince & R. Marsland (Eds.), *Making and unmaking public health in Africa: Ethnographic and historical perspectives* (pp. 208–230). Athens: Ohio University Press.

Prince, R. J., & Marsland, R. (Eds.). (2014). *Making and unmaking public health in Africa: Ethnographic and historical perspectives.* Athens: Ohio University Press.

Procuraduría General de la Nación. (2014). *Respuesta Resolución #120-2014, 2014.* Response to specific request for this volume.

Radoff, K. A., Thompson, L. M., Bly, K. C., & Romero, C. (2013). Practices related to postpartum uterine involution in the Western Highlands of Guatemala. *Midwifery, 29*(3), 225–232.

Red de Jóvenes para la Incidencia Política (REDLAC). (n.d.). *Prevenir con educación.* Guatemala City, Guatemala: REDLAC.

Redfield, R. (1950). *A village that chose progress: Chan Kom revisited.* Chicago, IL: University of Chicago Press.

Reilly, C. A. (1995). Topocrats, technocrats and NGOs. In C. A. Reilly (Ed.), *New paths to democratic development in Latin America: The rise of NGO-municipal collaboration* (pp. 247–272). Boulder, CO: Lynne Rienner.

Reilly, S., Reid, J., Cahir, P., Mei, C., & Bunik, M. (2013). Academy of breastfeeding medicine clinical protocol #17: Guidelines for breastfeeding infants with cleft lip, cleft palate, or cleft lip and palate. *Breastfeeding Medicine, 8*(4), 349–353.

Rivera Alvarez, J. R. (1985). *Evolución de la Salud Pública en Guatemala.* Guatemala City, Guatemala: Departamento de Artes Graficas, Ministerio de Salud Pública y Asistencia Social.

Rivers, W. H. R. (1924). *Medicine, magic, and religion.* New York, NY: Harcourt Brace.

Robinson, W. I. (2000). Neoliberalism, the global elite, and the Guatemalan transition: A critical macrosocial analysis. *Journal of Interamerican Studies and World Affairs 42*(4): 89–107.

Robinson, W. I. (2003) *Transnational conflicts: Central America, social change, and globalization.* London: Verso.

Rodríguez, J. (2010). Mental health care systems in Latin America and the Caribbean. *International Review of Psychiatry, 22*(4), 317–324.

Rodriguez, J., Barrett, T., Narváez, S., Caldas, J. M., Levav, I., & Saxena, S. (2007). [Mental health systems in El Salvador, Guatemala, and Nicaragua: Results of a WHO-AIMS evaluation]. *Revista Panamericana de Salud Pública, 22*(5), 348–357.

Rodríguez, J., Kohn, R., & Aguilar-Gaxiola, S. (2009). *Epidemiología de los trastornos mentales en America Latina y el Caribe. Publicación Científica y Tecnica No. 632.* Washington DC: Pan American Health Organization.

Rodríguez Rouanet, F. (1969). Prácticas médicas tradicionales de los indígenas de Guatemala. *Guatemala Indigena, 4*(2), 51–86.

Rogoff, B. (with Perez Gonzalez, C., Chavajay Quiacain, C., & Chavajay Quiacain, J.) (2011). *Developing destinies: A Mayan midwife and town.* New York, NY: Oxford University Press.

Rohloff, P., & Kraemer Diaz, A. (2013). Guatemala. In M. J. Krasnoff (Ed.), *Building partnerships in the Americas: A guide for global health workers.* Hanover, NH: Dartmouth University Press.

Rohloff, P., Kraemer Diaz, A., & Dasgupta, S. (2011). "Beyond development": A critical appraisal of the emergence of small health care non-governmental organizations in rural Guatemala. *Human Organization, 70*(4), 427–437.

Rostow, W. W. (1960). *The stages of economic growth: A non-communist manifesto.* Cambridge, England: Cambridge University Press.

Rutebemberwa, E., Muhamadi, L., Katureebe, S., Oundo, A., Kiweewa, F., & Mukanga, D. (2013). Use of traditional medicine for the treatment of diabetes in Eastern Uganda: A qualitative exploration of reasons for choice. *BMC International Health and Human Rights, 13,* 1.

Sabin, M., Lopes Cardozo, B., Nackerud, L., Kaiser, R., & Varese, L. (2003). Factors associated with poor mental health among Guatemalan refugees living in Mexico 20 years after civil conflict. *JAMA, 290*(5), 635–642.

Sanford, V. (2003). *Buried secrets: Truth and human rights in Guatemala.* New York, NY: Palgrave Macmillan.

Sansone, R. A., & Sansone, L. A. (2012). Doctor shopping: A phenomenon of many themes. *Innovations in Clinical Neuroscience, 9*(11–12), 42–46.

Sargent, C., & Davis-Floyd, R. (Eds.). (1997). *Childbirth and authoritative knowledge: Cross-cultural perspectives.* Berkeley: University of California Press.

Sargent, C. F., & Johnson, T. M. (Eds.). (1996). *Medical anthropology: Contemporary theory and method* (Revised ed.). Westport, CT: Praeger.

Saving Mothers. (2012). *Guatemala.* Retrieved from: http://www.savingmothers.org/guatemala

Scaling Up Nutrition (SUN). (2012, September). Scaling Up Nutrition (SUN) movement strategy [2012-2015]. Retrieved from http://scalingupnutrition.org.

Scaling Up Nutrition (SUN). (2014, February). An introduction to the Scaling Up Nutrition Movement. Retrieved from http://scalingupnutrition.org/sun-countries/guatemala

Scheper-Hughes, N. (1995). The primacy of the ethical: Propositions for a militant anthropology. *Current Anthropology, 36*(3), 409–440.

Scherz, C. (2014). *Having people, having heart: Charity, sustainable development, and problems of dependence in Central Uganda.* Chicago, IL: University of Chicago Press.

Schieber, B., & Stanton, C. (2000). *Estimates of maternal mortality in Guatemala 1996–1998.* Guatemala City: GSD Consultores/Guatemala; Chapel Hill, NC: MEASURE Evaluation.

Schirmer, J. G. (1998). *The Guatemalan military project: A violence called democracy.* Philadelphia: University of Pennsylvania Press.

Schlesinger, S., & Kinzer, S. (1982). *Bitter fruit: The untold story of the American coup in Guatemala.* Garden City, NY: Doubleday.

Schneider, S. (2010). *Mexican community health and the politics of health reform.* Albuquerque: University of New Mexico Press.

Schneider, S. D. (2006). Variations on marginalization—on the periphery of midwifery: A critical analysis of a community-based cancer screening program in Mexico. *Human Organization, 65*(4), 362.

Schuller, M. (2012). *Killing with kindness: Haiti, international aid, and NGOs*. New Brunswick, NJ: Rutgers University Press.

Scrimshaw, S. C. M., & Hurtado, E. (1988). Anthropological involvement in the Central American Diarrheal Disease Control Project. *Social Science & Medicine, 27*(1), 97–105.

Scott, M. A. (2010). *La mujer se va pa'bajo: Women's health at the intersections of nationality, class, and gender* (Doctoral Dissertation). Retrieved from http://uknowledge.uky.edu/gradschool_diss/15/.

Scott-Smith, T. (2013). The fetishism of humanitarian objects and the management of malnutrition in emergencies. *Third World Quarterly, 34*(5), 913–928.

Segura-Ubiergo A. (2007). *The political economy of the welfare state in Latin America: Globalization, democracy, and development*. Cambridge, UK: Cambridge University Press.

Sen, G., Iyer, A., & George, A. (2007). Systematic hierarchies and systemic failures: Gender and health inequities in Koppal district. *Economic and Political Weekly, 42*(8), 682-690.

Sethi, R. (2014). A study of direct selling in India with special reference to Amway. *International Journal of Economics and Management, 1*(1), 43–55.

Shaffer, E. R., & Brenner, J. E. (2009). A trade agreement's impact on access to generic drugs. *Health Affairs, 28*(5), 957–968.

Shafiq, Y., Shaikh, B. T., & Kumar, R. (2011). Availability and affordability of essential medicines: Exploring the health seeking behaviours and health service utilisation for children under-five years living in squatter settlement of Karachi, Pakistan. *Journal of Ayub Medical College Abbottabad, 23*(1), 132–138.

Sheehan, H. E. (2009). Medical pluralism in India: Patient choice or no other options? *Indian Journal of Medical Ethics, 6*(3), 138–141.

Sibley, L., & Sipe, T. A. (2006). Transition to skilled birth attendance: Is there a future role for trained traditional birth attendants? *Journal of Health, Population and Nutrition, 24*(4), 472–478.

Sieder, R. (2011). Contested sovereignties: Indigenous law, violence and state effects in postwar Guatemala. *Critique of Anthropology, 31*(3), 161–184.

Smith, C. A. (Ed.) (with Moors, M. M.). (1990). *Guatemalan Indians and the state, 1540 to 1988*. Austin: University of Texas Press.

Smith, T. J., & Adams, A. E. (Eds.). (2011). *After the coup: An ethnographic reframing of Guatemala, 1954*. Urbana-Champaign: University of Illinois Press.

Smith-Nonini, S. C. (2010). *Healing the body politic: El Salvador's popular struggle for health rights--from civil war to neoliberal peace*. New Brunswick, NJ: Rutgers University Press.

Solien de Gonzales, N. L. (1966). Health behavior in cross-cultural perspective: A Guatemalan example. *Human Organization, 25*, 122–125.

Sollis, P. (1996). Partners in development? The state, NGOs, and the UN in Central America. In T. G. Weiss & L. Gordenker (Eds.), *NGOs, the UN and Global Governance* (pp. 189–206). Boulder, CO: Lynne Rienner.

Sridhar, A. (2007). Tax reform and promoting a culture of philanthropy: Guatemala's "third sector" in an era of peace. *Fordham International Law Journal, 31*(1), 186-229.

Stampini, M., & Tornarolli, L. (2012). *The growth of conditional cash transfers in Latin America and the Caribbean: Did they go too far?* (Policy Brief No. IDB-PB-185). Inter-American Development Bank. Retrieved from http://publications.iadb.org.

Stewart, K. (2007). *Ordinary affects*. Durham, NC: Duke University Press.

Stiglitz, J. (2002). *Globalization and its discontents*. New York, NY: W.W. Norton.

Stoeckle, J. D. (2000). From service to commodity: Corporization, competition, commodification, and customer culture transforms health care. *Croatian Medical Journal 41*(2), 141–143.

Stoll, D. (1999). *Rigoberta Menchú and the story of all poor Guatemalans*. Boulder, CO: Westview Press.
Stoll, O. (1938). *Etnografía de Guatemala*. Guatemala: Tipografia Sanchez y de Guise.
Stracuzzi Ramirez, L. B. (2009). *Proyecto de implementación de un nuevo modelo de negocio dentro de la estrategia de crecimiento de Omnilife-Ecuador* (Masters thesis). Escuela Superior Politécnica del Litoral de Ecuador, Guayaquil, Ecuador.
Stuesse, A., Manz, B., Oglesby, E., Olson, K., Sanford, V., Snow, C. C., & Walsh-Haney, H. (2013). Sí hubo genocidio: Anthropologists and the genocide trial of Guatemala's Ríos Montt. *American Anthropologist, 115*(4), 658–663.
Sussman, R. W., & Cloninger, C. R. (Eds.). (2011). *Origins of altruism and cooperation*. New York, NY: Springer.
Tax, S. (1963). *Penny capitalism: A Guatemalan Indian economy*. Chicago, IL: University of Chicago Press.
Tessaro, I., Smith, S. L., & Rye, S. (2005). Knowledge and perceptions of diabetes in an Appalachian population. *Preventing Chronic Disease, 2*(2), A13.
The Hope Alliance. (2014). Guatemala – 2012 midwife training. Retrieved from http://www.thehopealliance.org/what-we-do/midwife-training
Thomas, K. (2013). Brand "piracy" and postwar statecraft in Guatemala. *Cultural Anthropology, 28*(1), 144–160.
Thompson, L., Diaz, J., Jenny, A., Diaz, A., Bruce, N., & Balmes, J. (2007). Nxwisen, ntzarrin or ntzo'lin? Mapping children's respiratory symptoms among indigenous populations in Guatemala. *Social Science & Medicine, 65*(7), 1337–1350.
Thousand Days. (2014). *1,000 days*. Retrieved from http://www.thousanddays.org
Torri, M. C. (2012). Traditional midwives in Tamaulipas: The difficult negotiation between traditional child-birth knowledge & the biomedical system in Mexico. *Women's Health and Urban Life, 11*(2), 42–63.
Towghi, F. (2004). Shifting policies toward traditional midwives: Implications for reproductive health care in Pakistan. In A. Castro & M. Singer (Eds.), *Unhealthy health policy: A critical anthropological examination* (pp. 79–95). Lanham, MD: AltaMira Press.
Triolo, N. (1994). Fascist unionization and the professionalization of midwives in Italy: A Sicilian Case Study. *Medical Anthropology Quarterly, 8*(3), 259–281.
Tronto, J. (1993). *Moral boundaries: A political argument for an ethic of care*. New York, NY: Routledge.
Turshen, M. (1989). *The politics of public health*. New Brunswick, NJ: Rutgers University Press.
Unger, J. P., De Paepe, P., Cantuarias, G. S., & Herrera, O. A. (2008). Chile's neoliberal health reform: An assessment and a critique. *PLoS Medicine, 5*(4), 542–547.
United Nations Development Program (UNDP). (2010). *Guatemala: Hacia un estado para el desarrollo humano: Informe nacional de desarrollo humano 2009-2010*. Guatemala City, Guatemala: UNDP.
United Nations Population Fund [UNFPA]. (2013). "Protégeme del embarazo" campaña llama a prevenir embarazos en niñas y adolescentes. Retrieved from http://www.unfpa.org.gt/content/%E2%80%9Cprotegeme-del-embarazo%E2%80%9D.
United Nations Statistics Division (UNSD). (2014). Births attended by skilled health personnel, percentage. Retrieved from http://mdgs.un.org/unsd/mdg/SeriesDetail.aspx?srid=570
United States Agency for International Development (USAID). (2008). ¿Quién financia el sistema de salud en Guatemala? Retrieved from: http://www.proyectodialogo.org/documents/salud/politica_salud_01.pdf.
United States Agency for International Development (USAID). (2014, March). Proyecto USAID/Reforma Educativa en el Aula, Educación de la niña de 1992 a 2013: 20 años de política, Avances y retos pendientes. Retrieved from http://pdf.usaid.gov/pdf_docs/PA00JWJT.pdf.
Universidad Rafael Landívar, & Pan American Health Organization. (2009). Estudio: Información Sobre Recursos Humanos de Salud en Guatemala. Retrieved from

http://mspas.gob.gt/decap/files/descargas/bibliotecaVirtual/RRHH/Informaci%C3%B3n sobre recursos humanos de salud.pdf.
University of San Carlos, Guatemala (USAC). (2009). [*National mental health survey: Epidemiological description of mental health disorders in men and women age 18 to 65 years, completed in the Guatemalan Republic*]. Guatemala City: Universidad de San Carlos de Guatemala.
Valladares, L. A. (1952). *El hombre y el maíz: Etnografía y etnopsicología de Colotenango.* Guatemala City, Guatemala: Universidad de San Carlos.
van der Geest, S. (1991). Marketplace conversations in Cameroon: How and why popular medical knowledge comes into being. *Culture, Medicine, and Psychiatry, 15*(1), 69–90.
van der Geest, S., & Hardon, A. (1990). Self-medication in developing countries. *Journal of Social and Administrative Pharmacy, 7*(4), 199–203.
Vargas, I., Vázquez, M. L., Mogollón-Pérez, A. S., & Unger, J.-P. (2010). Barriers of access to care in a managed competition model: Lessons from Colombia. *BMC Health Services Research 10*, 297.
Vaux, A. (2001). *The selfish altruist: Relief work in famine and war.* Sterling, VA: Earthscan.
Villatoro, E. M. (1986). El baño de vapor tradicional: Un recurso terapéutico en el altiplano guatemalteco. *La Tradición Popular, 59*, 1–16.
Villatoro, E. M. (2001). *Promoción de la medicina y terapias indígenas en la atención primaria de salud: El caso de los Maya de Guatemala.* Washington, DC: Pan American Health Organization.
Vogt, E. (1976). *Tortillas for the gods: A symbolic analysis of Zinacanteco rituals.* Cambridge, MA: Harvard University Press.
Vogt, E. (1994). *Fieldwork among the Maya: Reflections on the Harvard Chiapas Project.* Albuquerque: University of New Mexico Press.
Waitzkin, H., Jasso-Aguilar, R., & Iriart, C. (2007). Privatization of health services in less developed countries: An empirical response to the proposals of the World Bank and Wharton School. *International Journal of Health Services, 37*(2), 205–227.
Walsh, L. V. (2006). Beliefs and rituals in traditional birth attendant practice in Guatemala. *Journal of Transcultural Nursing, 17*(2), 148–154.
Warren, K. B. (2001). Pan-Mayanism and the Guatemalan peace process. In C. Chase-Dunn, S. Jonas, & N. Amaro (Eds.), *Globalization on the ground: Postbellum Guatemala democracy and development* (pp. 145–166). Lanham, MD: Rowman and Littlefield.
Watanabe, J. M. (1990). From saints to shibboleths: Image, structure, and identity in Maya religious syncretism. *American Ethnologist 17*(1), 131–150.
Way, J. T. (2012). *The Mayan in the mall: Globalization, development, and the making of modern Guatemala.* Durham, NC: Duke University Press.
Weaver, T. (Ed.). (2002). *The dynamics of applied anthropology in the twentieth century.* Oklahoma City, OK: Society for Applied Anthropology.
Weller, S. C., Baer, R. D., de Alba Garcia, J. G., Glazer, M., Trotter, R., Pachter, L., & Klein, R. E. (2002). Regional variation in Latino descriptions of susto. *Culture, Medicine, and Psychiatry, 26*(4), 449–472.
Wendland, C. (2010). Moral maps and medical imaginaries: Clinical tourism at Malawi's college of medicine. *American Anthropologist, 114*(1), 108–122.
Whyte S. R., Whyte, M. A., Meinert, L., & Twebaze, J. (2013). Therapeutic clientship: Belonging in Uganda's projectified landscape of AIDS care. In J. Biehl & A. Petryna (Eds.), *When people come first: Critical studies in global health* (pp. 140–165). Princeton, NJ: Princeton University Press.
Whyte, S. R. (2014a). The publics of the new public health: Life conditions and "lifestyle diseases" in Uganda. In R. J. Prince & R. Marsland (Eds.), *Making and unmaking public health in Africa: Ethnographic and historical perspectives* (pp. 187–207). Athens: Ohio University Press.
Whyte, S. R. (Ed.). (2014b). *Second chances: Surviving AIDS in Uganda.* Durham, NC: Duke University Press.

Wiedman, D. (2012). Native American embodiment of the chronicities of modernity: Reservation food, diabetes, and the metabolic syndrome among the Kiowa, Comanche, and Apache. *Medical Anthropology Quarterly, 26*(4), 595–612.

Williams, R. (1977). *Marxism and literature*. Oxford, England: Oxford University Press.

Wilson, C. H. (2010). *The commodification of health care in Kerala, South India: Science, consumerism and markets* (Doctoral Dissertation) Retrieved from ProQuest Dissertations and Theses. (Accession No. 4577225).

Wisdom, C. (1952). The supernatural world and curing. In S. Tax (Ed.), *Heritage of conquest: The ethnology of Middle America* (pp. 119–141). Glencoe, IL: Free Press. (Republished in 1968 by Cooper Square Publishers, New York).

World Bank. (1993). *World development report: Investing in health*. New York: Published for the World Bank, Oxford University Press.

World Bank. (2013). Towards better expenditure quality: Guatemala public expenditure review. May 2013. Retrieved from: http://www-wds.worldbank.org/external/default/WDSContentServer/WDSP/IB/2013/06/07/000356161_20130607145317/Rendered/PDF/780000ESW0P1230LIC00ENGLISH04257297.pdf.

World Bank. (2014a). GINI index (World Bank estimate). Retrieved from http://data.worldbank.org/indicator/SI.POV.GINI?page=1

World Bank. (2014b). Maternal mortality ratio (modeled estimate, per 100,000 live births). Retrieved from: http://data.worldbank.org/indicator/SH.STA.MMRT?order=wbapi_data_value_2010+wbapi_data_value+wbapi_data_value-first&sort=desc.

World Health Organization (WHO). (2006). *Comprehensive cervical cancer control: A guide to essential practice*. Geneva, Switzerland: WHO Press.

World Health Organization (WHO). (2011). Global status report on noncommunicable diseases 2010. Retrieved from http://www.who.int/nmh/publications/ncd_report_full_en.pdf.

World Health Organization (WHO). (2011). *Mental health atlas: Guatemala*. Geneva: Department of Mental Health and Substance Abuse. Retrieved from http://www.who.int/mental_health/evidence/atlas/profiles/gtm_mh_profile.pdf?ua=1.

Yu, C. H., & Zinman, B. (2007). Type 2 diabetes and impaired glucose tolerance in aboriginal populations: A global perspective. *Diabetes Research and Clinical Practice, 78*(2), 159–170.

Index

About the Contributors

Anita Chary, MA, is an MD/PhD Candidate in Anthropology at Washington University in St. Louis. She is the editor of Global Health Hub (globalhealthhub.org), an online platform that publishes and aggregates content related to global health for public health professionals. She is also the Research Director of Wuqu' Kawoq | Maya Health Alliance, a health services NGO working in Guatemala.

Peter Benson, PhD, is an Associate Professor of Sociocultural Anthropology at Washington University in St. Louis. After graduate studies at Harvard University, Dr. Benson was a post-doctoral fellow at Yale University. Dr. Benson is the author of the monograph *Tobacco Capitalism: Growers, Migrant Workers, and the Global Face of a Changing Industry*, published in 2012 by Princeton University Press, and co-author with Edward Fischer of the book *Broccoli and Desire: Global Connections and Maya Struggles in Postwar Guatemala.*

Alejandra Colom, MA, is Associate Professor of Anthropology at University del Valle of Guatemala. She is a PhD Candidate in anthropology at the Catholic University of Leuven, Belgium, and the Senior Program Director for the Guatemalan branch of Population Council, an NGO working to promote reproductive rights, education, and health care.

Shom N. Dasgupta-Tsikinas, MD, MPH, MA is the Director of Social Medicine at St. John's Well Child and Family Center in Los Angeles, California. Dr. Dasgupta-Tsikinas trained as a pediatrician, public health practitioner, and medical anthropologist at UCLA, Northwestern, and Harvard, respectively, and conducts field research in Guatemala as a staff physician for Wuqu' Kawoq | Maya Health Alliance.

David Flood, MD, MSc, is an internist and pediatrician at the University of Minnesota. He trained in medicine at Harvard University and in international health policy at the London School of Economics and Political Science. Dr. Flood oversees chronic disease clinical programs for Wuqu' Kawoq | Maya Health Alliance.

Rachel Hall-Clifford, PhD, MPH, MSc, is Assistant Professor of Anthropology and Public Health at Agnes Scott College in Decatur, Georgia.

Her current research is funded by the U.S. National Institutes of Health and investigates effective training of community health workers in oral rehydration therapy and zinc supplementation in Guatemala. She has also held medical anthropology research positions at Oxford University, Harvard University, and the London School of Hygiene and Tropical Medicine. Dr. Hall-Clifford is In-Country Director of the NAPA-OT Field School in Guatemala.

Nora King, MD, is an obstetrician/gynecologist at the University of Minnesota. She trained in medicine at Mayo Medical School. Dr. King oversees women's health programming of Wuqu' Kawoq | Maya Health Alliance. She is currently managing a regional midwife training initiative in the Western highlands of Guatemala.

Jonathan Maupin, PhD, is an Assistant Professor in the School of Human Evolution and Social Change at Arizona State University. He received his PhD from the University at Albany, SUNY. In addition to operating an ethnographic field school in medical anthropology in Guatemala, he conducts field research in Guatemala and the U.S. focused on community participation in health and development programs as well as variation and change in health-related beliefs.

Carla Pezzia, PhD, MPH, is an Assistant Professor at University of Dallas in the Human Sciences of the Contemporary World Department. Dr. Pezzia has worked in Guatemala since 2006 as the co-Director for the Ethnographic Field School of North Carolina State University and has research affiliations with the University of Texas Health Science Center at San Antonio and the South Texas Veterans Health Care System. Her dissertation in Anthropology at the University of Texas at San Antonio won the 2014 Kurt M. Landgraf Outstanding Dissertation Award, co-sponsored by the American Association of Hispanics in Higher Education and the Educational Testing Service.

Peter Rohloff, MD, PhD is Faculty of Medicine at Harvard University. He is an internist at Brigham and Women's Hospital and a pediatrician at Children's Hospital Boston. Dr. Rohloff is the founder and Medical Director of Wuqu' Kawoq | Maya Health Alliance. He has conducted extensive field research about ethnomedicine, health, and chronic disease in indigenous communities of Guatemala. He has also edited and published the bilingual (Kaqchikel/Spanish) monograph *Tiqaq'omaj qi'* (2008) with Magda Sotz Mux.

Paul H. Wise, MD, MPH is the Richard E. Behrman Professor of Child Health and Society, Professor of Pediatrics and Senior Fellow in the Freeman-Spogli Institute for International Studies, Stanford University. Dr.

Wise has published more than 175 articles focused on health inequalities, child health policy, and global health care delivery in areas of poor governance and political instability.

www.ingramcontent.com/pod-product-compliance
Ingram Content Group UK Ltd.
Pitfield, Milton Keynes, MK11 3LW, UK
UKHW041630031026
15587UKWH00001B/185

9 781498 505376